Constituent Structure

OXFORD SURVEYS IN SYNTAX AND MORPHOLOGY

GENERAL EDITOR: Robert D. Van Valin, Jr, Heinrich-Heine Universität Düsseldorf & University at Buffalo, State University of New York

ADVISORY EDITORS: Guglielmo Cinque, University of Venice; Daniel Everett, Illinois State University; Adele Goldberg, Princeton University; Kees Hengeveld, University of Amsterdam; Caroline Heycock, University of Edinburgh; David Pesetsky, MIT; Ian Roberts, University of Cambridge; Masayoshi Shibatani, Rice University; Andrew Spencer, University of Essex; Tom Wasow, Stanford University

Constituent Structure

Second Edition

ANDREW CARNIE

OXFORD
UNIVERSITY PRESS

OXFORD
UNIVERSITY PRESS

Great Clarendon Street, Oxford OX2 6DP

Oxford University Press is a department of the University of Oxford.
It furthers the University's objective of excellence in research, scholarship,
and education by publishing worldwide in

Oxford New York

Auckland Cape Town Dar es Salaam Hong Kong Karachi
Kuala Lumpur Madrid Melbourne Mexico City Nairobi
New Delhi Shanghai Taipei Toronto

With offices in

Argentina Austria Brazil Chile Czech Republic France Greece
Guatemala Hungary Italy Japan Poland Portugal Singapore
South Korea Switzerland Thailand Turkey Ukraine Vietnam

Oxford is a registered trade mark of Oxford University Press
in the UK and in certain other countries

Published in the United States
by Oxford University Press Inc., New York

First published 2007
This edition 2010

British Library Cataloguing in Publication Data
Data available

Library of Congress Cataloging in Publication Data
Data available

Typeset by SPI Publisher Services, Pondicherry, India
Printed in Great Britain
on acid-free paper by
the MPG Books Group, Bodmin and King's Lynn

ISBN 978-0-19-958345-4 (Hbk.)
      978-0-19-958346-1 (Pbk.)

1 3 5 7 9 10 8 6 4 2

Contents

Acknowledgements

This book has benefited from the input, advice, and feedback from a number of people, ranging from answering simple email queries to reading all or some of the manuscript. Here's a partial list, in alphabetical order: Anne Abeillé, Ash Asudeh, Andy Barss, Bob Berwick, Tom Bever, Sherrylyn Branchaw, Jean Carnie, Fiona Carnie, Morag Carnie, Robert Carnie, Robert Chametzky, Noam Chomsky, John Davey, Andrea Dauer, Malcolm Elliott, Yehuda Falk, Georgia Green, Heidi Harley, Michael Hammond, Richard Hudson, Peter Kahrel, Tibor Kiss, Simin Karimi, Tracy Holloway-King, Terry Langendoen, Shalom Lappin, Howard Lasnik, Tel Monks, David P. Medeiros, Stefan Müller, David Pesetsky, Massimo Piatelli-Palmarini, Chloe Plummer, Carl Pollard, Geoff Pullum, Sumayya Racy, Ivan Sag, Maggie Shade, Yosuke Sato, Robert Van Valin, Steve Wechsler. Thanks to you all. Special thanks go to my family who let me work on this book while ignoring them over the 2006 winter holidays.

AC

Tucson, February 2007

Preface to the Revised Edition

A word of explanation is due as to why a revised edition of this book has been brought out so soon after the publication of the original. Unfortunately a sad confluence in events led to the first edition being filled with an unacceptable number of errors, particularly in some of the formal definitions. In the months between the submission of this manuscript and its publication, my father's health showed a rapid decline. My main focus during this time was on helping my family look after him. The proofs for this book arrived in my inbox on the very day that my father passed away. Knowing that I would not be able to give them my full attention for a long time, I returned them to the Press essentially without looking at them, hoping for the best. Many technical errors and typos made it through the process, all of which have now been corrected, along with a number of additional changes, for this new edition. For people who own the first edition, a complete errata sheet can be found on my website at <http://dingo.sbs.arizona.edu/~carnie>. If (heaven forbid) there should be any errata to this revised edition, they will also be found at that website.

While the circumstances surrounding the need for this new edition were unhappy, it has brought with it a unique opportunity for me to update the material in the book with information about new advances in the study of constituent structure and to fill in a few gaps that I had missed before. This version contains an entirely new chapter (Chapter 12) with some of the latest information about constituent structure. I hope that the addition of this material makes the revised edition a valuable addition to your bookshelves.

I'd like to thank Dirk Bury, Mark Baltin, and Fredrik Heinat for writing encouraging reviews of the original edition (which appeared in *Journal of Linguistics, Lingua,* and *Linguist List* respectively). I will attempt the ambitious goal of revising the work in the ways they suggest in the event of a third edition. I greatly appreciate their feedback. In addition to the people mentioned above and in the first edition's acknowledgements, I'd like to add my thanks to Dirk Bury, Ben Fletcher, Adam Przepiórkowski, and Denis Ott, all of whom helped track down many of the corrections presented in this revised edition. Thanks also to John Davey and Julia Steer for allowing me a second stab at this work and to Elmandi du Toit, Jess Smith and Jill Bowie for helping in the production phase.

Andrew Carnie, May 2009, Tucson, Arizona

General Preface

Oxford Surveys in Syntax and Morphology provides overviews of the major approaches to subjects and questions at the centre of linguistic research in morphology and syntax. The volumes are accessible, critical, and up-to-date. Individually and collectively they aim to reveal the field's intellectual history and theoretical diversity. Each book published in the series will characteristically contain: (1) a brief historical overview of relevant research in the subject; (2) a critical presentation of approaches from relevant (but usually seen as competing) theoretical perspectives to the phenomena and issues at hand, including an objective evaluation of the strengths and weaknesses of each approach to the central problems and issues; (3) a balanced account of the current issues, problems, and opportunities relating to the topic, showing the degree of consensus or otherwise in each case. The volumes will thus provide researchers and graduate students concerned with syntax, morphology, and related aspects of grammar, communication, and cognition with a vital source of information and reference.

Andrew Carnie's *Constituent Structure* surveys one of the most fundamental areas of syntax. It encompasses a variety of views and proposals, both within the Chomskyan tradition and outside of it, and in this regard it is a quite unique and valuable contribution to the study of syntax.

Robert D. Van Valin, Jr
General Editor

University at Buffalo, The State University of New York
Heinrich Heine University, Düsseldorf

Abbreviations

3rd	third person
A movement	Argument movement (same as NP movement)
A	answer
A-bar movement	non-argument movement (typically the same as wh-movement)
Adj'	"Adjective bar", intermediate adjective category
Adj	Adjective
AdjP	Adjective Phrase
Adv'	"Adverb bar", intermediate adverb category
Adv	Adverb
AdvP	Adverb Phrase
AFD	in RRG, actual focus domain
AGREEMENT	agreement feature
AgrIO	Indirect object functional projection
AgrIOP	Indirect object Agreement Phrase
AgrO	Object agreement functional projection
AgrOP	Object agreement Phrase
AgrS	Subject agreement functional projection
AgrSP	Subject agreement Phrase
ARG	in RRG, arguments
Aux	Auxiliary
AVM	attribute value matrix
BAR	bar-level feature
BPS	Bare Phrase Structure
C'	"Complementizer bar", intermediate complementizer category
C	Complementizer
CATEGORY	category feature
CF	context free
chô	chômeur (relational grammar)
COMPS	complement feature
Condition A	the requirement that an anaphor must be bound in a local domain
Condition B	the requirement that a pronoun must not be bound in a local domain

Condition C	the requirement that an R-expression must not be bound
Conj	Conjunction
COP	copula
CP	Complementizer Phrase (= S')
CS	context sensitive
D'	"Determiner bar", intermediate determiner category
D	Determiner
DAG	directed acyclic graphs
DEF	definiteness
DOM	Domain-of-word-order feature in HPSG
DP	Determiner Phrase
DTRS	daughters feature in HPSG
ECPO	Exhaustive Constant Partial Ordering
EPP	Extended Projection Principle
EST	Extended Standard Theory
FCR	Feature Co-occurence Restriction
FFP	Foot-Feature Principle
FIN	Finite
Foc	Focus
FSA	finite-state automata
FSD	feature-specification defaults
GB	Government and Binding Theory
GENDER	gender feature
GKPS	Gazdar, Klein, Pullum, and Sag (1983)
GPSG	Generalized Phrase Structure Grammar
GT	generalized transformation
HFC	Head Feature Convention
HPSG	Head-driven Phrase Structure Grammar
IC	immediate constituent
ID/LP	immediate dominance/linear precedence
IDC	immediate dominance c-command
IF	in RRG, Intentional Force
Infl	the functional category of Inflection, later replaced by Agr, AgrS, AgrO, TP
INV	inversion feature
IP	Inflectional Phrase (often the same as TP or S)
LABEL	set of category labels

LCA	Linear Correspondence Axiom
LCS	in RRG, the layered structure of the clause
LF	Logical Form
LFG	Lexical-Functional Grammar
LSLT	*Logical Structure of Linguistic Theory*
M	mothership relation/immediate domination
MAX	set of XP categories
MP	Minimalist Program
MSO	Monadic Second Order
MTS	Model-Theoretic Syntax
MUB	Minimal Upper Bound
N′	"Noun bar", intermediate noun category
N	Noun
Neg	Negation
NP	Noun Phrase
NUC	in RRG, the nucleus of the CORE
NUM	number feature
OBJ	in LFG, object function
OSV	Object-Subject-Verb order
OVS	Object-Verb-Subject order
P′	"Preposition bar", intermediate preposition category
P	Preposition
P&P	Principles and Parameters Theory
PERSON	person feature
PF	Phonetic/Phonological Form
PFD	in RRG, potential Focus Domain
PM	phrase marker
PP	Prepositional Phrase
PRED	in RRG, the predicate; in LFG, the predicative content of the f-structure
PSG	phrase structure grammar
PSR	phrase structure rule
Q	Question
QP	Quantifier Phrase
R-expression	referring expression (most nouns, excluding pronouns, anaphors, and other elements that typically get their reference from linguistic context)
RG	Relational Grammar
RRG	Role and Reference Grammar

S	Sentence (often = IP or TP)
S′	"S-bar" (= CP)
SAI	Subject-Aux Inversion
SCT	structure-changing transformation
SLASH	"slash feature" (indicates a gap in structure)
SOV	Subject-Object-Verb order
SUBCAT	subcategorization feature
SUBJ	in LFG, subject function
SVO	Subject-Verb-Object order
T′	"Tense bar", intermediate tense category
T	Tense functional projection
TAG	Tree-Adjoining Grammar
TG	Transformational Grammar
Tns	in RRG, tense
Top	Topic
TP	Tense Phrase (often the same as S)
UB	upper bound
v	"little v" or "light v"
V′	"Verb bar", intermediate verb category
V	verb
VOS	Verb-Object-Subject order
vP	"little v" phrase
VP	Verb Phrase
VPISH	VP-internal Subject Hypothesis
VSO	Verb-Subject-Object order
X′	some intermediate category headed by category X
X″	"X double bar", usually equivalent to XP or X_{max}
X⁰	head (word) indicating category X
XCOMP	in LFG, predicate complement
X^{max}	maximal (usually phrasal) category associated with category X, usually equal to X″ and XP
X^P	a node of category X, of indeterminate phrasality
XP	some maximal/phrasal category headed by category X, often equivalent to X″ and X^{max}

Symbols Used

#	Before an example sentence, indicates semantic oddity Or pragmatic infelicity.
&	Conjunction (and)
∨	Disjunction (or)
¬	Negation ("it is not the case that")
→	Two uses: (a) in logical formula: conditional (if... then); (b) in phrase structure grammars → means "rewrites as", "projects from", "consists of" or "is licensed by", depending upon the approach.
↔	Biconditional (if and only if)
∀	Universal quantifier (every)
∃	Existential quantifier (some)
⊕	List addition
( )	In phrase structure rules indicates optionality. In syntactic forms may indicate structure. In logical forms may indicate functional application or structure, as in the usual usages.
(↑SUBJ)=↓	In LFG, metavariable indicating node bears subject role of dominating category (similarly for (↑OBJ)=↓, etc.)
↑=↓	In LFG, metavariable indicating featural identity between node and dominating category
*	Kleene star. In phrase structure rules, indicates zero or more. Before an example, indicates ungrammaticality.
/ _____	In phrase structure rules, "_____ is in the context of"
?	Before an example sentence, indicates marginal grammaticality.
[]	Constituent boundaries
^	Span; in the right-wrap rule, indicates linear concatenation
{NP/CP}	In phrase structure rules, indicates choice between NP and CP.
{x, y}	Unordered set of x and y
|	Such that (in set descriptions); boundary in immediate constituent analysis
~	Approximately

+	Kleene plus. In phrase structure rules, indicates one or more. In other contexts, indicates addition.
<A	Rule of Backward Application (Combinatorial Categorial Grammar)
$\langle x, y \rangle$	Ordered set of x and y
$\prec$	Precedence
$\prec_s$	Sister precedence
=	Equals
$=_{def}$	Is defined as
>	Greater than
>A	Rule of forward application (Combinatorial Categorial Grammar)
$\pm$	Plus or minus in binary feature values
$\in$	Element of (set membership)
$\cup$	Set union
$\approx$	"Is a" relation
$\neq$	Does not equal
$\leq$	Lesser than or equal too
$\geq$	Greater than or equal to
$\supset$	Used in feature coocurrence restrictions (FCRs) for "entails" or "requires"
$\triangleleft$	Immediate domination
$\triangleleft^\star$	Domination
$\triangleleft^+$	Proper domination
$\Rightarrow$	In TG, this indicates a structure changing transformation; in GPSG it indicates the application of a meta-rule or a meaning postulate.
$a, b, c, \ldots$	Constants
$i, j, k, l, \ldots$	Indices
$w, x, y, z, \ldots$	Variables
$\mathbb{N}$	Set of non-terminals
NP$\downarrow$	Substitute an NP in this position. (Tree-Adjoining Grammar)
$\mathbb{P}$	Set of production rules
$\mathbb{S}$	Start symbol
S/NP	In Combinatorial Categorial Grammar, look right for an NP to form an S.
S\NP	In Combinatorial Categorial Grammar, look left for an NP to form an S.

$\mathbb{T}$	Set of terminals
λx	Lambda operator (indicates following string is an open function unspecified for x)
Π	Projection path
ΣP	Polarity Phrase

Part 1
Preliminaries

1

Introduction

1.1 What this book is about

The study of phrase or constituent structure explores the combination of words into phrases and sentences. Constituent structure provides the roadmap that determines which words can be combined with which other words. This book is about the many, and varied, attempts to explain how word combination occurs.

An old, but important, observation about sentences is that they are not merely linear strings of words. There appears, even at an intuitive level, to be some organization that links some words more closely together than others. Take, for example, the sentence in (1):

(1)   My cat eats at really fancy restaurants.

In terms of interpretation, the relationship between *really* and *fancy* seems to be closer than that between *eats* and *at*. The word *really* tells us about how fancy the restaurants are, whereas the semantic relationship between *eat* and *at* seems to be mediated by the more distant words *fancy* and *restaurants*—this despite the fact that in terms of linear order the relationship between *eat at* and *really fancy* is identical—in each case the words are adjacent. In the structuralist tradition, whether instantiated in a formalist or functionalist framework, this kind of closeness is indicated by "phrase" (or "constituent") structure. The graphic representation of phrase structure has about as many variants as there are theories about syntax, but roughly converge on structures like those given in (2) as a tree (a) or a bracketed diagram (b):

(2)   (a)

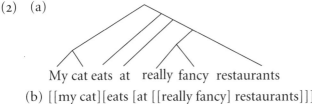

My cat eats at really fancy restaurants

(b) [[my cat][eats [at [[really fancy] restaurants]]]]

Although there is a great deal of controversy over even these simple diagrams (whether there is a verb phrase category, what the nature of each of the larger groups of words is, what labeling mechanisms are appropriate, etc.) these structures capture the fact that there is some closer relationship between *really* and *fancy* than between *eats* and *at*.

As first observed by Bloomfield (1933), such semantically based grouping of words seems to correlate with the way these groups function with respect to syntactic processes. Compare, for example, the grouped constituent [*eats at really fancy restaurants*] to the non-constituent [*eats at really*]. The first group can stand alone in answer to a question. The second cannot:

(3)   Q. What does your cat do when you're on vacation?
    (a)   Eat at really fancy restaurants.
    (b)   *Eat at really.

The first group can be replaced by *do so*, the second cannot:

(4)   My cat eats at really fancy restaurants...
    (a)   ...and my goldfish [does too].
    (b)   *...and my goldfish [does too] fancy restaurants.

Finally, the first group can be dislocated in the sentence, but the second cannot:

(5)   (a)   Eating at really fancy restaurants, that's what my cat likes to do.
    (b)   *Eating at really, that's what my cat likes to do (fancy restaurants).

These facts are fairly robust and require an account.

1.2 Organizational notes

In this book, I survey the current thinking, both cross-linguistically and cross-theoretically, on the topic of constituent structure. In the next few chapters, I review some fundamentals of constituent structure. In Chapter 2, I present the basic empirical evidence for constituent structure (constituency tests), and I discuss the related notions of compositionality and ambiguity. We will see that simple theories of concatenation fail to capture the basic facts about phrase structure and that a hierarchical approach is necessary. However, we will also see that constituency tests do not always give uniform results about what the structure of a particular sentence is. Chapters 3 and 4 also cover some fundamentals and describe in simple terms a uniform vocabulary for describing phrase structure. Chapter 3 focuses on the primitive relations of precedence and dominance. Chapter 4 looks at the higher-order relations of c-command and government, which are largely restricted to theories operating in the Principles and Parameters (P&P) framework.

In order to facilitate discussion of complex questions and controversies, the second section of the book gives an explicit and detailed history and description of two popular and widely adopted approaches to phrase structure. Chapter 5 addresses the basics of phrase structure grammars (PSGs). Chapter 6 looks at the wide variety of extensions to PSGs that have been proposed, including transformations, metarules, functional equations, feature structures, meaning postulates, and lexical rules. Finally, Chapter 7 addresses the origins and forms of, and the motivations for one particular extension to, PSGs, namely, X-bar theory.

The last section of the book examines critical controversies in treatments of constituent structure. Three of these chapters (8, 11 and 12) focus almost exclusively on recent proposals in the Minimalist Program variety of P&P. Chapter 8 traces the development of Bare Phrase Structure and related notions including Antisymmetry and derived X-bar theory. Chapter 11 addresses questions about the categorial and structural content of constituent systems. It discusses a tripartite view of the clause, with an emphasis on an approach that uses functional categories. There is also a fair amount of discussion as to whether there is a verb phrase (VP) category or not. Chapter 12 discusses some of the most recent advances in minimalist thinking on the topic of constituent structure. Chapters 9 and 10, by contrast, emphasize non-Minimalist controversies. Chapter 9 looks at alternatives to constituency based systems, looking at systems based in semantic relations, dependencies, Categorial Grammars, and constructional schemata. Chapter 10 questions some of the basic assumptions of Chapter 2, and considers approaches that allow the crossing of lines in trees. It also looks at cases where a single node in the tree is dominated by multiple nodes (multidomination), approaches where there is a single constituent system, but it branches multidimensionally, and approaches with multiple planes of constituent structure.

1.3 Apples, oranges, and pears

Most books on syntax, textbooks aside of course, are designed to promote a single theory or convince the reader about an innovation of recent syntactic theorizing. Readers picking up this book and looking for a well-argued coherent proposal about phrase structure are likely to be disappointed. This is due to the nature of the series this book appears in. The surveys in this series are not supposed to isolate a single viewpoint, but instead should provide a survey of the thinking on a particular topic. In this case, this means surveying a wide variety of theoretical approaches with a wide variety of underlying assumptions. For the reader this means that sometimes the discussion will be dizzying in the way I shift from one set of assumptions to another– sometimes with little argument. Except where I feel strongly about a topic, I try to avoid presenting too much evaluation and concentrate on presenting the ideas in what I hope is a coherent way.

Throughout the book, I will be surveying and discussing many concepts that are controversial. I will do my best to provide an even-handed presentation of alternative points of view. In some cases, I will just describe all the sides of a question and leave it open to the reader to judge the question on their own. In others, my own biases[1] will emerge, and I will argue for one particular view or another. No doubt proponents of other views will be frustrated with my presentation both when I present their ideas and when I leave them out. Even if I do not discuss alternatives in detail, I have tried to provide sufficient citations so that the interested reader will be able to follow up. I know this is frustrating, but the constraint that I not write a multi-volume encyclopedia on constituent structure requires that I limit the discussion in some ways. Comparing theories and frameworks of syntax is a dangerous game. On one hand, one might be comparing theoretical tools that appear the same but are different on some deep ontological way. On the other hand, one can easily miss similarities between approaches when they are couched in distinct formalisms. I am well aware that my discussion in this book occasionally suffers from both these flaws. I hope the reader will be patient with me when this happens.

The theories I address at various levels of detail here include, obviously, the main line of Chomskyan theorizing, including Transformational Grammar (TG), The Standard Theory, The Extended Standard Theory (EST), and the class of theoretical proposals known as Principles and Parameters (P&P), which includes Government and Binding Theory (GB) and the Minimalist Program (MP). Five other generative

[1] I am a generative (minimalist) syntactician, so my biases tend in the direction of that general theoretical approach. This is reflected in the heavy emphasis in this book on generative grammar. Even within minimalism, I have my own particular take on many issues.

theories are considered in some detail: Relational Grammar (RG), Lexical-Functional Grammar (LFG), Tree-Adjoining Grammar (TAG), Generalized Phrase Structure Grammar (GPSG) and Head-driven Phrase Structure Grammar (HPSG). The structuralist–functionalist theory of Role and Reference Grammar (RRG) and the new Simpler Syntax model also receive some attention. On a much more limited scale, I also briefly discuss relevant parts of many theories that do not have a phrase structure component per se, such as Dependency Grammar (including Word Grammar), Categorial Grammar, Functional Grammar, Cognitive Grammar, and Construction Grammar. The discussion of these latter approaches is largely limited to Chapter 9.

1.4 Who I assume you are

Since this book covers a wide variety of topics in a wide variety of frameworks, I think it is worth spending a few words about what I have assumed you know as I write this book.

In some parts of this book (e.g. Chs. 2 and 3), I start at very first principles and work up to a higher level of understanding. I do this to ensure that the discussion is thorough and grounded. Despite this, this book is not meant to be an introduction to the material. I am assuming that readers have at least a basic course in general syntactic analysis (see for example my 2006c textbook), and ideally have a more detailed background in some major version of generative grammar.

I hope that the presentation here will give both the beginning syntactician and the experienced old hand pause to think about the nature of the relationship between words and the representation of these relationships in terms of constituent structure.

2

Constituent Structure

2.1 Constituent structure as simple concatenation

Let us start our consideration of constituent structure by considering a few simple hypotheses about the nature of our grammars' word-combination mechanisms. Outside of linguistics, there is a well-established tradition governing combinatorics: mathematics. So consider preliminarily the possibility that some already well-motivated mechanisms from arithmetic or other mathematical disciplines might be carried over to the domain of sentence structure. Perhaps the simplest theory of phrase structure would be one of linear concatenation. On such an approach, phrase structure simply corresponds to the order of speech from the beginning of the utterance to the end (or from left to right on the printed page.) Consider the following sentence:

(1)   Nemo ate Dory's seaweed.

In our concatenation approach, the structure would be that in (2):

(2)   Nemo + ate + Dory's + seaweed.

Let us assume, not uncontroversially, that we as linguists have an intuitive notion of semantic relatedness between words reflecting which words "modify" other words. For example, we can intuit that *Dory's* is more closely related to *seaweed* (it tells us whose seaweed is being eaten, thus modifies *seaweed*) than it is to either *Nemo* or *ate*. Ultimately, of course, we will want something more scientific than this heuristic (and will return to empirical tests for structure later in this chapter), but for the moment this intuitive notion of "closeness" of words will suffice to make some simple points about our straw-man proposal of simple concatenation.

It is not hard to see how simple concatenation fails to capture a native speaker's intuitions about this sentence. First, let us consider what might be meant by the + signs in (2); let us take them literally, and assume that they are equivalent to the algebraic addition function. We might call this the concatenation-as-addition hypothesis. Addition is commutative; that is, $2 + 4 = 4 + 2$. But if we compute the meaning of the structure in (2) using addition, we might predict that the sentence means the same thing as any of the sentences in (3):

(3)   (a) Dory's seaweed ate Nemo.
      (b) Dory ate Nemo's seaweed.
      (c) Seaweed ate Dory's Nemo.
          etc.

Clearly this is not true: (2) means something quite distinct from any of the sentences in (3). One might reasonably object that this is because the important relation here is not one of addition per se, but rather the relationship mediated by the meanings of the words. That is, you know that the word *ate* expresses a relation between two nouns and that relationship is not symmetric or commutative: *ate* requires that the first noun does the eating, and the second one is the eatee; the lexical semantic relationships between the words limit the combinatorics, but the mechanism of combination itself is simple addition. While semantic relationships do indeed play an important role in governing combinatorics,[1] this revised hypothesis misses the point about simple addition. By claiming that *ate* has some privileged status in the sentence, we are essentially abandoning the idea that the words combine by simple concatenation in a manner similar to addition (it would be like claiming that the number 4 has some special property that governs which other numbers it can be combined with and in what order). In the end, this idea that certain words have a privileged semantic status—i.e. headedness—is ultimately adopted by almost every syntactician today; we will discuss this in detail in Chapters 7 and 9. However, enriching the system with semantic notions does not allow us to maintain the concatenation-as-addition hypothesis as the simplest possible approach to word combination: it becomes an entirely different kind of theory.

    Consider another possibility, which is only one step removed from our simple concatenation-as-addition hypothesis. Perhaps, unlike simple addition, the order in which the structure is built is important. That is, we have something like addition, but that is not commutative.

---

[1] See Farrell (2005) and Ch. 9 for discussions of the semantic or grammatical relations among words.

Moving from left to right on the page, we combine two elements creating a new object, then we combine[2] this new structure with the next word to the right, and so on.

(4) (a) Nemo ⊕ ate
     (b) (Nemo ⊕ ate) ⊕ Dory's
     (c) ((Nemo ⊕ ate) ⊕ Dory's) ⊕ seaweed
     (d) (((Nemo ⊕ ate) ⊕ Dory's) ⊕ seaweed)

Let us call this the structured-concatenation hypothesis. This approach does not suffer from the problem of (2), in that any subpart of (4d) is not identical to a subpart of any of the strings in (3). For example, the first concatenation in (4) is not identical to the first concatenation of (3b):

(5) (Nemo ⊕ ate) ≠ (Dory ⊕ ate)

This is what we want, since we do not want sentence (2) to mean the same thing as (3b). Nevertheless, the structured concatenation hypothesis suffers in a different, important, way. If you look closely at the brackets in (4d), you will note that *Dory's* is structurally closer to *ate* than it is to *seaweed*. We can capture this more precisely by counting the number of parentheses enclosing each item. If we were to number matching opening and closing parens, we get the annotated structure in (6):

(6) $(_1(_2(_3$Nemo ⊕ ate$)_3$ ⊕ Dory's$)_2$ ⊕ seaweed$)_1$

You will note that all of {Nemo, ate, Dory's} are enclosed in the $(_2)_2$ parentheses. *Seaweed* is excluded from this set. In this set-theoretic sense then, *Dory's* is closer to *ate* than it is to *seaweed*. However, this flies in the face of native-English-speaker intuitions about what words go together with one another. On an intuitive level, we know that *Dory's* has a closer semantic relationship to *seaweed* than it does to *ate*. You might think we could get around this problem by reversing the order of concatenation and starting at the right. Indeed, for the example sentence (1), this gives us a structure corresponding to the intuition about the closeness of *Dory* and *seaweed*:

---

[2] I use the symbol ⊕ here *roughly* in the sense in which it is used in Head Driven Phrase Structure Grammar (HPSG): as a list-addition operator which is not commutative: a ⊕ b ≠ b ⊕ a. Though technically speaking ⊕ operates over set-theoretic objects, I abstract away from this here. Also, the brackets in (4) are not actually part of the representation, I put them in this diagram as a heuristic for the reader. The symbol ⊕ is meant here as the *rough* equivalent of $^\wedge$ in Chomsky's *Logical Structure of Linguistic Theory* (1975).

(7)   (Nemo ⊕ (ate ⊕ (Dory's ⊕ seaweed)))

However, it gives us the wrong result if the subject of the sentence is contains more than one word:

(8)   (The ⊕ (fish ⊕ (ate ⊕ (Dory's ⊕ seaweed))))

This structure misses the intuition that *fish* is more tightly linked to *the* than to *ate*. Judgments about what goes together indicate that the Structured-Concatenation hypothesis cannot be right, and that the sentence in (8) is probably structured more like (9):

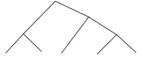

(9)   The fish ate Dory's seaweed.

Note that the structure represented in (9) cannot be created by a procedure that relies strictly and solely on linear order (such as the concatenation-as-addition and the structured-concatenation procedures). Instead, we need a richer hierarchical structure (such as that in (9)) to represent which words go together. This hierarchical structure must represent the intuition that *the* bears a closer relationship to *fish* than it does to *eat* or *seaweed*, and that *fish* bears a closer relationship to *the* than it does to *eat*, etc.

On the other side of the scale, human syntax seems to be filled with relationships that are not obviously "close." Take, for example, the contrast between (10a and b):[3]

(10)   (a)   The men that John saw are tall.
       (b)   *The men that John saw is tall.

Either of the two addition hypotheses fail immediately with such sentences. The noun that the verb *are* agrees with in (10a) (i.e. *the men*) is nowhere near the verb itself. Worse, there is a closer noun for the verb to agree with (i.e. *John*). Accounting for these facts is easy if one takes a hierarchical approach to combinatorics.

The focus of this book is on capturing the nature, mechanics, and forms of both "closeness" relationships and relationships that are more distant like the agreement facts in (10).

---

[3] Thanks to Massimo Piatelli Palmarini for pointing out these examples to me.

2.2 Regular grammars

It is worth briefly discussing the long tradition in linguistics and psychology of treating sentence structure as a kind of concatenation similar to that we rejected above. In particular, consider the case of a regular grammar (so called because in one formulation it makes use regular expressions, including concatenation). Regular grammars are also sometimes formulated as Finite State Automata[4] (FSA), also known as Markov Processes. Chomsky (1957) describes a machine that represents a regular grammar:

Suppose we have a machine that can be in any one of a finite number of different internal states, and suppose that this machine switches from one state to another by producing a certain symbol (let us say, an English word). One of these states is the initial state; another is a final state. Suppose the machine begins in the initial state, runs through a sequence of states (producing a word with each transition and ends in the final state. Then we call the sequence of words that has been produced a sentence).   (Chomsky 1957: 18–19)

An example (also taken from Chomsky 1957) of such a machine is seen in (11).

(11)

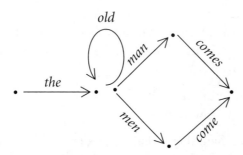

---

[4] In their original conceptions in modern generative grammar, grammars were viewed as structure generators, and automata functioned as machines that accepted structures and checked to see if they were part of the language. This distinction relies on the metaphor that descriptions of sentences are "built up" by grammars and "knocked down" by automata. This derivational metaphor is now widely rejected by practitioners of most varieties of syntax, except followers of the Principles-and-Parameters framework (a.k.a "GB theory" and "Minimalism") and even then it is largely viewed as a metaphor (cf. Epstein et al. 1998). As such, the distinction between automata and grammars is blurred. Although they are not technically the same thing, for the purposes of this book we will treat them as if they are notational variants.

Each dot represents a state, the words are functions from state to state. This machine generates sentences such as those in (12) (but not limited to them):

(12) (a) The man comes.
      (b) The old man comes.
      (c) The old old man comes.
      (d) The old old old man comes.
      (e) The old old old old man comes.
           etc.
      (f) The old men come.
      (g) The old old men come.
      (h) The old old old men come.
      (i) The old old old old men come.
           etc.

More sophisticated versions of regular grammars are found in Stratificational Grammar (Lamb 1966) and in connectionist/neural net/ Parallel Distributed Processing models (see e.g. Rumelhart and McClelland 1987).[5]

Chomsky (1957) argued that simple regular grammars are insufficient descriptions of human language. (For a transparent retelling of Chomsky 1957's results, see Lasnik 2000).[6] Chomsky enumerates four problems with regular grammars:

Problem 1. regular grammars have no memory. This can be illustrated by making up a "mirror image" language. Example "sentences" in this language are seen in (13), where the *a*s and *b*s are words in the language:

(13)   (i)   ab
      (ii)   aabb
     (iii)   aaabbb
      (iv)   aaaabbbb
             etc.

---

[5] One finds relics of concatenative regular grammars as parts of more mainstream generative grammars. Building on Curry (1961), Dowty (1982, 1989) distinguishes the processes that generate hierarchical structure (tectogrammatical structure) from the linear order (phenogrammatical structure) which can be constructed by concatenation (see Chapter 9). Langendoen (2003) presents a similar analysis in Minimalist syntax, Reape (1994) and Kathol (2000) do the same in HPSG.

[6] The discussion in this section draws heavily on Lasnik (2000) and, obviously, on Chomsky (1957).

This "language" has a grammar where the number of *a*s is identical to the number of *b*s. ($a^n b^n$, n > o). Since finite state automata cannot "remember" old states, (they only have access to the current state), the grammar cannot remember how many *a*s were present, and thus will not necessarily stop when the correct number of *b*s are produced.

We know that human languages do have a "memory". Lasnik (2000:15) gives a real language example, which he attributes to Morris Halle. This mini "language" is seen in (14). Given a noun like *missile*, it is possible to "circumfix" the expression *anti... missile*. So an *anti missile missile* is a missile that attacks missiles. This circumfixation can be applied an infinite number of times: an *anti anti missile missile missile*, is a missile that attacks missiles that attack other missiles.

(14)   (i)   missile
       (ii) anti missile missile
       (iii) anti anti missile missile missile

In this language, then, we have a pattern where the number of times the word *missile* is found is exactly one more than the number of times the word *anti* is found ($anti^n\ missile^{n+1}$). Another example might be the correspondence between subjects and verbs in Subject-Object-Verb (SOV) order languages like Japanese. If we have three nouns marked as subjects [NP_1, NP_2, NP_3...] we must also have three verbs which agree with those subjects [... V_3, V_2, V_1].

It is interesting to note that, while it is difficult to find other examples of cases where the grammar of a human language needs to have a memory of the number of times an operation has applied, non-local relationships are common. These too require a kind of memory that is not available in the machine that Chomsky describes in the above quote.

Problem 2. In a pure regular grammar, there can only be dependencies between adjacent elements, non-local dependencies can not be expressed.[7] However, non-local dependencies abound in human language. Take, for example, the cases in (15). *If* and *then* must co-occur even though they are not adjacent to each other (15i); *Either* and *or* are

---

[7] This is particularly extreme in SOV languages that allow center embedding, as the main clause subject is separated from its verb by the embedded clause. Japanese is a typical example:

(i)   Gakusei-ga   sensei-ga   odotta-to   itta.
      student-NOM   teacher-NOM   danced-   that said
      "The student said that the teacher danced." (From Uehara 2003)

similarly linked (15ii); and verb agreement can be sensitive to a non-local subject (15iii).

(15)   a + S$_1$+ b   where there is a dependency between a and b
    (i) If S$_1$, then S$_2$ *If S$_1$, or S$_2$
    (ii) Either S1 or S2   *Either S1 then S2
    (iii) The boy, who said S$_1$, is arriving today (Chomsky 1957: 22)

Examples which Chomsky does not mention are cases such as that in (16), where the verb *insist* requires that the embedded verb *be* be a bare infinitive.

(16)   I insist that John be honest.

Another example of non-local dependencies is the structure of embedded clauses in the Züritüütsch variety of Swiss German discussed by Shieber (1985) (and the related facts from Dutch discussed in Bresnan et al. (1982), Huybregts (1984)[8]). In Züritüütsch, as in many Germanic languages, some verbs, such as *hälfen* 'help', require that their objects take the dative case (marked, among other mechanisms by the determiner *em*); other verbs, such as *aastriichen* "paint" require that their objects take accusative case (marked in the sentence below by *es*). When there is a complex embedded clause that has both of these verbs, there is an interleaving of the objects and verbs (17):

(17)   Jan   säit   [das   mer em   Hans ess
       John   says   [that   we   the-DAT   Hans the-ACC
       huus   hälfed   aastriiche]
       house   helped   paint]
       "John says that we helped Hans paint the house."

In this example, the datively marked object of the verb *hälfed* (*em Hans*) is separated from the verb by the accusative *es huus*, which in turn is separated from the verb that governs its case (*aastriche*) by the verb *hälfed*. This is a cross-serial dependency. The grammar for these constructions requires a string $wa^m b^n xc^m d^n y$, where w,x,y are variables ranging over strings of words, a and b are nouns and c and d are verbs, and $n,m \geq 0$). The relationships here are non-local and thus require memory of the kind that a simple regular grammar or finite-state

---

[8] See also the survey of the literature on the non-context-freeness of human language in Pullum (1986).

automaton cannot provide. These constructions also provide examples of the kind of counting dependency described in (13) in that the number of subjects and the number of verbs have to correspond, but are added to the structure non-locally.

While it is true that in traditional regular grammars and finite-state automata we have no access to anything other than the immediately preceding state, we should note that in modern connectionist modeling it is possible to encode such information. The networks are considerably more complex (with parallel rather than serial connections) and each state is weighted to reflect statistical frequency (determined by exposure to a training regimen); these two factors combined can mimic the effects we are describing here (Rumelhart and McClelland 1987).

Chomsky also shows that grammars of human languages are structure dependent, a fact that cannot be expressed in a finite-state grammar which merely reflects concatenation.[9] This is *Problem 3*. He illustrates this with the phenomenon of subject-aux inversion (SAI):

(18)   (a) Mary has gone.
       (b) Has Mary gone?

As a first hypothesis, we might argue that the general procedure here is to invert the first two words in the sentence (such a formalization would be consistent with concatenation view of syntax). But this hypothesis is easily disproved:

(19)   (a) The man has gone.
       (b) *Man the has gone?

So instead, we might hypothesize that what happens is that we move the first auxiliary verb to the beginning of the sentence. Note that by introducing a notion of "auxiliary verb" (and other categories) we have already moved beyond the system of a simple finite-state grammar into one where the states are categorized. This hypothesis still fails on empirical grounds:

(20)   (a) The man who was reading the book is leaving.
       (b) *Was the man who reading the book is leaving?
            (cf. Is the man who was reading the book leaving?)

---

[9] Again, a properly trained parallel/connectionist model can mimic constituency although it does not refer to it directly.

What is important for SAI is not linear order (as would be predicted by the concatenation function of a regular grammar), but the depth of embedding of the various auxiliaries. To account for the ungrammaticality of (18b), we need to be able to distinguish between an auxiliary that is embedded in the subject (*was*) from the main clause auxiliary (*is*). This involves a notion of hierarchical structure not available to a simple regular grammar (or any concatenative approach). The correct description of SAI refers to the highest[10] auxiliary, where "highest" is defined in terms of hierarchical structure.

The final problem with regular grammars has to do with the fact that there are many processes in syntax that refer to some linear strings of words, but not to others. This is *Problem 4*, the problem of constituency. The next section is devoted to this question.

2.3 Constituent structure and constituency tests

In section 2.1, we discussed the fairly vague idea that certain words go together—on an intuitive level—pointing towards the claim that sentences are organized hierarchically, rather than linearly. In section 2.2, we saw that one typical approach to a purely linearly organized sentence structure (regular grammars) seems to fail on conceptual and empirical grounds. Instead, a richer, hierarchical, structure is needed. The fact that such hierarchical structures can be referred to by other grammatical processes provides not only evidence for their existence, but also drives the final nail into the coffin of a concatenation/finite state[11] account of word combinatorics.

The hierarchical organization of sentences represents constituents.[12] The idea of constituent analysis of sentences dates back at least to

---

[10] Defined, perhaps, as the auxiliary with the fewest brackets around it.

[11] However, it does not disprove the approaches of connectionism/neural networks or stratificational grammar, which all involve enriched networks that have been claimed to be able to mimic the empirical effects of constituency. For example, in Stratificational Grammar, the network connections themselves using a special node type (downward AND) represent constituency (see Lamb 1966 or Lockwood 1972 for details). One way of capturing constituency effects in Connectionist modeling is by enriching the system with a semantic role network as proposed in Hinton (1981). This kind of approach imports the insights of various versions of Dependency Grammar (see Chapter 9 for discussion of these approaches).

[12] It is worth clarifying a bit of terminology at this point. People frequently use the terms "constituent" and "phrase" interchangeably. The reason for this is quite simple: all phrases are constituents and most constituents are phrases. However, as we will see later in

Thomas de Erfurt's *Grammatica Speculativa* (*c.* AD 1300), and perhaps earlier, although it appears in a more modern form in the "immediate constituent" analyses of the American Structuralists in the early part of the twentieth century (e.g. Bloomfield 1933; for a history of the idea, see Seuren 1998 and Newmeyer 1986).

We can tentatively define constituents as in (20):

(21)   Constituents are groups of words that function as units with
       respect grammatical processes.

The expression "function as units" in this definition means that grammatical processes can refer to the group of words as if it were a single item or unit.

There are a number of phenomena that are standardly assumed to test for constituency. I provide a partial list of these here. As we progress through this book, however, we will find many instances where these tests can give false results and results that are contradictory with the output of other tests. For a critical evaluation of tests such as these, see Croft (2001). As such, the list below should be taken lightly; these tests should be viewed more as heuristic tools than absolute determinants of constituent structure.

Perhaps the simplest constituent test is whether the string of words can stand alone as a fragment of sentence (such as in the answer to a question).[13] To see this at work, let us compare two strings of words in the following sentence:

(22)   Bruce loves to eat at really fancy restaurants.

Compare the strings in (23):

(23)   (a) eat at really fancy restaurants (constituent)
       (b) eat at really fancy (not a constituent)

If we were answering the question in (24), (25a) is an acceptable response but (25b) feels "incomplete":

---

the chapter on X-bar theory, it is not the case that *all* constituents are phrases. The term "phrase" is limited to a particular kind of constituent: one where all the modifiers of the word heading the constituent (the most semantically prominent word) have been attached. As we will see in detail in Chapter 7, there is evidence for constituent structure smaller than that of phrases (that is, we will see that some phrases contain sub-constituents that are not themselves phrases). For this reason, I will use the term "constituent" to refer to all groups of words that function as units, including single word units, and reserve the name "phrases" for those constituents that are completed by their modifiers.

[13]   For more on this test, see Barton (1991).

(24)   What does Bruce love to do?

(25)   (a)   Eat at really fancy restaurants.
      (b)   *Eat at really fancy.

The opposite of the fragment test is checking to see if the string of words can be omitted or deleted in some way. Starting again with (22), compare the strings in (26):

(26)   (a) really fancy (constituent)
      (b) at really (not a constituent).

If we delete (26a) from (22), we get a meaningful sentence, but if we delete (26b) we get something very odd-sounding indeed:

(27)   (a)   Bruce loves to eat at restaurants.
      (b)   *Bruce loves to eat fancy restaurants.

Not all constituents can be deleted; for example, in this sentence, verb-phrase constituents (such as the string [*eat at really fancy restaurants*], proven to be a constituent by the fragment test) are not omissible:

(28)   *Bruce loves to.

This is presumably because there are additional requirements at work here (such as the fact that *loves* requires a verbal predicate, or the structure is meaningless).

However, it is frequently the case that constituents can be substituted for by a single word instead (the replacement test) (Harris 1946). Usually, a pro-form[14] (pronoun, proverb, or proadjective, propreposition) is used (29):

(29)   (a) eating at really fancy restaurants (constituent)
      (b) eating at really fancy (not a constituent)

Using the proverb *too*, the fragment test yields:

(30)   (a) Bruce loves [eating at really fancy restaurants] and Dory
          loves to [too].

---

[14] The earliest form of the replacement or substitution test (e.g. Harris 1946), allowed freer equivalences. So, for example, one could substitute *the man* for *John* in *Yesterday, John left*. From this we were allowed to conclude that not only is *the man* a constituent it is a constituent of the same type as *John*. But this free substitution operation frequently gives false results (as pointed out to me by Dave Medeiros). For example, given the adverb *really* in *John really stinks*, we can substitute the non-constituent, non-adverb string *thinks that the fish*. For this reason we limit replacement to pronominal replacement with the additional proviso that there has to be some (vaguely defined) similarity in meaning between the replaced item and its replacement.

(b) *Bruce loves [eating at really] fancy restaurants and Dory loves to [too] fancy restaurants.

In the second part of (30a) *too* stands in for [*eating at really fancy restaurants*]; but it can not stand for [*eat(ing) at really*] as shown by the unacceptability of (30b). We get similar results with pronouns. The pronoun *he* can stand for [*the compulsive shark*] in (30a) but not [*compulsive shark*] (30b) or [*the compulsive shark ate*] in (30c):

(31) (a) [The compulsive shark] ate the angelfish, but [he] did not eat the tuna.

(b) *The [compulsive shark] ate the angelfish, but the [he] did not eat the tuna.

(c) *[The compulsive shark ate] the angelfish, but [he] the tuna.

The proadjective *so* can replace certain kinds of adjective constituents:[15]

(32) Nemo is quite [thoroughly independent minded] but Dory is less [so].

Contrast this with a situation where *so* replaces a non-constituent:

(33) *Nemo is quite [thoroughly independent] minded but Dory is less [so] minded.

Finally, the propreposition *there* can stand for a whole prepositional phrase constituent[16] (34a), but not a non-constituent (34b).

(34) (a) Dory dropped the goggles [in the sub], but Nemo couldn't find them [there].

(b) *Dory dropped the goggles [in the] sub, but Nemo couldn't find them [there] sub.

A different class of constituency tests looks at the displacement[17] of strings of words. There are many different types of syntactic displacement including clefting, pseudoclefting, topicalization, fronting, passivization, raising, scrambling, *wh*-movement, and right-node raising. I give a single example here using a passive; for other examples, one can consult any good introductory syntax textbook such as Carnie (2006c) or Radford (1988). The active sentence in (35a) contains the two strings

---

[15] *So* can only replace smaller-than-phrase adjective constituents that are used after a copular verb, such as *is* or *seem*.

[16] *There* can also function as a pronoun.

[17] Also called the movement test or the permutability test.

(35b) and (35c). However, only (35b) can be put in the subject position of the passive (36a, b):

(35)   (a)   The current swept away the little brown turtle.
       (b)   [the little brown turtle]
       (c)   [little brown turtle]

(36)   (a)   The little brown turtle was swept away by the current.
       (b)   *Little brown turtle was swept away (the) by the current.

Perhaps the most difficult class of constituency tests to apply are those involving coordination. In the simplest cases, only constituents may be coordinated:

(37)   (a)   Bruce [ate at really fancy restaurants] but [drank at seedy bars].
       (b)   *Bruce [ate at really fancy] but [drank at seedy] establish-
             ments.

However, this test is prone to false positives. For example, it would appear as if the subjects and the verbs form constituents as distinct from the object in the following right-node-raising sentence:

(38)   [Bruce loved] and [Dory hated] tuna salad sandwiches.

However, evidence from other constituency tests, such as movement or replacement, suggests that the verb and the object form a constituent distinct from the subject:

(39)   (a)   [Eating tuna fish salad] is what Bruce was famous for doing.
       (b)   Bruce [loved tuna fish salad] and Dory [did so too].

The constituency tests are in conflict over this; we will discuss this controversy at length in Chapters 8 and 9 (see also Steedman 1989, Blevins 1990, and Phillips 2003) for further discussion.

Despite some conflicts and contradictions, constituency tests most often converge on structures that correspond to our intuitive notion of what words go together, which is at least partially evidence that there is some kind of hierarchically organized constituent structure.

2.4 Compositionality, modification, and ambiguity

Aristotle and his contemporaries believed that at least some of the meaning of a sentence could be "composed" from the meanings of the individual words that it includes. In more recent times, Frege (1891, 1923) argued that this composition involved saturated (completed) and unsaturated meanings (saturated meanings are "arguments" in the sense used in formal logic; unsaturated meanings are functions). To take a simple example, the expression *is swimming* represents an unsaturated predicate, it is composed with an argument (a saturated meaning), say *Bruce*, to form a sentence *Bruce is swimming*, which is true precisely when the person called "Bruce" is performing the action of moving through water by agitating his arms and legs at the time of speech. The hypothesis of compositionality holds that the syntactic tree is the road map for this semantic computation. That is, semantic composition applies precisely in the order specified by the hierarchical constituent structure. If two elements x and y form a constituent excluding z, then the meaning of the (x, y) pair is computed before z is added into the mix.

This is a strong hypothesis not held by all syntacticians. For example, the entire line of research of Lexical-Functional Grammar (LFG), where there are correspondences between constituent structure and semantic interpretation, but the mapping is not direct, denies this correspondence. In Chapter 9 we consider the possibility that, rather than semantic relationships being dependent on compositional constituent structure, the reverse is true—an idea known as a dependency grammar (discussed in Ch. 9). However, let us take as a starting point the compositionality hypothesis as it makes some interesting predictions about how constituent structure is put together. For example, it requires that if one word modifies another (that is, restricts the meaning of another), then they must be composed together in the constituent structure. This greatly limits the range of possible structures assigned to a given sentence. Take a simple example:

(40)   The fish from the reef ate tuna.

If the hierarchical structure of this sentence has the PP *from the reef* as part of a constituent with *fish* (41a), then this sentence is about fish from the reef, not fish from the deep ocean. However, if we were to try to make it part of a constituent with the verb (41b), we would get the very odd (and for most speakers of English, unacceptable) meaning where the eating was from the reef, but the fish could be from somewhere else.

(41)   (a)   [The fish [from the reef]] [ate algae].
       (b)   #[The fish] [[from the reef] ate algae].

The semantic intuition that the meaning associated with (41b) is odd has a direct correlate in syntax, which we see by applying constituency tests. The string [*from the reef ate algae*] cannot be a sentence fragment (42a), nor can it be moved (42b):

(42) (a) Q. What did the fish do?
             A. *From the reef ate algae.

      (b) *From the reef ate/eat algae is what the fish did.

If we adopt the compositionality hypothesis, we thus see a striking correspondence between our syntactic evidence and our semantics. This is not to say that there is always a one-to-one relationship between constituent structure and semantics.

Another advantage to adopting both a hierarchical constituent structure and the compositionality hypothesis is that it allows a straightforward account of many syntactically ambiguous sentences. The sentence in (43) can have either of the meanings in (44):

(43) Dory kissed the man with an open mouth.

(44) (a) Dory kissed a man; the man had (or has) his mouth open.
      (b) Dory kissed a man using her open mouth.

If different meanings correspond to different constituent structures, then the meaning in (44a) corresponds to a constituent structure where the PP *with an open mouth* is part of the same constituent as *man*:

(45)

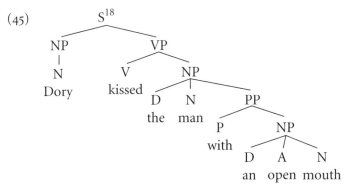

The meaning in (44b) corresponds to the structure where the PP composes with the verb, not the noun:

[18] To aid the reader in reading these trees, I use labels such as S (Sentence), NP (noun phrase), VP (verb phrase), and PP (prepositional phrase) here. Nothing in particular rides on the content or names of these labels. What is important in these diagrams is the constituent structure.

(46)

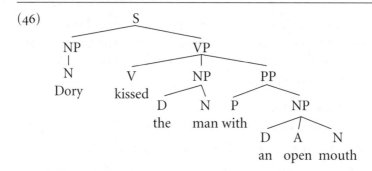

Under the compositionality hypothesis, hierarchical constituent structure thus also allows us to provide an explanation for syntactic ambiguity.

2.5 Some concluding thoughts

In this chapter, I started with the hypothesis that sentences may be
structured linearly from left to right by some operation of concatenation. There were three versions of this hypothesis: the concatenation-
as-addition hypothesis, the structured-concatenation hypothesis, and
traditional regular grammars. I presented Chomsky's (1957) arguments
that these failed to capture the basic facts of constituency, non-local
dependencies, and structure dependencies. They fail to account for
native-speaker's intuitions about what words go together. Finally, they
miss the important results from semantics about compositionality,
modification relations and ambiguity that can be drawn when a hierarchical constituent structure is assumed.

For much of the rest of this book, I assume as a common point of
departure that there is a hierarchical constituent structure. This does
not mean, however, that I will not question from time to time many of
the assumptions that underlie the discussion in this chapter. Indeed,
several of the later chapters address the deeper assumptions that
underlie the idea that we have constituent-based syntax.

3

Basic Properties of Trees: Dominance and Precedence

3.1 Introduction

In the last chapter, we looked at some preliminary evidence that syntactic structure is organized hierarchically into constituents. In this chapter we look at many of the terminological issues and structural properties of a hierarchical constituent structure. We will look primarily at the formal description of trees and the basic structural relations of dominance (also known as domination) and precedence. I start by giving some definitional descriptions—some formal, some intuitive— in terms of the graphic representation of each relation, then I provide a more precise description in terms of axiomization in first-order logic and set theory.

At first blush, such formalization might appear to be pedantic, baroque, or a needless exercise in symbolism. However, it serves both a practical purpose in this book and a more important purpose in terms of theory creation. In this book, we examine a number of different approaches to constituent structure, most of which have similar notational conventions. Often, however, these approaches rest on vastly different sets of assumptions about what these notations mean. It is worth having a precise, framework-neutral, definition of the properties of syntactic descriptions to serve as a reference point for the more intricate theory-internal notions. Axiomization into logical notation can serve us in this primarily definitional role. For example, if a particular theoretical perspective suggests that linear precedence relations are derived from something else (say headedness parameters (Travis 1984) or a secondary relation like c-command (Kayne 1994), or are "relaxed", as in McCawley 1982, 1987, 1989), it is useful to have a precise characterization of what the relationship being relaxed or derived is.

In terms of theory construction, there is at least one approach that suggests that axiomization of constituent relations is itself the foundation of the theory. Following the insights of Rogers (1994, 1998), Pullum and Scholz (2005) have suggested that one might approach framework construction using truth-conditional statements about the properties of syntactic structures (extending far beyond the structural relations that are the focus of this chapter).[1] An implementation of this idea within Minimalist assumptions is found in Palm (1999) and Kolb (1999). I am not going to pursue this line of thought further in this book, but the axiomizations given in this chapter can be interpreted in those terms.

This chapter focuses solely on the two basic relations of dominance and precedence. These two relations, taken together, can provide us with a total description of a constituent tree. That is, we can express the relationships among all the elements of a tree using only these two notions (i.e. dominance and precedence taken together provide us with a total ordering of every possible pairing of nodes in a tree). Of these two relationships, dominance is taken to be more basic. As we will see, it is extremely difficult to define precedence relationships without referencing domination. In later chapters (in particular Chs. 8 and 10), I will present arguments that the precedence relation is really a secondary or derived part of grammar.

In addition to dominance and precedence, the Chomskyan Principles-and-Parameters framework (encompassing both GB and MP) makes frequent reference to two other structural relations: c-command and, to a lesser degree, government (absent from MP). We will treat these separately in Chapter 4, as they are specific to one particular framework and are derived from the dominance relation.

3.2 Tree structures

I assume that most readers of this book are already familiar with basic syntactic notions, including trees and bracket notations. Nevertheless I'm going to quickly review the parts of the tree and related definitions

---

[1] Pullum and Scholz (2005) present arguments showing that a Model Theoretic Syntax (MTS) approach naturally captures gradience in ill-formedness judgments and explains the unfixed nature of the lexicon. See the original work for further arguments.

simply to ensure a common starting point for the discussion of tree geometrics. Take the tree in (1):

(1)

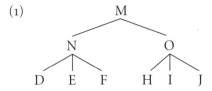

The lines in the tree are branches. The end of any branch is a node. Any time two or more branches come together, this is also a node. Nodes in a tree are labeled. Even though the label is written between the branches, we assume that, for example, the node labeled N is both the bottom of the branch above it, and the top of the branches below it.

The root node doesn't have any branch on top of it. At the opposite end of the tree are the terminal nodes with no branches underneath them. Any node that is not a terminal node is called a non-terminal node. Those nodes that are neither root nodes nor terminals (e.g. N and O in (1)) are intermediate nodes.

In some early works in generative grammar (and the practice survives to some degree today), a distinction was made between terminals and preterminals. Consider the following simple tree:

(2)

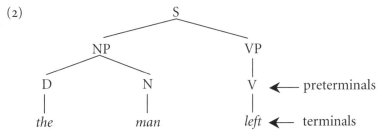

As we will see in Chapter 5, this kind of tree is at least partly an artifact of the way individual words came to be associated with their category in phrase structure grammar theories. In this kind of tree, we distinguish between the words, which are the terminals, and the categories of the words (D, N, V, etc.), which are the *preterminals*. In this kind of tree, syntactic rules, principles, and constraints make reference only to the preterminals nodes. In more recent work (starting in Gruber 1967), it is frequently assumed that the preterminal category and the word itself are identical (more on this below), so we need no distinction between preterminals and terminals and call both the word and its category the terminal node.

(2′)

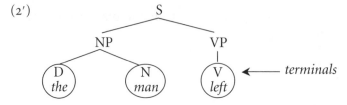

The intuition behind this view is that categories are properties of the words, and so they should be represented as a single object.

Constituent-structure trees are graphs in the mathematical sense of the word and, as such, can be formally described in terms of graph theory. Graphs are typically described by referring to two sets. The first set is the vertex set. Vertices are the labeled nodes in the trees. In the tree in (1) the vertex set is {M, N, O, D, E, F, H, I, J}. The branches of the tree form the other set, the edge set, which is defined in terms of the pairs of the nodes that are connected by branches. As we will see below when we look at dominance, there is an ordering to these pairs, such that one node is more prominent in the hierarchical structure than the other; so the pairs of nodes in the edge set are ordered pairs. The edge set for tree (1) is {⟨M,N⟩, ⟨M,O⟩, ⟨N, D⟩, ⟨N, E⟩, ⟨N, F⟩, ⟨O, H⟩, ⟨O, I⟩, ⟨O, J⟩}, where in each pair the first member is higher in the tree than the second member. Vertices (nodes), which are members of each pair in the edge set, are said to be adjacent to each other (so in (1) M and N are adjacent to each other; M and O are adjacent to each other; N and D are adjacent to each other, etc. A graph that has only ordered pairs in its edge set is said to be directed. Syntactic trees are all thus directed graphs.[2]

The definitions given in this chapter are either tree-theoretic or graph-theoretic (that is, set theoretic) descriptions of trees. As we will see in later chapters, not all theories of phrase structure use constituent trees, although they may make reference to the notions defined in this chapter. For the most part, the tree-theoretic definitions I give can be translated into set-theoretic or bracket-theoretic definitions with little difficulty.[3]

---

[2] More accurately, they are directed acyclic graphs; see below for arguments for the claim that they are acyclic (in the sense that they do not loop). Rayward-Smith (1995) captures this nicely as "A tree is a graph with a special vertex [the root], from which there is a unique path to every other vertex."

[3] The main exception to this are the loosened versions of the non-tangling constraint and the exclusivity condition, found in section 3.4.2, which can be defined only in terms of trees.

3.3 Dominance

Within a two-dimensional geometric object such as a constituent tree, we can describe relationships from left to right (and right to left), and from top to bottom (and bottom to top). The former of these relations is precedence; the latter is dominance (sometimes called domination). We start here with dominance.

3.3.1 Simple dominance

Informally, a node that sits atop another and is connected to it by a branch is said to dominate that node.

(3)   *Dominance* (◁*) (*informal definition*).

Node A dominates node B if and only if A is higher up in the tree than B and if you can trace a line from A to B going only downwards.

In (1), M dominates all the other nodes (N, O, D, E, F, H, I, J). N dominates D, E, and F, and O dominates H, I, J. O does not dominate F, as you can see by virtue of the fact that there is no branch connecting them.

Dominance is essentially a containment relation. The phrasal category N contains the terminal nodes D, E, and F. Containment is seen more clearly when the tree is converted into a bracketed diagram:

(4)   [$_M$ [$_N$ D E F] [$_O$ H I J]]

In (4) the brackets associated with N ([$_N$ D E F]) contain the nodes D, E, and F. The same holds true for O, which contains H, I, and J. M contains both N and O and all the nodes that they contain.

Graph-theoretically, the general relation of simple dominance is fairly difficult to define, although the ordering relations expressed in the pairs hint at how we might go about it. The more specific immediate dominance, which we discuss below, is easier to deal with. We return to the general description of simple dominance in graph theory below.

Dominance allows us to properly define the notions of root nodes, terminal nodes, and non-terminals:

(5)   (a) *Root node*: The node that dominates everything, but is dominated by nothing except itself.[4]

---

[4] The "except itself" and "other than itself" parts of these definitions will become clear below as we discuss the axioms constraining dominance, but rely on the assumption that dominance is a reflexive relation.

(b) *Terminal node*: A node that dominates nothing except itself.
(c) *Non-terminal node*: A node that dominates something other than itself.

3.3.2 Axiomization of dominance

In an early article on the mathematics of constituent trees, Zwicky and Isard (1963) sketch a series of definitions and axioms that specify the properties of structural relations. These axioms were updated in Wall (1972) and Partee, ter Meulen, and Wall (1990) (and discussed at length in Huck 1985, Higginbotham 1982/1985, and McCawley 1982); more recent axiomizations can be found in Blevins (1990),[5] Blackburn, Gardent, and Meyer-Viol (1993), Rogers (1994, 1998), Backofen, Rogers, and Vijay-Shanker (1995),[6] Kolb (1999), and Palm (1999).[7] The axioms, while not universally adopted, provide a precise characterization of the essential properties of the dominance relation.

Trees are taken to be mathematical objects with (at least) the following parts (based on Huck 1985):

(6) (a) a set N of nodes;
     (b) a set L of labels;
     (c) the binary dominance relation D ($\lhd^*$)[8] on N ($x\lhd^*y$ represents the pair $\langle x, y \rangle$, where x dominates y);
     (d) the labeling function Q from N into L.

---

[5] Blevin's axioms actually exclude some of the principles discussed below, especially those that disallow multidomination and tangling (line crossing). We will discuss Blevin's proposals in Chapter 10.

[6] Backofen, Rogers, and Vijay-Shanker (1995) actually argue that first-order axiomization is impossible for finite (but unbounded) trees; they propose a second-order account that captures the relevant properties more accurately. The proposal there is too complex to repeat here; and since for the most part, first-order description will suffice to express the intuitive and basic properties of trees, we leave it at this level.

[7] In this book, I have kept the logical notation to familiar first-order logic. These latter citations make use of a more expressive logic, namely, weak monadic second-order logic (MSO), which allows quantification not only over variables that range over individuals, but also over variables that range over finite sets. The importance of this is made clear in Rogers (1998) and discussed at a very accessible level by Pullum and Scholz (2005). MSO characterizations are important for describing such things as feature-passing principles, all beyond the scope of this chapter, which is why I've limited the descriptions here to first-order predicate logic.

[8] For McCawley (1982) the symbol is ρ and the relation is direct (i.e. immediate) dominance. Others use the symbol $\leq$ (unfortunately this symbol is also sometimes used for "precede"). I use Backofen, Rogers, and Vijay-Shanker's (1995) unambiguous notation ($\lhd^*$).

At the moment we will have nothing to say about the labeling function
Q, but will return to it Chapter 8 when we discuss the Bare Theory of
Phrase Structure. Our interest here lies in the relationship between
nodes (N) and their labels (L) as they are connected by the dominance
relation (D or ◁*). The axioms we propose over this relation can be
taken to be a formal definition of dominance.

The first axiom that constrains the dominance relation is:

A1.   *D is reflexive*:[9] $(\forall x \in N)\ [x \lhd^* x]$.

This means that all nodes dominate themselves. This axiom is important for two reasons, both indirect. First, it will allow us to write a
definition that excludes a multiply rooted tree such as that in (7):

(7)   *

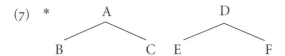

In mathematics such trees are allowed; in syntax, by contrast, we want
our trees to be connected (however, compare the discussion of Bare
Phrase structure in Ch. 8, and the discussion of multidimensional
tree structures in Ch. 10). We must also exclude trees like that in (8)
(where arrows indicate a downwards dominance relation, even when
the relation is not downwards on the page), where, even though
the tree is connected, there is not a single root:

(8)   *

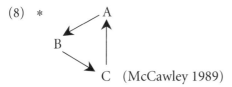

C   (McCawley 1989)

In order to disallow structures such as (7) and (8), we need the axiom
in (A2):[10]

A2.   *The Single-Root Condition*: $(\exists x\ \forall y \in N)\ [x \lhd^* y]$.

[9] This definition is based on that of Higginbotham (1982/1985), although the idea dates
back to at least Wall (1972), who changed Zwicky and Isard's asymmetric dominance to
dominance, which is both reflexive and antisymmetric.

[10] This definition is based on that in Partee, ter Meulen, and Wall (1990). McCawley
(1982) distinguishes two distinct conditions, one that requires that the structure be rooted,
and the other requires that the structure be connected. These are collapsed into this single
condition. See Collins (1997), who argues that this condition follows from Kayne's (1994)
Linear Correspondence Axiom. A2 does not rule out (8) by itself, it only does so in
combination with Axiom 4 (discussed below). Thanks to Adam Przepiórkowski for
pointing this out to me.

This axiom requires that there be some single node that dominates every node in N. Since the variable notation here allows $y = x$, it must be the case that x can dominate itself for this to be true. So domination must be reflexive for this to work. Graph-theoretically, (A2) has also the effect that syntactic trees are never cyclic.[11] Cyclic graphs are ones where the edges form a loop, as in (8). Take a graph with some number of distinct vertices (v, an integer, where $v \geq 3$). If the edge set contains the pairs $\langle 1, 2 \rangle$ and $\langle v, 1 \rangle$, the graph is cyclic. Syntactic trees are never cyclic because the single-root condition precludes any (other) node from dominating the root, which is the initial symbol in the ordering relationships expressed in the edge set. This means that all syntactic trees are directed acyclic graphs (DAGs).

Second, (A1) allows us to restrict the form of terminals in a tree. In many early forms of generative grammar (as mentioned above), all terminal nodes consisted of a word hanging from a category node, as in (9a) distinguishing preterminals from terminals. In the earliest versions of Chomsky's phrase structural approach (i.e. (1957), see Ch. 5 for more discussion), lexical items were inserted by rules. They substituted for and replaced their category label. As such, a notation like that in (9a) was appropriate.[12] Gruber (1967) was the first to note the inaccuracy of (9a) for these approaches; the matter has been discussed at length in Richardson (1982), Speas (1990), Freidin (1992: 29), Chomsky (1995a) and Chametzky (1995, 1996, 2000). Nevertheless many scholars continue to use, inaccurately[13] in my opinion, the notation in (9a) even when they assume principles that would actually generate (9b).

---

[11] The term "cyclic" is commonly used in the Principles-and-Parameters framework and its ancestor, the Revised Extended Standard Theory, to refer to transformational operations. It's worth noting that cyclicity in transformations and the cyclicity of graphs are unrelated.

[12] This notation is also crucial for the Antisymmetry approach of Kayne (1994). In more recent conceptions of generative grammar, the category of the terminal is part of the terminal itself, (14b). Under this view, lexical items are not inserted as the last step in phrase structure, they either *are* the terminal nodes (as in strictly lexicalist theories) or they are inserted by a special transformational process (in late-insertionist models).

[13] In the GPSG and HPSG frameworks, structures like (9a) are often licensed by a special lexical rules, thus exempting them from this criticism. See, for example, the version of GPSG discussed in Bennett (1995), or the HPSG in Sag, Wasow, and Bender (2000). Another exception is the set of grammars described in Kornai and Pullum (1990), where terminals (the words) are distinguished from preterminals (the categories) and all the relevant relations are defined making reference to preterminals only.

(9) (a)

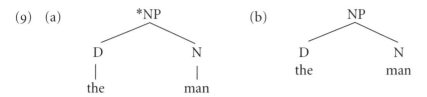

The opposite of domination is a sort of "part of" relation. So in (9a, b) the N is a part of NP. The reverse is not true, NP is not a part of N. So in (9a), we assert that *man* is a part of N, but that *N* is not a part of *man*. Every node is, of course, a part of itself (hence the intuition that domination is reflexive). N dominates N, so N is part of N. The part-of quality of domination tells us that when two nodes are part of each other, they dominate each other, and that is only possible when they are the same node. Consider now (9a). Under many current views (in a variety of theories including Minimalism, HPSG, Categorial Grammar, and LFG), the category of a word is the set of features that describe that word (i.e. they form a Saussurian sign for the conceptual and syntactic properties of the word itself). This information comes from the lexical entry for the word, and cannot be defined independently of the word.[14] Ontologically speaking, then, the category is actually part of the word. The category must dominate the word and the word must dominate the category. Structure (9a) lacks this crucial property, thus it is incoherent and ill-formed. If $x = y$, and x dominates y, but y does not dominate x, then axiom (A1) is violated. For (9a) to be well-formed, where N and *man* are the same thing, dominance would have to be irreflexive. So A1 rules out (9a) under this set of commonly held assumptions about the way in which words get into the tree.

As we will see below when we look at c-command (Ch. 4), there are circumstances where we may wish to relax the reflexivity axiom (A1). Dominance that is not reflexive is called "proper dominance" (or irreflexive dominance) and can be indicated with the symbol $\lhd^{+}$. Proper dominance has all the other properties of dominance, except those governed by axiom (A1).

The third axiom, (A3), states that the dominance relation is transitive:

A3. *D is transitive*: $(\forall xyz \in N)[((x \lhd^* y) \ \& \ (y \lhd^* z)) \rightarrow (x \lhd^* z)]$.

This should be obvious. In fact, it is impossible to draw a tree in two dimensions, where some x dominates y, and y dominates z, but x does

---

[14] Unlike in the old phrase structure system that underlay structures like (9a), where the N category came from the rule, not from the lexical entry of the word.

not also dominate *z*. Whether this is an empirically correct result or not is a matter of some debate. In Chapter 10, we look at theories of constituent structure which branch into three dimensions, where (A3) may or may not hold.

The relation of dominance is also antisymmetric;[15] this is formalized in axiom (A4).

A4.   *D is antisymmetric:* $(\forall xy \in N)[((x \lhd^* y) \,\&\, (y \lhd^* x)) \rightarrow (x = y)]$.

This means that the relation is unidirectional: *x* cannot both dominate *y* and be dominated by *y*, unless *x* and *y* are the same node. This allows us to rule out trees such as (10) (where again the arrow indicates "downwards", even though it is not downwards on the page.)

(10)   * A

B

Were the edge sets of trees not directed (using ordered pairs), such structures would be ruled out on general principles of set theory (the sets {A, B} and {B, A} being equivalent). However, since we are dealing with ordered pairs ($\langle A, B \rangle \neq \langle B, A \rangle$), we need (A4) to rule such structures out and guarantee acyclicity in the graph.

Finally, consider the tree in (11):

(11)

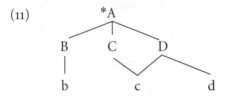

It is usually assumed (although not universally, see the discussion on multidomination in Ch. 10) that elements such as *c* cannot be dominated by more than one node that are not themselves related by dominance—In other words, a node can not have more than one mother. This is ruled out by (A5):[16]

A5.   *No multiple mothers:* $(\forall xyz \in N)\, [((x \lhd^* z) \,\&\, (y \lhd^* z)) \rightarrow ((x \lhd^* y) \lor (y \lhd^* x))]$.

---

[15] Zwicky and Isard's original axiom held that the relation was asymmetric $((\exists xy \in N)\,[(x \lhd^* y) \rightarrow \neg(y \lhd^* x)])$ but this, of course, contradicts (A1)—which was not part of Zwicky and Isard's original set of axioms (see n. 9).

[16] Based on Higginbotham (1982/1985). See Sampson (1975) and Blevins (1990), who argue that the single-mother requirement should be relaxed and multidomination allowed.

Below, we will see that a different axiom (the non-tangling condition, A9) rules out (11) as well as some other ill-formed trees, so we will be able to eliminate (A5); I list it here for completeness. Trees such as (11) will be a recurring theme throughout this book.

3.3.3 Immediate dominance

Because of transitivity (A3, above), M in (1)—repeated here—dominates *all* of the nodes under it.

(11)

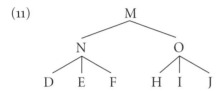

In certain circumstances, we might want to talk about relationships that are more local than this: a node immediately dominates another if there is only one branch between them.

(12)   *Immediate dominance* (◁)

Node A immediately dominates node B if there is no Intervening node G that is properly dominated by A and properly dominates B. (In other words, A is the first node that dominates B.)

$\forall xz \ [(x \triangleleft z) \leftrightarrow \neg \exists y[(x \triangleleft^+ y) \ \& \ (y \triangleleft^+ z)]].$[17]

In (1), M dominates all the other nodes in the tree but it only immediately dominates N and O. It does not immediately dominate any of the other nodes because N and O intervene. Immediate dominance is the same thing as the informal notion of motherhood.

(13)   (a) *Mother:* A is the mother of B iff A immediately dominates B.
       (b) *Daughter:* B is the daughter of A iff B is immediately dominated by A.

Immediate dominance also allows us to define the useful notion of sisterhood:

(14)   *Sisters:* A is a sister of B if there is a C, such that C immediately dominates both A and B.[18]

---

[17] Pullum and Scholz (2005) define this without explicit reference to proper dominance: $x \triangleleft y =_{\text{def}} (x \triangleleft^* y) \ \& \ (x \neq y) \ \& \ \neg \exists z[(x \triangleleft^* z) \ \& \ (z \triangleleft^* y) \ \& \ (x \neq z) \ \& \ (z \neq y)].$

[18] Chomsky (1986b) gives a much broader description of sisterhood, where sisters include all material dominated by a single phrasal node (instead of a single branching

The relationship of immediate dominance is the relationship expressed by the ordered pairs in the edge set of the graph. It is the stipulated ordering of certain vertices in the tree to represent hierarchical structure. As mentioned above, the more general relationship of simple dominance is difficult to express in graph-theoretic terms.[19]

3.3.4 Exhaustive dominance and "constituent"

In the previous chapter, I presented an intuitive characterization of constituent. The relation of dominance actually allows a little more rigorous formal characterization of constituency. In order to do this, we need yet another definition, namely, exhaustive dominance:

(15)   *Exhaustive dominance*

> Node A exhaustively dominates a *set* of terminal nodes {b, c, ..., d}, provided it dominates all the members of the set (so that there is no member of the set that is not dominated by A) *and* there is no terminal node g dominated by A that is not a member of the set.

Consider:

(16)

In (16) all members of the set {b, c, d} are dominated by A; there is no member of the set that is not dominated by A. Furthermore, A dominates *only* these nodes. There is no node g dominated by A that is not a member of the set. We can therefore say of the tree in (16) that A exhaustively dominates the set {b, c, d}. This set of terminals, then, is a constituent. Now consider the set {b, c, d} again but this time with respect to (17):

node); the reasons for this have to do with a theory-internal requirement on how theta-roles are assigned; we will leave it aside here. See Fukui (1995) for a critical evaluation of Chomsky's (1986b) definition and a reanalysis of the phenomenon in terms of the more normal sisterhood as defined here.

   [19] One possible solution is to simply define dominance as uninterrupted sequences of immediate dominance relations (essentially axiom A3, using immediate dominance, rather than the dominance relation). Such a characterization, however, runs afoul of axiom A1, where dominance is defined as reflexive. Since, from a set-theoretic perspective, the edge set cannot contain pairs of the form $\langle x, x \rangle$, we will never be able to capture the reflexive character of dominance using graph-theoretic terms. I leave this problem aside here.

(17)

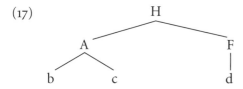

In (17), one member of the set, *d*, is not dominated by A. As such the set {b, c, d} is *not* exhaustively dominated by A and not a constituent. The reverse situation is seen in (18):

(18)

While it is the case that in (18) *b*, *c*, and *d* are all dominated by A, there is also the node *g*, which is not a member of the {b, c, d}, so the set {b, c, d} is not exhaustively dominated by A and is again not a constituent (although the set {b, c, d, g} is). On a more intuitive level, exhaustive domination holds between a set of nodes and their mother. Only when the entire set and only that set are immediately dominated by their mother can we say that the mother exhaustively dominates the set. Constituency[20] can then be defined in terms of exhaustive domination:

(19)   *Constituent*
       A set of nodes exhaustively dominated by a single node.

This ends our discussion of the up and down dominance axis of syntactic trees. We now turn to the precedence (left-to-right relation) in trees.

3.4 Precedence

3.4.1 *Intuitive characterizations of precedence*

In some approaches, syntactic trees do not only encode the hierarchical organization of sentences, they also encode the linear order of the constituents. Linear order refers to the order in which words are spoken or written (left to right, if you are writing in English) or precedence. While precedence is intuitively "what is said first" or "what is written on the left" (assuming one writes from left to right), formalizing this relationship turns out to be more difficult. First,

---

[20] The term "constituent" must be distinguished from "constituent of", which boils down to domination: B is a constituent of A if and only if A dominates B.

consider two nodes that are in a dominance relation, but one appears physically to the left of the other on the page:

(20)

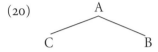

A appears to the left of B, but we wouldn't want to say that A precedes B. The reason for this should be obvious on an intuitive level. Remember, domination is a containment relation. If A contains B, there is no obvious way in which A could be to the left of B. If you have a box, and the box has a ball in it, you can not say that the box is to the left of the ball—that is physically impossible! The box surrounds the ball. The same holds true for dominance. You can not both dominate and precede/follow.[21] Part of any formal definition of precedence will have to exclude this possibility. For the moment we will call this restriction the exclusivity condition:

(21)   *The exclusivity condition*
        If A and B are in a precedence relation with each other, then A cannot dominate B, and B cannot dominate A.

We'll integrate this into our definition of precedence shortly.

The second problem with an intuitive left to right definition has to do with badly drawn trees like (22):

(22)

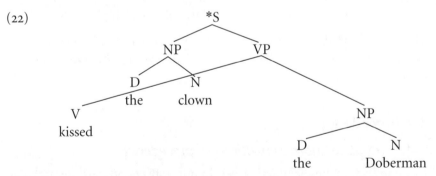

If we ignore the dominance relations, the verb *kissed* actually appears to the left of the noun *clown*. However, we wouldn't want to say that

---

[21] A simpler way to encode this would be to replace the exclusivity condition with the requirement that only terminals participate in the precedence relations. However, if we did this then we would have no way to, for example, say that the subject NP precedes the VP, as these are non-terminal nodes. Since making reference to the precedence relations among non-terminals is useful, I will stick to the more complicated definition based on exclusion of dominance between sets of nodes that hold the precedence relation.

kissed precedes *clown*; this is clearly wrong. The sentence is "The clown kissed the Doberman," where *kissed* follows *clown*. A related problem occurs in well-drawn trees such as (23):

(23)

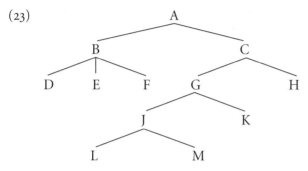

Does J precede F? It is not to the right of F nor to the left of it. L is similar to *kissed* in (22). It appears to the left of F, but most syntacticians would understand it to follow F. Precedence appears to be at least partly dependent upon the dominance relation, and cannot be defined without dominance. To see this is true, take the tree in (23) again, but this time draw a box[22] from L all the way up to the root node, surrounding only the lines and nodes that dominate L. This box represents all the nodes that dominate L; as such they aren't in a precedence relation without L. All the nodes to the left of this box precede L; all the nodes to the right of the box follow L.

(23′)

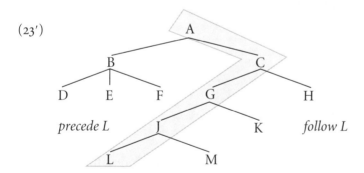

Clearly, the dominance relation plays a crucial role in defining precedence. You need to know what nodes dominate some node A in order to tell what nodes precede or follow A. For example, L follows F in (23) because G and C, which are dominators of L, follow F. The easiest way to define precedence is by appealing to the most local of dominance

---

[22] Thanks to Dave Medeiros for suggesting this heuristic technique to me.

relations (immediate dominance) in combination with the orderings of elements among sisters. We will assume that sisters are always ordered left to right on a single line, so problems like those in trees like (22) will not arise. This ordering is a primitive.[23] We might call the relation in question here sister-precedence.[24]

(24) *Sister Precedence* ($\prec_s$)
      Node A sister-precedes node B if and only if both are immediately dominated by the same node M, and A emerges from a branch from M that is to the left of the branch over B.

General precedence, then, can be defined parasitically on sister precedence:

(25) *Precedence* ($\prec$) Node A precedes node B if and only if
      (i) neither A dominates B nor B dominates A *and*
      (ii) some node E dominating A sister-precedes some node F dominating B (because domination is reflexive, E may equal A and F may equal B, but they need not do so).

Recall our badly drawn tree in (22). There is a node, NP (= E in the definition above), which dominates the N *clown*, and that NP sister-precedes the VP (= F), which in turn dominates V *kissed* (NP). Therefore N *clown* precedes V *kissed*.

This definition (in particular part ii) also derives a typical restriction on syntactic structure: branches may not cross. So trees like that in (26) are disallowed.

(26)

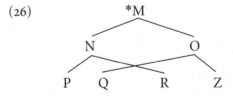

In this tree, Q is written to the left of R, apparently preceding R, but by the definition of precedence given above, this tree is ruled out. Q is to the left of R, but O, *which dominates* Q, is sister-preceded by N. In other words, branches may not cross. We will revisit this issue in Chapter 10.

---

[23] But might be due to the ordering in the phrase structure rule or other generative principle of linearization.

[24] Sister-precedence is a relation that captures the exhaustive constant partial ordering (ECPO) insight of GPSG (Gazdar, Klein, Pullum, and Sag 1983), where precedence relations hold only in local trees and between local trees.

3.4.2 Immediate precedence

There is also the local form of precedence: immediate precedence:[25]

(27)   *Immediate precedence*

A immediately precedes B if A precedes B and there is no node G
that follows A but precedes B.

Consider the string given in (28) (assume that the nodes dominating
this string meet all the criteria set out in (25)):

(28)   A   B   G

In this linear string, A immediately precedes B, because A precedes B
and there is nothing in between them. Contrast this with (29):

(29)   A   G   B

In this string, A does *not* immediately precede B. It does precede B, but
G intervenes between them, so the relation is not immediate.

Note that immediate precedence and sister precedence are different
relations. This can be seen by looking at the tree in (30):

(30)

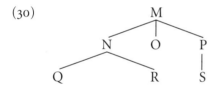

Each of the following pairs of nodes expresses a sister precedence
relation: $\prec_s = \{\langle Q, R\rangle, \langle N, O\rangle, \langle N, P\rangle, \langle O, P\rangle\}$. The set of immediate
precedence relations is different: $\{\langle Q, R\rangle, \langle N, O\rangle, \langle O, P\rangle, \langle R, O\rangle,$
$\langle O, S\rangle\}$. R immediately precedes O, but it does not sister-precede it.
Similarly, N sister-precedes P but does not immediately precede it.

3.4.3 Axioms of precedence

With these definitions in mind, we can now define the properties of
these trees axiomatically using first-order logic. First, we need to add

---

[25] To my knowledge there is no standard symbol for the immediate precedence relation.
One might extend the * notation so that $\prec^*$ means "general precedence" and $\prec$ is limited
to "immediate precedence". For the purposes of this book, we will keep with the standard
usage of $\prec$ as general precedence. See Zwicky (1986b) for an argument from Finnish that
immediate precedence is the more important relation.

the precedence relation[26], [27] to the parts of the mathematical description of trees (6):

(6) (e) the binary precedence relation P ($\prec$) on N.

This relation is, of course, constrained by several axioms. First, like dominance, the relation is transitive:

A6. *P is transitive*: ($\forall xyz \in N$) [(($x \prec y$) & ($y \prec z$)) → ($x \prec z$)].

That is, if A precedes B and B precedes C, then A precedes C. This rules out graphs such as (31), where the arrow means "appears to the left of" even though on the page it actually appears to the right:

(31) * A → B → C

This would be the impossible situation where A is said before B; B is said before C, yet C is said before A.

We also need to exclude the possibility that a node A both precedes and follows another B. (I am assuming that we can not say two different words at the same time[28]), as in (32) where the arrows indicate "appear to the left of":

---

[26] As we will see in Chapter 8, Kayne (1994) argues that the precedence relation can be reduced to asymmetric c-command, and thus need not be part of our formal description of tree structures. We leave this aside here.

[27] Terry Langendoen (p.c.) has suggested that a different characterization of precedence than the one given here actually allows one to derive a certain number of these axiomatic statements. Langendoen's proposal is that terminal nodes are specified for a *span*. This consists of a pair of numbers, the first is the "begin" integer, the second is the "end" integer. The two numbers are linked with the symbol $^\wedge$. The left-most terminal is specified for the span $0{^\wedge}1$, the next to its immediate right is $1{^\wedge}2$, etc. The rightmost terminal is $(n-1){^\wedge}n$. A node N with k daughters spans $m_0{^\wedge}m_k$ if and only if N's daughters span $m_0{^\wedge}m_1 \ldots m_{k-1}{^\wedge}m_k$. The no-crossing constraint is the requirement that every node in the tree have a span in this sense. Immediately precedes is defined as the relation that holds between nodes A and B, when the *end*(A) = *begin*(B). Precedes is simply the case where *end*(A) $\leq$ *begin*(B). The fact that precedence represents a strict ordering (i.e. is irreflexive, asymmetric and transitive) falls out naturally from this definition. Langendoen even suggests that domination can be defined in terms of these spans, where the span of a dominator contains the spans of the daughters. For example, if A dominates B, then *begin* (A) $\leq$ *begin*(B) & *end*(A) $\leq$ *end*(B). This proposal is an interesting alternative. I do not have the space here, however, to consider what empirical advantage (if there is one) it has over the more usual relation specified in the main body of the text.

[28] This assumes, of course, a purely acoustic medium for language. In principle, although it doesn't appear to happen in practice (Senghas p.c.), in a signed language one might be able to sign two words simultaneously.

(32)   *   A ⇄ B

As such, precedence is asymmetric:

A7.   *P is asymmetric:* $(\forall xy \in N)[((x \prec y) \rightarrow \neg(y \prec x)]$.

It follows from this, then, that precedence is not reflexive (T1), because if you were allowed to precede yourself, then you would also be allowed to follow yourself. This situation would be contradictory to (A7).

T1.   *P is irrreflexive:* $(\forall x \in N) [\neg(x \prec x)]$.

One hypothesis about the relations P and D is that they, taken together, represent a total ordering of the elements in the set N. As such, we claim that P and D are mutually exclusive (if *x* precedes *y*, *x* cannot dominate *y* and vice versa). This was encoded in part (i) of the definition of precedence given in (25), we restate this here as (A8):

A8.   *Exclusivity condition:*[29] $(\forall xy \in N) [((x \prec y) \lor (y \prec x)) \leftrightarrow \neg$
       $((x \vartriangleleft^* y) \lor (y \vartriangleleft^* x))]$.

The second part of the definition of precedence given in (25) can also be viewed axiomatically. This is the so-called non-tangling condition of Wall (1972), which derives a basic assumption of Chomsky (1975): there are no discontinuous constituents.[30]

A9.   *Non-tangling condition:* $(\forall wxyz \in N) [((w \prec_s x) \,\&\, (w \vartriangleleft^* y)$
       $\&\, (x \vartriangleleft^* z)) \rightarrow (y \prec z)]$.

Schematically, (A9) represents a structure like that in (33a), not the one in (33b), thus ruling out crossing lines.[31]

---

[29] Zwicky and Isard (1963) originally state this as a condition whereby precedence is defined only over sisters.

[30] Higginbotham (1985) states this constraint over terminals (I have rephrased his formulation slightly here):

(i) $x \prec y \leftrightarrow x \vartriangleleft^* u$ and $y \vartriangleleft^* v$ jointly imply $u \prec v$ for all terminals *u, v*.

In Carnie (2006c), I informally present the non-tangling constraint as the no-crossing-branches constraint:

(ii) *No-crossing-branches constraint*

   If one node X precedes another node Y then X and all nodes dominated by X must precede Y and all nodes dominated by Y.

   See also Gärtner (2002) and references therein.

[31] The prohibition against crossing lines is also found in autosegmental phonology. See Goldsmith (1976), McCarthy (1979), Pulleyblank (1983), Clements (1985), Sagey (1986, 1988), and Hammond (1988, 2005) for discussion.

(33) (a) 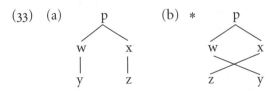 (b) *

Interestingly, this condition also rules out multiply mothered nodes such as that represented in (34) (which we ruled out using (A5) in in section 3.3.2):

(34) *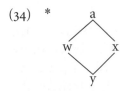

For the purposes of (A9), $y = z$ in (34) (that is, y is dominated by w, y is dominated by x, and w precedes x). According to (A9) then, this entails that $y \prec y$ for (34). However, this is in direct contradiction to (T1), which disallows nodes from preceding themselves. Therefore, (34) is ruled out by a combination of (A9) and (T1) (which itself follows from the more basic (A7)). As such, (A5) is a superfluous part of the description of tree structures and can be omitted from our axiomization.

3.5 Concluding remarks

The discussion in this chapter has characterized the two most basic relations in tree-based constituency representations, dominance and precedence, using an axiomization cast in terms of first order logic and set theory. This gives us a precise starting point for comparing various approaches to constituency. The primary relation is dominance, which expresses the containment properties of hierarchical constituency. Precedence is defined relative to dominance relations. We looked at a number of axiomatic properties of these relations. While many of these are universally assumed, some are not. For example, we will see in later chapters that the requirements of single rootedness, single motherhood, the ban on crossing lines, the ban on acyclic graphs all have their detractors. Indeed, it is the issue of interpreting these basic notions that often lies at the heart of the fundamental differences among syntactic frameworks. In the later chapters of this book, we examine the various mechanisms at work in determining constituent structure, and we will see all of these properties questioned.

The next chapter continues the investigation of the structural properties of trees. In particular, it looks at the relations of c-command and government, which are parasitic on dominance. These relations are mostly used by the Chomskyan Principles and Parameters framework, but the generalizations they express are common to many other approaches as well.

4

Second Order Relations:
C-command and Government

4.1 Introduction

The previous chapter dealt with the basic structural relations of dominance and precedence, which gave the tree a total ordering. The focus of this chapter is on two structural relations that are derived from dominance: c-command and its local variant, government.

For the most part, this book is not limited to a single theoretical approach and c-command and government are for the most part limited to versions of Chomskyan generative grammar (in particular Government and Binding theory and Minimalism). Nevertheless, these are influential ideas about the role of constituent structure, so it is worth discussing them here.

4.2 Command, kommand, c-command, and m-command

We start by looking at several versions of the command relation. These relations are generally motivated by various kinds of antecedent–anaphor and filler–gap (e.g. a displaced item and its trace) relationship.

Let us stage the discussion first in terms of antecedent-anaphor and antecedent pronoun-relations. Again, I assume some basic knowledge of the theory of binding.[1] The discussion is phrased in terms of Chomsky's (1981) binding theory, although it could easily be recast in other theoretical frameworks. The term "bound" is taken to mean that the element under consideration is coindexed with some other NP that bears some particular structural relation to it. Which structural relation is relevant lies at the heart of this section of this chapter.

---

[1] A quick review of the chapters on binding theory in any beginning-syntax book should suffice to bring the reader up to speed for this discussion.

I assume a filter (well-formedness) constraint version of the binding theory, very loosely construed with the following conditions:

(1) *Condition A*: Anaphors must be bound within their binding domain (roughly clause and NP).
Condition B: Pronouns must not be bound within their binding domain.
Condition C: Referential expressions (R-expressions) must not be bound.

These conditions are, without a doubt, gross oversimplifications of the complex phenomena of NP interpretation (see, for example, the discussion in the papers contained in the recent collection edited by Barss 2002), but they suffice for the purposes of explicating the various structural relations we will examine. For the most part, the conditions that will be most helpful to us here are conditions B and C.

4.2.1 Command and kommand (cyclic command)

Langacker[2, 3] (1966) observed an asymmetry between complex NPs in subject and object position. When dealing with simple NPs, R-expressions are disallowed in object position when they are coreferent to any kind of subject NP (2) (i.e., speaking anachronistically, they constitute a condition-C violation.)

(2) (a) *He$_i$ loves Sam$_i$.
(b) *Sam$_i$ loves Sam$_i$.
(c) *The man$_i$ loves Sam$_i$.

When the antecedent is embedded inside a relative clause on the subject NP, however, the coreference becomes acceptable (3):

(3) Anyone who meets him$_i$ instantly loves Sam$_i$.

To explain this phenomenon, Langacker observes that there is a structural distinction between the position of the antecedent *him* in the sentences in (2) and (3). He couches this in the notion of command:

(4) *Command*: Node A commands B, if the first S (Sentence) node dominating[4] A also dominates B.

---

[2] See also Ross (1967) who extends command to scope of negation.

[3] Langacker was actually discussing the transformational rule of pronominalization. The differences between a rule-based and constraint-based approach need not concern us here; see Chomsky and Lasnik (1977) for discussion.

[4] Or, more accurately, properly dominating.

To see how this explains the contrast between (2) and (3), consider the two trees in (5) and (6):

(5)

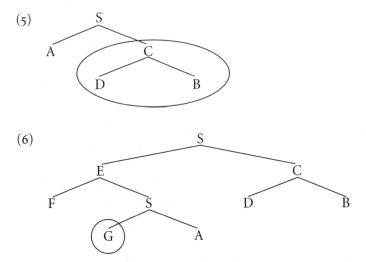

(6)

Abstractly, (5) represents the sentences in (2). Tree (6) represents the sentence in (3). The circled nodes represent those commanded by A. We can see that in (5), B is commanded by A. If A = *he*, and B = *Sam*, we see the difference between the two sentences. In the ungrammatical sentences in (2), A commands B. In the grammatical (3), A does not command B. There seems to be a restriction that R-expressions may not be commanded by a coreferent antecedent, but R-expressions that are not in this configuration are okay.

Command by itself is not sufficient, however. Consider the nodes commanded by B in (7):

(7)

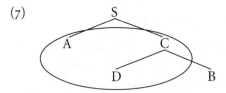

The set of nodes commanded by B according to the definition in (4) include A. This means that just as A commands B, B also commands A. This would predict that R-expressions would not be allowed in subject position when coreferent with an object either, contrary to fact:

(8)   Sam$_i$ loves himself$_i$.

To explain this,[5] Langacker combines command with the precedence relation: R-expressions must not be both preceded by and commanded by a coindexed NP. Anachronistically speaking, we can say that the binding conditions under this view use this compound "command and precede" relation.

Wasow (1972) and Jackendoff (1972) both observed that the command relationship must be expanded to include other possible dominators than S. The asymmetries found with relative clauses are also found in complex NPs. While an R-expression may not corefer to a nominative pronoun in subject position (9a), it may corefer to a genitive pronoun (9b). *His* in (9b) commands *Sam* according to the definition in (4), as they are both dominated by the same S node:

(9)   (a)   *He$_i$ loves Sam$_i$.
      (b)   His$_i$ father loves Sam$_i$.

In the Extended Standard Theory of the 1970s, the nodes S and NP were considered to define *transformational cycles*, which were domains of application of certain rules, and which derived certain kinds of rule ordering. Wasow and Jackendoff both extend command to include NP as well as S in defining the command relationship. This special kind of cyclic command was called **kommand** by Lasnik (1976).

(10)   *Kommand*: Node A kommands B, if the first cyclic node (S or NP) dominating A also dominates B.

Kommand explains (9b), in that the NP dominating *his* does not dominate *Sam*, so *his* does not kommand *Sam*.

4.2.2 C-command (constituent command)

In her influential (1976) dissertation, Reinhart suggests that an entirely different notion of command is relevant to the study of nominal interpretation. Her proposal removes the reference to categories (S and NP) in command, and at the same time eliminates the need to refer to precedence in conjunction with command. Reinhart observes that the compound relation "command and precede" (or, more accurately, "kommand and precede") fails to account for the acceptability of

---

[5] More accurately, to predict the behavior of the reflexivization and pronominalization rules that Langacker uses.

co-reference when there is any kind of branching above the antecedent that does not also dominate the R-expression (Reinhart 1983):

(11)   Near him$_i$, Dan$_i$ saw a snake.

In this sentence, the NP *him* is not dominated by another NP, so the first cyclic node dominating [$_{NP}$ *him*] is the S node; this node also dominates *Dan*. *Dan* is thus kommanded and preceded by *him*.

(12)

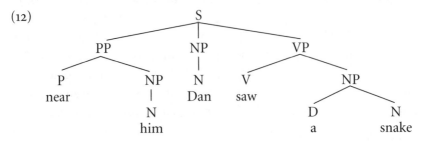

Such a configuration should trigger a condition C violation. However the sentence is grammatical. It appears as if any branching—not just NP or S nodes—above the antecedent blocks the kommand relation.

The fact that kommand is typically used in combination with precedence is also suspicious. In English, the trees branch to the right. This means that material lower in the tree is usually preceded by material higher in the tree. Consider the following facts of Malagasy, a VOS language, where the branching is presumably leftwards (data from Reinhart 1983: 47, attributed to Ed Keenan):

(13)   (a)   namono   azy   ny   anadahin-dRakoto
              kill   him   the   sister-of-Rakoto
              "Rakoto$_i$'s sister killed him$_i$."

        (b)   *namono   ny   anadahin-dRakoto   izy
               kill   the   sister-of-Rakoto   he
               "He$_i$ killed Rakoto$_i$'s sister."

Under the "kommand and precede" version of the binding conditions we predict the reverse grammaticality judgments. In (13a), *azy* "him" both precedes and kommands *Rakoto*, so by condition C, coreference here should be impossible, contrary to fact. The unacceptability of (13b) is not predicted to be a condition C violation under the 'kommand and precede' either, since *izy* does not precede *Rakoto*.[6]

---

[6] Nor is it a condition B violation, since *Rakoto* is in a different cyclic domain (NP) than the pronoun.

These kinds of facts motivate Reinhart's "c-command" (or constituent command[7]), which eliminates reference to both precedence and cyclic nodes. I give first an informal definition here.

(14)   *C-command (informal)*
        A node c-commands its sisters and all the daughters (and grand-daughters and great-granddaughters, etc.) of its sisters.

Consider the tree in (15). The node A c-commands all the nodes in the circle. It doesn't c-command any others:

(15)

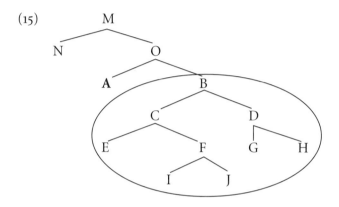

That is, A c-commands its sister (B) and all the nodes dominated by its sister (C, D, E, F, G, H, I, J). Consider the same tree, but look at the nodes c-commanded by G:

(16)

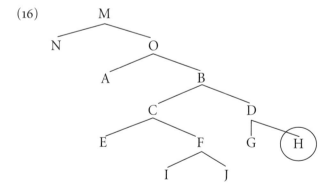

G c-commands only H (its sister). Notice that it does not c-command C, E, F, I, or J. C-command is a relation that holds between sisters and among the daughters of its sister (nieces). It never holds between cousins (daughters of two distinct sisters) or between a mother and daughter.

---

[7] Barker and Pullum (1990) attribute the name to G. N. Clements.

The c-command relation is actually composed of two smaller relations (which we will—somewhat counter-intuitively—define in terms of the larger relation). The first is the sisterhood relation or symmetric c-command:

(17)   *Symmetric c-command*
        A symmetrically c-commands B, if A c-commands B and B c-commands A.

Asymmetric c-command is the kind that holds between an aunt and her nieces:

(18)   *Asymmetric c-command*
        A asymmetrically c-commands B if A c-commands B but B does not c-command A.

Consider again the tree in (16) (repeated here as (19)):

(19)

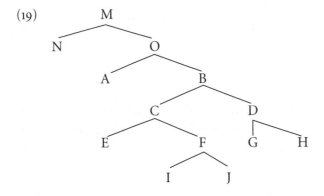

In this tree, N and O symmetrically c-command each other (as do all other pairs of sisters). However, N asymmetrically c-commands A, B, C, D, E, F, G, H, I, and J, since none of these c-command N.

Now that we have established the basic flavor of the c-command relation, let us consider the proper formalization of this configuration. Reinhart's original definition is given in (20):[8]

---

[8] Chomsky's (1981: 166) actual formulation is:

A c-commands B if
(i) A does not contain B;
(ii) Suppose that $s_1, \ldots, s_n$ is the maximal sequence such that
    (a) $s_n = A$;
    (b) $s_i = A^j$;
    (c) s_i immediately dominates s_{i+1}.
Then if C dominates A, then either (I) C dominates B, or (II) $C = s_i$ and s_1 dominates B.

(20)   Node A c-commands node B if neither A nor B dominates the
       other and the first branching node dominating A dominates
       B. (Reinhart 1976: 32)

There are a couple things to note about this definition. First observe
that it is defined in terms of (reflexive) domination. It should be
obvious that non-reflexive proper domination is necessary. Consider
again the tree in (19), this time focusing on the node C. If domination
is reflexive, then the first node that dominates C is C itself. This means
that C would *not* c-command D, G, and H, contrary to what we want.
As such, c-command needs to be cast as proper domination, so that the
first branching node dominating C is B, which correctly dominates D,
G, and H. Following Richardson and Chametzky (1985) we can amend
(20) to (21):

(21)   Node A c-commands node B if neither A nor B dominates the other
       and the first branching node properly dominating A dominates B.

   Next consider how we formalize the notion of aunt/sisterhood. In
Reinhart's definition the terminology "first branching node" is used.
As Barker and Pullum (1990) note, neither the notions of "first" nor
"branching" are properly (or easily) defined. But let us assume for the
moment that we give these terms their easiest and intended meaning:
"first" means nearest in terms of domination relations, "branching"
means at least two branches emerge from the node. Somewhat surprisingly, under such a characterization in the following tree, A
c-commands C, D, and E:

(22)

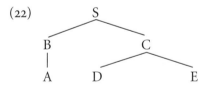

Because B does not branch binarily, S is the first branching node dominating A, and S also dominates C. There is at least one theory-internal
reason why we would want to restrict A from c-commanding C. Assume,
following Travis (1984), that head-movement relations (movement from a
head into another head) are subject to a constraint that the moved element
must c-command its trace. If the configuration described in (20) is a
c-command relation, then verbs, tense, etc., should be able to head-move
into the head of their subject NPs (i.e. A), since this position c-commands

the base position of these elements. In order to limit the scope of c-commanded relations to the more usual notion based on sisterhood and aunthood, the definition in (23) is closer to common current usage:

(23)   *C-command*
        Node A c-commands node B if every node properly dominating A also properly dominates B, and neither A nor B dominate the other.

This definition corresponds more closely to our intuitive definition above, and is consistent with (the inverse of) Klima's (1964) "in construction with" relation (Barker and Pullum 1990).

There is one additional clause in (23) that we have not yet discussed. This is the phrase "and neither A nor B dominate the other." Assume for the moment that this clause was not part of the definition. Even with the condition that c-command is defined in terms of proper domination rather than domination, in (19), C c-commands its own daughters. The mother of C, B, dominates not only D, G, and H, but also C, E, F, I, and J, so C c-commands its own daughters. This again goes against our intuitive aunt/sister understanding of c-command. It also has negative empirical consequences. Consider the situation where the antecedent of an NP is inside the NP itself (such as *[NP *his*$_i$ *friend*]$_i$). Under this definition of c-command, [*his friend*] binds [*his*]. There is a circularity here that one wishes to avoid. This kind of sentence is typically ruled out by a different constraint in Chomsky's Government and Binding (GB) framework (the *i*-within-*i* condition). However, we can rule it out independently with the condition "neither A nor B dominate the other." This restriction was not originally in place to limit i-within-i constructions, but to limit the behavior of government—a structural relation parasitic on c-command (see below). Nevertheless it also has the desired effect here.

Notice that although they both seem to restrict the same kind of behavior (induced by reflexivity), both the proper domination and "neither A nor B dominate the other" restrictions are independently necessary. The proper dominance restriction is required to ensure that a node can c-command out of itself (this is true whether the neither/nor restriction holds or not, since what is at stake here is not a restriction on what nodes A cannot dominate, but a means of ensuring that A c-commands more than its own daughters). By contrast, the neither/nor restriction limits a node from c-commanding the nodes it dominates, and from c-commanding its own dominators. Put another way, there are really three distinct entities involved in c-command, the c-commander, the c-commandee, and the branching dominator. Proper dominance is a condition on the nature of only the last of these: the branching dominator (proper dominance excluding the c-commander from this role). By contrast, the neither/nor restriction limits the other two (the c-commander and the c-commandee), by insuring they are not related to each other via domination. In other words, these two parts of the definition work in tandem: proper dominance is required to *allow* a branching node to c-command outside of itself; the neither/nor restriction, on the other hand, *prevents* that node from commanding either the nodes that dominate it or the nodes it dominates.

4.2.3 Deriving and explaining c-command

C-command seems to be a very different beast from the relations of precedence and dominance. It is a second-order relation, defined through dominance; one must have a notion of dominance before it is possible to define c-command.[9] Next observe that while the underlying motivations for precedence and dominance are clear (precedence reflects the necessary ordering of speech, and dominance reflects the compositional function of phrase structure), c-command is more mysterious. Why would language refer to such a notion? There are, to my knowledge, four attempts in the literature to "derive" or "explain" the c-command relation in terms of other parts of the grammatical system: Kayne's (1984) unambiguous paths; Chametzky's (1996) complete factorization; and Epstein's c-command-as-merge approach and Medeiros' (2008) account in terms of packing. We look at the first three of these here, and return to the fourth in chapter 12.

Kayne (1984) proposes that the c-command relation reduces to a special kind of bi-directional dominance called a "path". Look at the tree in (24). You will see that there is a direct path up and down the tree starting at E and ending at A, with a change of direction at B. This path is indicated by the dotted line.

(24)

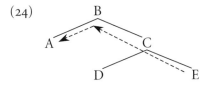

The path in (24) is unambiguous: assuming that paths cannot backtrack on themselves, when the path starts its downwards direction at node B it has no choice but to continue to A. Contrast this with the tree in (25)

(25)

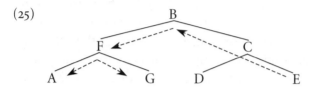

The path from E is ambiguous, at node F we have a choice between continuing the path to A or on to G. In (24) A c-commands E; this is equivalent to saying that there is an unambiguous path from E to A. In (25), A does not c-command E; there is no unambiguous path from E to A. Kayne suggests recasting all c-command relationships in terms of unambiguous paths. The formal definitions of path is as follows (Kayne 1984:132):

(26) *Path*
     Let a path P (in tree T) be a sequence of nodes $(A_0, \ldots, A_i, A_{i+1}, \ldots A_n)$ such that:
     (a) $\forall ij, n \geq i, j \geq 0, A_i = A_j \rightarrow i = j$.
     (b) $\forall i, n > i \geq 0, A_i$ immediately dominates A_{i+1} or A_{i+1} immediately dominates A_i.

Part (a) stipulates that paths cannot double back on themselves; the path is a sequence of distinct nodes. Part (b) requires that the path be a sequence of adjacent (or more accurately sub- and superjacent) nodes.
    The formal definition of unambiguous path is given in (84) (Kayne 1984:134):

(27) *Unambiguous Path*
     An unambiguous path T is a path $P = (A_0, \ldots, A_i, A_{i+1}, \ldots A_n)$ such that $\forall i, n > i \geq 0$:
     (a) if A_i immediately dominates A_{i+1}, then A_i immediately dominates no node in T other than A_{i+1}, with the exception of A_{i-1};
     (b) if A_i is immediately dominated by A_{i+1}, then A_i is immediately dominated by no node in T other than A_{i+1}.

In other words, if, when tracing a path, one is never forced to make a choice between two unused branches, both pointing in the same direction, then you have an unambiguous path.

Kayne notes that c-command and unambiguous paths differ in how many branches are allowed in constituent structure. In the tree in (28), all the nodes c-command one another, but there is no unambiguous path between any of them, due to the ternary branching.

(28)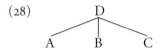

If the unambiguous paths approach is correct, then tree structures—at least those that require reference to paths—must be binary. Binarity is a common assumption in most versions of X-bar theory (see Ch. 7).[10]

Epstein (1999) and Epstein, Groat, Kawashima, and Kitahara (1998)[11] develop a closely related explanation for c-command (although seemingly in ignorance of Kayne 1984, since they never cite him, even when discussing other explanations for c-command). Epstein et al.'s approach is couched in a hyperderivational version of minimalist Bare-Phrase Structure theory. In this theory, as we will discuss at length in Chapter 8, there is a binary operation of "merge" that operates cyclically from the bottom of the tree upwards. Merge takes two sets of nodes and combines them together into a single set. For example, given the words *ate* and *geraniums*, the merge operation forms the set {*ate, geraniums*} (corresponding to the [$_{VP}$ *ate geraniums*]). Given the words *the* and *puppy*, merge forms the set {*the, puppy*} (=[$_{NP}$ *the puppy*]). These two larger sets can be merged to form the set { {*the, puppy*}, {*ate, geraniums*}} (=[$_S$ [$_{NP}$ *The puppy*] [$_{VP}$ *ate geraniums*]]). For Epstein et al., c-command is a reflection of this derivational structure-building operation. A node only c-commands those nodes that are dominated by nodes it is merged with during the course of the derivation. The whole NP [*the puppy*] c-commands *geraniums*, since it is merged with the set containing *geraniums*. But the node *puppy* does not c-command *geraniums*, because it is never directly merged with *geraniums*. This appears to be a notational variant of Kayne's approach, but one where the unambiguous path is determined by the derivation that creates the structure. More particularly, the c-command relationship represents the inputs to the merger

---

[10] Binarity finds a different origin in both Minimalism and Categorial Grammar. The operations that define constituency in these systems take an open function and find an argument to complete it. This pairwise derivation of compositionality naturally results in binarity. See Chametzky (2000) and Dowty (1996) for discussion.

[11] See also the related work of Kaneko (1999).

operation, and the dominance relationship represents the structure built from the merger operation.

Chametzky (1996) and Richardson and Chametzky (1985) provide a very different explanation for c-command in terms of the minimal factorization of the constituent structure of a sentence. In (29) (taken from Chametzky 2000: 45), the nodes B, E, and F are the only nodes that c-command G:

(29)

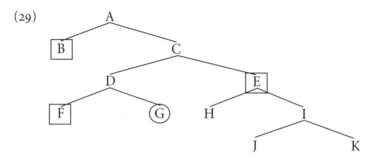

Chametzky (2000: 45) describes the approach as follows:

> {F, E, B} provides the minimal factorization of the phrase-marker [AC: phrase marker = tree] with respect to G. That is, there is no other set of nodes which is smaller than . . . {F, E, B} which when unioned with G provides a complete non-redundant constituent analysis of the phrase marker.

In other words, given any node in the tree, the set of all nodes that c-command it represent the other constituents in the tree and exclude no part of the tree. C-command thus follows from the fact that trees are organized hierarchically.

I am not going to try to choose among these explanations of c-command here. It is not clear to me that we will ever be able to empirically distinguish among them. It seems that the criteria for distinguishing these approaches are either metatheoretical or theory-internal. I leave it to the readers to decide for themselves whether the issue is an important one, and which of the approaches meets their personal tastes.

4.2.4 M-command

There is one other variation on c-command that I mention here for completeness. This version was introduced by Aoun and Sportiche (1983) (for a dissenting voice see Saito 1984), and has come to be known as m-command.[12] It differs from the standard definition in

---

[12] However, Aoun and Sportiche call it "c-command".

replacing "branching node" or "every node" with "maximal category":

(30) *M-command*
      Node A c-commands node B if every maximal category (XP)
      node properly dominating A also dominates B, and neither A
      nor B dominate the other.

This distinction becomes relevant with X-bar theory (ch. 7), where not
all branching categories are "maximal"—only full complete phrases
obtain this status. Haegeman (1994) gives the following example that
distinguishes c-command from m-command:

(31) I presented Watson$_i$ with a picture of himself$_i$.

Assuming that the constituent structure of the VP in this sentence is
the partly binary branching structure in (32) (the V′ notation will be
explained in Chapter 6):

(32)

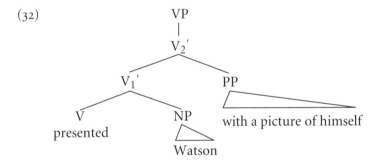

Watson does not c-command *himself* (the node dominating [$_{NP}$ *Watson*]
is V$_1$′, which does not dominate *himself*). However, *Watson* does
m-command *himself*. The maximal category dominating [$_{NP}$ *Watson*]
is the VP, which does dominate *himself*. Haegeman also notes that,
unexpectedly, the c-command relationships between *quit* and *in autumn*
in the following pair of sentences is quite different:

(33) (a) John [$_{VP}$ [$_{V2'}$ [$_{V1'}$ quit [$_{NP}$ his job]] [$_{PP}$ in autumn]]].
      (b) John [$_{VP}$ [$_{V2'}$ [$_{V1'}$ quit] [$_{PP}$ in autumn]]].

In (33a), V$_1$′ branches, so *quit* does not c-command the PP; in (33b) by
contrast, V$_1$′ doesn't branch, and the node dominating it (V$_2$′) also
dominates the PP, meaning *quit* does c-command the PP. This seems
like an unlikely asymmetry. With m-command, however, the relationship between the verb and the PP is identical. The verb m-commands
the PP in both sentences.

Within the Government and Binding (GB) and minimalist approaches to syntactic theory, NPs are licensed by structural Case, which is assigned under a local version of c-command (government; see section 4.3) by some particular node. This is one of the primary motivations for Aoun and Sportiche to introduce m-command. Nominative case is assigned by Infl in the configuration in (34a); genitive case, by a noun in the configuration in (34b).

(34) (a)

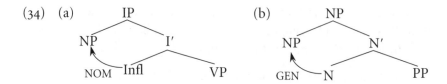

If Case licensing does indeed occur under a c-command-like structural relation, then clearly m-command is most appropriate. In the trees in (34) the case assigning node m-commands—but does not c-command— the NP it assigns case to.

4.2.5 Barker and Pullum (1990): A unified approach to command relations

Barker and Pullum (1990)[13, 14] offer an important contribution to our understanding of command relations and their underlying similarities and differences. They observe that many of the definitions, like those given above of command, are vague and imprecise (such as what precisely is meant by "first" in first branching node). They provide a unified account of all command relationships, and precise typology of the various kinds of command relationships.

Barker and Pullum define all command relationships in terms of various kinds of "upper bounds" determined by various relationships or properties.[15]

---

[13] For a detailed discussion of the mathematical properties of Barker and Pullum's proposal, see Kracht (1993).

[14] In addition, Barker and Pullum also observe a number of formal properties of command relations, including the interrelationships between various kinds of command. See the original work for details.

[15] Note that Barker and Pullum's definitions do not include the neither/nor condition discussed in section 4.5.3. They claim to see no empirical reason for it. They do not discuss the i-within-i facts. It is a relatively minor change to fix their definitions so that it includes this condition.

(35)   The set of upper bounds for *a* with respect to a property *P* (writ-
        ten UB(a, P)) is given by UB(a, P) = { b | b ◁⁺ a & P(b) }

That is, some node *b* is an upper bound for *a*, if *b* properly dominates
a, and satisfies property *P*. Most command relationships actually refer
to the minimal upper bounds (MUB):

(36)   MUB(a, P) ={ b | b ∈ UB(a, P) & ∀x [(x ∈ UB(a, P) & b ◁* x)
        → (b = x)] }

(This is an antisymmetricity requirement: *b* is a minimal upper bound
for *a* if *b* is an upper bound for *a* satisfying *P*, and if for all nodes *x* that
are upper bounds for *a*, if *b* (reflexively) dominates *x*, then *b* is
identical to *x*.) As such, command relations will be defined in terms
of types of relationships between that node and some (minimal)
dominator of that node.

    Command relations are defined as pairs of nodes, both of which are
dominated by the same upper bounds relative to some property P:

(37)   C_P = { <a, b>: ∀x [(x ∈ MUB(a, P)) → x ◁* b] }

The command domain of some node *a* is the set of nodes with which it
is paired, relative to some MUB as defined by property P. What is left to
define is the nature of the property P. This will vary depending upon
the type of command relationship that is involved.

    Langacker's command is defined in terms of S nodes. So the defining
relation is:

(38)   S-command is the command relation C_{P1}, where P1 is given by:
        P1 = {a | LABEL(a) = S}

Although no one has ever limited command to the NP node, Barker
and Pullum state the equivalent relation defined in terms of NPs for
completeness sake:

(39)   NP-command is the command relation C_{P2}, where P2 is given by:
        P2 = {a | LABEL(a) = NP}

Lasnik's kommand is the combination of S-command and NP-command:

(40)   K-command is the command relation C_{P3}, where P3 is given by:
        P3 = {a | LABEL(a) ∈ {S, NP} }

M-command (Barker and Pullum's max-command) assumes the
existence of the set MAX, which is the set of XP categories.

(41)   M-command is the command relation C_{P4}, where P4 is given by:
$$P4 = \{a \mid \text{LABEL}(a) \in \text{MAX}\}$$

Reinhart's original definition of c-command referenced branching nodes, rather than labeled nodes. Barker and Pullum's definition of branching is rather involved. In order to describe branching, one has to reference a treelet—that is, a structure consisting of a mother node and at least two distinct daughters. The mother in this treelet does not have to be the immediate dominator of the c-commanding node, but it does have to reference immediate domination in order to establish the branching relation. Barker and Pullum's definition of immediate dominance (M for mothership) is given in (42):

(42) $M = \{<a, b> \mid (a \vartriangleleft^{+} b) \ \& \ \neg\exists x \ [a \vartriangleleft^{+} x \vartriangleleft^{+} b \ ]\}$
(*a* properly dominates *b*, and there is no node *x*, such that *a* properly dominates *x* and *x* properly dominates *b*).

Branching is defined in the relation P5, where the dominator must be the mother of two distinct nodes:

(43)   C-command is the command relation C_{P5}, where P5 is given by:
$$P5 = \{a \mid \exists xy \ [x \neq y \ \& \ M(a, x) \ \& \ M(a, y)]\}$$

Note that neither *x* nor *y* here must be the c-commander or c-commandee. The node *a* need not immediately dominate these nodes (although it must dominate them), however, *a* must immediately dominate *x* and *y*, which themselves dominate (potentially reflexively) the c-commander and the c-commandee. Note, however, that while c-command is frequently defined in terms of branching nodes, most scholars do not, in practice, require binary (or n-ary) branching. This intuition is captured in the informal definition of c-command given in section 4.2.1.

Barker and Pullum provide an alternative definition based on dominating node, not necessarily branching ones. This is the relationship that Emonds calls "minimal c-command", and is actually the most frequent usage in the literature (although it is the least common definition). Barker and Pullum call this IDC-command (immediate dominance c-command).

(44)   IDC-command is the command relation C_{P6}, where P6 is given by:
$$P6 = N \ (N \text{ the set of nodes})$$

This corresponds to our definition in (23).

4.3 Government

In Chapter 3, we provided local or immediate variants of the structural relations of precedence and dominance. One interpretation of the term "government" provides the local variant of c-command. Government, unsurprisingly, was the central notion in the Government and Binding (GB) framework (Chomsky 1981). It was perhaps the most important structural relation in that theory until the paradigm shift in Chomskyan linguistics known as the Minimalist Program (MP), which started in the early 1990s (however, a relation very similar to government has re-emerged in the Phase-theoretic version of minimalism (Chomsky 2000, 2001, 2004a, b)).

Somewhat confusingly, the term "govern" really has two quite distinct usages in GB theory. The first usage is as a structural relation (essentially local c-command), the second usage is as a licensing condition. In GB theory, all the nodes in a tree must be licensed in order to surface. Licensing occurs when the licensor stands in a government relationship to the element needing licensing. For example, an NP is licensed with Accusative Case, when it stands in a government relationship with a tensed transitive verb (the licensor). In the GB literature, the term "government" is thus used in two distinct (but interrelated ways). We will be concerned here only with the structural relation usage, although the licensing relationships defined using the structural relation serve as the primary evidence for the approach.

There are many definitions of government. I give a typical, but partly incomplete definition:

(45) *Government:* A governs B iff
    a) A c-commands B;
    b) There is no X, such that A c-commands X and X asymmetrically c-commands B.

The workings of this definition can be seen in the trees in (46).

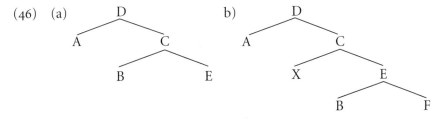

A governs B in (46a) but not in (46b). The node X intervenes blocking A's government of B. The relevant question, of course, is what X is. X can vary depending upon the type of licensing relationship.

This is the "minimality" approach to government (see Rizzi 1989); in earlier versions of government, condition (b) of the definition was given in terms of intervening "barrier" nodes, rather than intervening potential c-commanders. The barrier nodes dominated the c-commanded node rather than c-commanded it. The difference between the two has to do with whether a head can govern into the specifier of its complement (these notions will be explained in Ch. 7; for a textbook treatment of such definitions, see ch. 2 of Haegeman 1994 or, for a more formal definition, see Chomsky 1981).

In early versions of GB theory, X was usually defined as either a lexical head (giving the licensing relationships known variously as head government, lexical government or theta government, depending on the particular restrictions on X) or a co-indexed antecedent element (known as antecedent government). Rizzi (1989) proposed that, for filler–gap dependencies (movement relationships) at least, the nature of X was relativized to the type of relationship that held between the filler and the gap or trace. If the filler and the gap were both heads, then X would be a head. If the filler and the gap were related by an argument relationship (i.e. A-movement, such as NP raising) then X would be an argument, and if the filler and gap were related by an A-bar chain, (such as *wh*-movement), then X is another A-bar element. For a survey of the function of the government relation, see any good GB theory textbook (such as Haegeman 1994 or Cowper 1992). For a discussion of the formal properties of this relation (and how it is technically *not* a c-command relation, narrowly construed) see Barker and Pullum (1990).[16]

---

[16] Their argument is as follows. They start with the assumption that all c-command relationships have the property of "descent". That is, if *a* commands *b* then *a* commands *b*'s descendants. Government by definition lacks this property, so according to Barker and Pullum it is not really a command relationship. It seems to me that this is a matter of terminology. The definitions of immediate relations (e.g. immediate domination) have related properties. That is, if A immediately precedes B, then it does not immediately precede B's followers (although it does precede them). We would not want to say that "immediate" precedence is not "really" precedence, just because it is not transitive; nor should we say that government is not a command relation because it is defined to be a local relation, and does not obey descent. We just need to distinguish between the general relation and the local one. We should also note that descent is a problem for any system (like Chomsky's Phase theory) that is strongly cyclic, since nodes in such a system are not allowed to c-command into lower cycles.

4.4 Concluding remarks

The relations of c-command and government, taken together with the varieties of precedence and dominance discussed in the last chapter, provide us with mechanisms for describing constituent structure in some detail. We have not yet, however, discussed the ways constituent structure might be constructed. Nor have we really discussed what kinds of information constituent structures represent. In the next chapter we turn to one simple mechanism for deriving constituent structures, namely, phrase structure grammars, and begin an investigation of what types of information are encoded in these structures.

Part 2
Phrase Structure Grammars and X-bar Theory

5

Capturing Constituent Structure: Phrase Structure Grammars

5.1 Before the Chomskyan revolution: Conflating semantic and structural relations

The analysis of sentences as structured entities is a very old idea. The discipline of pure logic is based on this intuition. Logic distinguishes between predicates (properties and the relations between entities) and arguments (the participants in the predicate relations). Since predicates and arguments can be represented by strings of words, it follows that a basic notion of constituency can be found in this semantic distinction. We can trace this at least as far back as Apollonius Dyscolus (*c.* AD 200), and probably much earlier to Aristotle.

This idea—that sentential units are defined according to their semantic function—is perhaps one of the most enduring concepts in syntactic analysis. Indeed, today we can observe modern syntactic equivalents of such analyses in the form of dependency or categorial grammars (see Ch. 9). Students learning grammar at schools throughout the Americas are trained to identify constituents according to their semantic function as "subjects", "predicates", or "modifiers". In both the European and American Structuralist traditions of the late nineteenth and early twentieth century, we find similar notions. For example, Saussure (1910; Eng. trans. 1959) discusses syntagmatic relations (which amount to semantically defined relations among words and linear strings of words). Perhaps the most influential analysis of constituency in this tradition[1] was Bloomfield (1933). Bloomfield proposed a system for analyzing sentences into their composite parts

---

[1] I leave aside the lexical bar-notation tradition of Z. Harris (1951), which we will return to in the chapter on X-bar theory.

called *immediate constituent analysis* (IC). IC was not so much a formalized algorithm for segmenting sentences, but was based on the native speaker and linguist's intuitions about semantic relatedness between elements. IC splits sentences into constituents based on how closely the modification relations among the words were. For example, take the diagram in (1) (adapted from Wells 1947: 84), where a sentence has been analyzed into immediate constituents. The greater the number of pipes (|) the weaker the boundary between the constituents (i.e. the more pipes, the more closely related the words).[2] The constituents in this diagram are listed below it.

(1)   The || King ||| of |||| England | open||| ed || parliament.

   Constituents:

   (a) The King of England
   (b) The
   (c) King of England
   (d) King
   (e) of England
   (f) of
   (g) England
   (h) opened
   (i) open
   (j) ed
   (k) opened parliament
   (l) parliament

Pike (1943) criticized Bloomfield's IC system for its vagueness (although see Longacre 1960 for a defense of the vaguer notions). Pike developed a set of discovery procedures (methodologies that a linguist can use to come up with a grammatical analysis), which are very similar to the constituency tests listed in Chapter 2. Harris (1946) (drawing on Aristotelian notions borrowed from logic) refined these tests somewhat by formalizing the procedure of identification of immediate constituents by making reference to *substitution*. That is,

---

[2] The number of pipes should not be taken relativistically. That is, the fact that there are three pipes between *open* and *ed* and four pipes between *of* and *England*, does not mean that *of* and *England* are more closely related than *open* and *ed*. The fact that there are four pipes in the first half has to do with the fact that there are four major morphemes in the NP, and only three in the VP. The number of pipes is determined by the number of ultimate constituents (i.e. morphemes), not by degree of relationship.

if one can substitute a single morpheme of a given type for a string of words, then that string functions as a constituent of the same type. Wells (1947) enriches Harris's system by adding a notion of construction—an idea we will return to in Chapter 9. Harwood (1955) foreshadows Chomsky's work on phrase structure grammars, and suggests that Harris's substitution procedures can be axiomized into formation rules of the kind we will look at in the next section.

Harris's work is the first step away from an analysis based on semantic relations like "subject", "predicate", and "modifier", and towards an analysis based purely in the structural equivalence of strings of words.[3] Harris was Chomsky's teacher and was undoubtedly a major influence on Chomsky's (1957) formalization of phrase structure grammars.

5.2 Phrase structure grammars

In his early unpublished work (the *Logical Structure of Linguistic Theory* (LSLT), later published in 1975), Chomsky first articulates a family of formal systems that might be applied to human language. These are phrase structure grammars (PSGs). The most accessible introduction to Chomsky's PSGs can be found in Chomsky (1957).[4] Chomsky asserts that PSGs are a formal implementation of the structuralist IC analyses. Postal (1967) presents a defense of this claim, arguing that IC systems are all simply poorly formalized phrase structure grammars. Manaster-Ramer and Kac (1990) and Borsley (1996) claim that this is not quite accurate, and there were elements of analysis present in IC that were explicitly excluded from Chomsky's original definitions of PSGs (e.g. discontinuous structures). Nevertheless, Chomsky's formalizations remain the standard against which all other theories are currently measured, so we will retain them here for the moment.

A PSG draws on the structuralist notion that large constituents are replaced by linear adjacent sequences of smaller constituents. A PSG thus represents a substitution operation. This grammar consists of four parts. First we have what is called an *initial symbol* (usually S (= sentence)), which will start the series of replacement operations. Second we have vocabulary of *non-terminal symbols* {A, B, ... }. These

---

[3] Harris's motivation was computerized translation, so the goal was to find objectively detectable characterizations and categorizations instead of pragmatic and semantic notions that required an interaction with the world that only a human could provide.

[4] See Lasnik (2000) for a modern recapitulation of this work, and its relevance today.

symbols may never appear in the final line in the derivation of a sentence. Traditionally these symbols are represented with capital letters (however, later lexicalist versions of PSGs abandon this convention). Next we have a vocabulary of *terminal symbols* {a, b,...}, or "words". Traditionally, these are represented by lower-case letters (again, however, this convention is often abandoned in much recent linguistic work). Finally, we have a set of replacement or production rules (called phrase structure rules or PSRs), which take the initial symbol and through a series of substitutions result in a string of terminals (and only a string of terminals). More formally, a PSG is defined as quadruple (Lewis and Papadimitriou 1981; Rayward-Smith 1995; Hopcroft, Motwani, and Ullman 2001):

(2) $PSG = \langle \mathbb{N}, \mathbb{T}, \mathbb{P}, \mathbb{S} \rangle$
   $\mathbb{N} =$ set of non-terminals
   $\mathbb{T} =$ set of terminals
   $\mathbb{P} =$ set of production rules (PSRs)
   $\mathbb{S} =$ start symbol

The production rules take the form in (3).

(3) $X \rightarrow W\ Y\ Z$

The element on the left is a higher-level constituent replaced by the smaller constituents on the right. The arrow, in this conception of PSG, should be taken to mean "is replaced by" (in other conceptions of PSG, which we will discuss later, the arrow has subtly different meanings).

   Take the toy grammar in (4) as an example:

(4) $\mathbb{N} =$ {A, B, S}, $\mathbb{S} =$ {S}, $\mathbb{T} =$ {a, b},
   $\mathbb{P} =$ (i) $S \rightarrow A\ B$
       (ii) $A \rightarrow A\ a$
       (iii) $B \rightarrow b\ B$
       (iv) $A \rightarrow a$
       (v) $B \rightarrow b$

This grammar represents a very simple language where there are only two words (*a* and *b*), and where sentences consist only of any number of *a*s followed by any number of *b*s. To see how this works, let us do one possible derivation (there are many possibilities) of the sentence *aaab*. We start with the symbol *S*, and apply rule (i).

(5) (a) S
    (b) A   B   rule i

Then we can apply the rule in (v) which will replace the *B* symbol with
the terminal *b*:

    (c) A   b   rule v

Now we can apply rule (ii) which replaces *A* with another *A* and the
terminal *a*:

    (d) A *a* b   rule ii

If we apply it again we get the next line, replacing the *A* in (d) with A
and another *a*:

    (e) A *a a* b   rule ii

Finally we can apply the rule in (iv) which replaces *A* with the single
terminal symbol *a*:

    (f) *a a a* b   rule iv

This is our *terminal string*. The steps in (5a–f) are known as a *derivation*.
   Let's now bring constituent trees into the equation. It is possible to
represent each step in the derivation as a line in a tree, starting at the top.

(6) (a)
    (b)
    (c)
    (d)
    (e)
    (f)

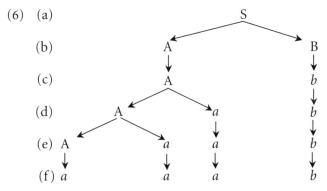

This tree is a little familiar, but is not identical to the trees in Chapters 2
to 4. However, it doesn't take much manipulation to transform it into a
more typical constituent tree. In the derivational tree in (6) the arrows
represent the directional "is a" relation ($\approx$). (That is, S $\approx$ A B sequence. In line (c), A $\approx$ A, and B $\approx$ b. By the conventions we developed in Chapter 3, things at the top of the tree have a directional
"dominance" relation, which is assumed but not represented by
arrows. If we take the "is a" relation to be identical to domination,
then we can delete the directional arrows. Furthermore, if we conflate

the sequences of non-branching identical terminals then we get the tree in (7):

(7)

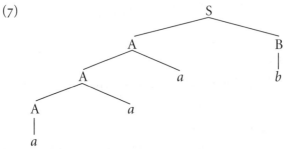

This is the more familiar constituency tree that we have already discussed. What is crucial to understanding this particular conception of PSGs is that the derivational steps of the production correspond roughly to the constituents of the sentence.

Ambiguity in structure results when you have two derivations that do not reduce to the same tree, but have the same surface string. Consider the more complicated toy grammar in (8):

(8) $\mathbb{N}$ = {A, B, S}, $\mathbb{S}$ = {S}, $\mathbb{T}$ = {a, b},
      $\mathbb{P}$ =   (i) S → A B
             (ii) S → A
             (iii) A → A B
             (iv) A → a
             (v) B → b

The sentence *ab* has many possible derivations with this grammar. However, at least two of them result in quite different PS trees. Compare the derivations in (9), (10), and (11):

(9)   (a) S
      (b) A B   (i)
      (c) *a* B   (iv)
      (d) *a* b   (v)

(10)   (a) S
       (b) A B   (i)
       (c) A b   (v)
       (d) *a* b   (iv)

(11)   (a) S
       (b) A   (ii)
       (c) A B   (iii)
       (d) *a* B   (iv)
       (e) *a* b   (v)

The derivations in (9) and (10) give different derivation trees (9′) and (10′), but result in the same constituent structure (12). The derivation in (11) however, reduces to quite a different constituent tree (13).

(9′) (a)

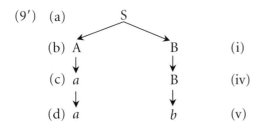

 (b) A   B   (i)

 (c) a   B   (iv)

 (d) a   b   (v)

(10′) (a)

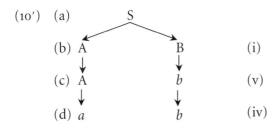

 (b) A   B   (i)

 (c) A   b   (v)

 (d) a   b   (iv)

(11′) (a)   S

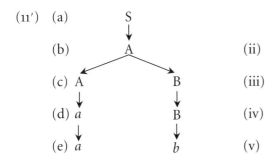

 (b)   A   (ii)

 (c) A   B   (iii)

 (d) a   B   (iv)

 (e) a   b   (v)

(12)

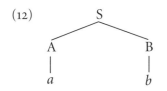

(13)

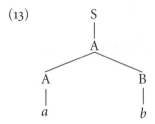

In (12) B is a daughter of S, but in (13) it is a daughter of the higher A. PSGs are thus capable of representing two important parts of sentential structure: constituency and ambiguity in structure.

To see how this works, let us consider an example with a real sentence: *A burglar shot the man with a gun.* A grammar that gives this structure is seen in (14):

(14) $\mathbb{N} = \{NP, N, VP, V, PP, P, S, D\}$, $\mathbb{S} = \{S\}$, $\mathbb{T} = \{the, man, shot, a,$
         burglar,gun, with}
         $\mathbb{P} = $ (a) $S \rightarrow NP\ VP$ (b) $NP \rightarrow D\ N$
              (c) $NP \rightarrow D\ N\ PP$ (d) $VP \rightarrow V\ NP$
              (e) $VP \rightarrow V\ NP\ PP$ (f) $PP \rightarrow P\ NP$
              (g) $D \rightarrow the, a$
              (h) $N \rightarrow man, burglar, gun,$ etc. . . .
              (i) $V \rightarrow shot, took,$ etc. . . .
              (j) $P \rightarrow with, in,$ etc. . . .

Let us first consider the meaning where the burglar used a gun to shoot the man. In this case, the prepositional phrase *with a gun* forms a constituent with the verb *shoot*. I will do one possible derivation here (although by no means the only one):

(15)   (i) S
        (ii) NP   VP   (a)
        (iii) D   N   VP   (b)
        (iv) *A*   N   VP   (g)
        (v) *A*   *burglar*   VP   (h)
        (vi) *A*   *burglar*   V   NP   PP   (e)
        (vii) *A*   *burglar*   *shot*   NP   PP   (i)
        (viii) *A*   *burglar*   *shot*   D   N   PP   (b)
        (ix) *A*   *burglar*   *shot*   *the*   N   PP   (g)
        (x) *A*   *burglar*   *shot*   *the*   *man*   PP   (h)
        (xi) *A*   *burglar*   *shot*   *the*   *man*   P   NP   (f)

(xii)	*A*	*burglar*	*shot*	*the*	*man*	*with*	NP		(j)
(xiii)	*A*	*burglar*	*shot*	*the*	*man*	*with*	D	N	(b)
(xiv)	*A*	*burglar*	*shot*	*the*	*man*	*with*	*a*	N	(g)
(xv)	*A*	*burglar*	*shot*	*the*	*man*	*with*	*a*	*gun*	(h)

This corresponds to the simplified derivation tree in (16), where all repetitive steps have been conflated.

(16)

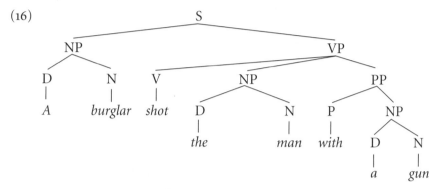

Compare this to a derivation for the other meaning, where the man was holding the gun, and the method of shooting is unspecified (i.e. it could have been with a slingshot, bow and arrow, or even a pea-shooter). In this case, we want *with a gun* to form a constituent with *man*.

(17)	(i) S									
	(ii) NP	VP								(a)
	(iii) D	N	VP							(b)
	(iv) *A*	N	VP							(g)
	(v) *A*	*burglar*	VP							(h)
	(vi) *A*	*burglar*	V	NP						(d)
	(vii) *A*	*burglar*	*shot*	NP						(i)
	(viii) *A*	*burglar*	*shot*	D	N	PP				(c)
	(ix) *A*	*burglar*	*shot*	*the*	N	PP				(g)
	(x) *A*	*burglar*	*shot*	*the*	*man*	PP				(h)
	(xi) *A*	*burglar*	*shot*	*the*	*man*	P	NP			(f)
	(xii) *A*	*burglar*	*shot*	*the*	*man*	*with*	NP			(j)
	(xiii) *A*	*burglar*	*shot*	*the*	*man*	*with*	D	N		(b)
	(xiv) *A*	*burglar*	*shot*	*the*	*man*	*with*	*a*	N		(g)
	(xv) *A*	*burglar*	*shot*	*the*	*man*	*with*	*a*	*gun*		(h)

This derivation differs from that in (15) only in lines (vi) and (viii) (with an application of rules (d) and (c) respectively instead of (e) and (b)). This gives the conflated derivation tree in (18):

(18)

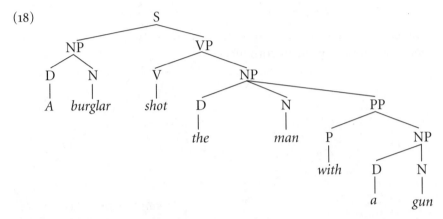

So this limited set of phrase structure rules allows us to capture two important parts of syntactic structure: both the constituency and ambiguity in interpretation.

5.3 Phrase markers and reduced phrase markers

Although tree structures are the easiest form for viewing constituency, Chomsky's original conception of constituent structure was set theoretic (see Lasnik 2000: 29–33 for extensive discussion).[5] The basic idea was that one took each of the unique lines in each of the possible derivations of a sentence and combined them into a set called the phrase marker or p-marker. Let's take the example given by Lasnik (2000: 30):

---

[5] To be historically accurate, the discussion in this section is fairly revisionist and is based almost entirely on Lasnik's (2000) retelling of the *Syntactic Structures* story. Careful reading of LSLT and Chomsky (1957) shows significantly less emphasis on the set vs. tree notational differences. Chomsky (1975: 183) does define P-markers set theoretically:

K is a P-marker of Z if and only if there is an equivalence class $\{D_p \ldots, D_n\}$ of r_1-derivations of Z such that for each i, $D_i = (A_{i1}, \ldots, A_{im(i)})$ and $K = \{A_{ij} \mid j \leq m(i), (i) \leq n\}$ [r_1-derivations are terminated phrase structure derivations].

However, Chomsky (1957) does not give a single example of a set-theoretically defined P-marker. Nevertheless, Lasnik's discussion of Chomsky's PSRs and P-markers is insightful and helpful when we return to Bare Phrase Structure in Chapter 8, so I include it here.

(19) $\mathbb{N}$= {NP, VP, V, S}, $\mathbb{S}$ = {S}, $\mathbb{T}$ = {he, left},
       $\mathbb{P}$ =   (i) S → NP VP
              (ii) NP → he
              (iii) VP → V
              (iv) V → left

The sentence *He left* can be generated by three distinct derivations:

(20)   (a)   S   (b)   S   (c)   S
        (i) NP   VP   NP   VP   NP   VP
        (ii) *He*   VP   NP   V   NP   V
        (iii) *He*   V   *He*   V   NP   *left*
        (iv) *He*   left   *He*   left   *He*   left

All three of these derivations reduce to the same tree:

(21)   S

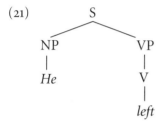

The P-marker for these derivations is (Lasnik 2000: 31):

(22)   {S, *he left, he* VP, *he* V, NP *left*, NP VP, NP V}

S, NP VP, and *he left* appear in all three of the derivations. *He* V appears
in (a) and (b), NP V appears in (b) and (c). *He* VP only appears in (a);
NP *left* only appears in (c). The set theoretic phrase marker (not the
tree, or the derivation) was the actual representation of the structure of
a sentence in LSLT and *Syntactic Structures*.

   One advantage to P-markers is in how they can explain the "is a" (≈)
relations among the elements in a derivation. It turns out that the easiest
way to explain these relations is to make use of a notion invented much
later by Lasnik and Kupin (1977) and Kupin (1978): the monostring.
Monostrings are those elements in the P-marker that consist of exactly
one non-terminal and any number (including Ø) of terminals. In other
words, the monostrings leave out any line with more than one non-
terminal (e.g. NP VP). The monostrings that appear in (22) are listed in
(23), which Lasnik and Kupin call the reduced P-marker (RPM).

(23)   {S, *he* VP, *he* V, NP *left*}

The ≈-relations can be calculated by comparing each of these mono-strings to the terminal string (example from Lasnik 2000):

(24) (a) *he left*
          he *VP*   therefore *left* ≈ VP

      (b) *he left*
          he V   therefore *left* ≈ V

      (c) *he left*
          NP *left*   therefore *he* ≈ NP

      (d) *he left*
          S   therefore *he left* ≈ S

Note that there are number of relationships not expressed in this notation. For example, it does not assert that V ≈ VP (nor VP ≈ V);[6] nor does it assert that NP VP ≈ S. The RPM simply does not contain this information. Despite what you might construe from the tree representations of such sentences, the only constituency relationships are between terminals and the nodes that dominate them.[7] The sentence is otherwise ordered by the precedence relations expressed in the monostrings. Trees, although helpful to the student and linguist, are not actually an accurate representation of the P-marker as it was originally conceived by Chomsky and later extended by Lasnik and Kupin. Indeed, Lasnik and Kupin (1977) and Kupin (1978) suggest we can do away with trees and the PSG component entirely (i.e. the sentences are not derived by a PSG, but rather are declaratively stated with the restriction that the RPM express all the relevant ≈-relations, and be ordered by dominance and precedence). As we will see when we look at Bare Phrase Structure in Chapter 8, a derivational version of this set theoretic idea returns to generative grammar in much more recent versions of the theory.

5.4 Regular grammars; context-free and context-sensitive grammars

There are a variety of types of phrase structure grammar. They vary in their power to make accurate empirical predictions and in the kinds of

---

6 This means that VP, V, and *left* are actually unordered with respect to one another in terms of immediate dominance. This is perhaps part of the motivation for abandoning non-branching structures from the theory of Bare Phrase Structure discussed in Ch. 8.

7 More precisely, simple dominance is an important relation in this theory but immediate dominance plays no role at all. This means that trees (and by extension, the derivations that create them) are not part of Lasnik and Kupin's system.

language systems they described. In this section, we look at a number of different kinds of PSG and what they can and cannot capture. See Chomsky (1963) for a more rigorous characterization.

5.4.1 Regular grammars

First, note that the class of regular grammars and finite state automata (discussed in Ch. 2, but not formalized) can, in fact, be captured with a phrase structure grammar formalism. Recall that finite state automata start (usually) at the left edge of the sentence and work their way to the right. It is relatively easy to capture this using a PSG. All we have to do is ensure that the only structure that is expanded in each rule application is the final element (that is, they branch only rightwards; there is never any branching on the left of a rule) or on the first element (that is, they only branch leftwards, there is never any branching on the right side of the rule). Such grammars are slightly more restricted than the kind we have above, in that on the left side of the arrow we may have exactly one terminal and exactly one non-terminal (restricted to one end). Take for example the finite state automaton in (25):

(25)

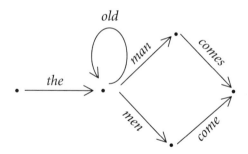

This can be defined by the following regular grammar.

(26) $\mathbb{N} = \{A, B, C, S\}$, $\mathbb{S} = \{S\}$, $\mathbb{T} = \{the, old, man, comes, men, come\}$,
$\mathbb{P} = $ (i)   S $\rightarrow$ *the* A
        (ii)   A $\rightarrow$ *old* A
        (iii) A $\rightarrow$ *man* B
        (iv)   A $\rightarrow$ *men* C
        (v)   B $\rightarrow$ *comes*
        (vi)   C $\rightarrow$ *come*

This generates a tree such as (27).

(27)

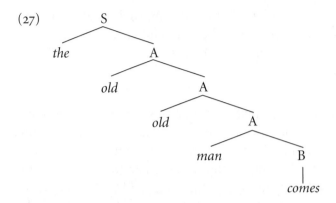

The problem with such a structure is, as we discussed in Chapter 2, that it does not accurately represent the constituency[8] (which is, of course [[the [old [old man]]][comes]], not [the [old [old [man [comes]]]]]). Furthermore, there is no possible ambiguity in the structures, all the trees in this grammar branch strictly rightwards and binarily. See Sag, Wasow, and Bender (2003) for careful discussion of these problems. So, such grammars aren't terribly useful in describing human language. The fact that it is possible to represent a FSA using the notation of PSG is not necessarily a bad thing, it just shows that we need to explore in more detail how the powerful PSG notation can be used and restricted. We can start this with one observation:

(28)   The grammars of human languages are not regular grammars (i.e. are not strictly limited to branching on one side or another.)[9]

The structures of human language clearly need more flexibility than this, but what kinds of limitations are there on PSGs? We deal with this question in the next chapter.

---

[8] See Langendoen (1975) for an attempt to force a regular grammar to produce correct constituency. This is accomplished by not identifying constituency with the derivation, but by having the regular grammar contain explicit rules for the insertion of constituency brackets. These kinds of rules, however, miss the fundamental distinction between the structures that the derivation is meant to represent, and the notational devices that are used to mark the structures. By adding brackets to the inventory of elements that can be inserted into the derivation, Langendoen blurs the line between the lexical items and their constituency, and the devices that we use to notate that constituency; essentially equating structural notions (right edge of constituent, left edge of constituent, etc.) with lexical items. This kind of approach also (intentionally) disrupts the constituent construction effects of the actual derivation.

[9] Interestingly, Kayne (1994) actually proposes that syntactic trees are universally rightward branching, but he derives the surface order from a very abstract structure using movement operations.

5.4.2 Context-free and context-sensitive phrase structure grammars

Let us distinguish between two distinct types of PSG system. The first kind can make reference to other material in the derivation (known as the context of the rule): *context-sensitive phrase structure grammars* (abbreviated either as CSG or CS-PSG). The rule in (29) is a typical example:

(29)   BAC → B*a*DC

This rule says that the symbol A is replaced by a sequence of a terminal *a* and non-terminal D, if it is preceded by a B and followed by a C. That is, it would apply in context (30a), but not (30b) (or any other context than (30a)):

(30)   (a)   . . . BAC . . .
       (b)   . . . BAE . . .

There are two common formalizations of CS-PSGs. The format in (29) is perhaps the most transparent. The format in (31) which expressed the same rule as (29) is borrowed from generative phonology, and uses the / and ___ notations, where / means "in the environment of" and ___ marks the position of the element to be replaced relative to the context:

(31)   A → *a* D / B ___ C

This notation says A is to be replaced by [*a* D] precisely when A appears in an environment where A is between B and C.

   The second kind of phrase structure rule (PSR) is the context-free phrase structure rule (the grammar containing such rules is abbreviated either CFG or CF-PSG). These rules disallow reference to any context. Manaster-Ramer and Kac (1990) refer to such rules as unisinistral ("one on the left") as they only allow one symbol on the left hand side of the rule (in the format in (29)).

(32)   A → *a* D

The rule in (32) says that at any given step in the derivation (regardless of context) A will be spelled out as . . . *a* D . . .

   It has long been the assumption of practitioners of phrase structure grammars that the syntax of human language is context-free (see e.g. Gazdar 1982). In Chapter 2, we discussed some evidence from Züritüütsch and Dutch presented by Shieber (1985) and Huybregts (1984), which shows that syntax is at least mildly context sensitive (see the original works for mathematical proofs). Interestingly, few researchers have reached for CS-PSGs as the solution to this problem (however, cf. Huck 1985 and Bunt 1996b); instead most have "extended" pure CF-PSGs in some way. In the next chapter, we will explore many of these extensions in detail.

5.5 The recursive nature of phrase structure grammars

Although not present in their earliest versions (Chomsky 1975, 1957) most PSGs since the 1960s have included rules of a type that allows a partial explanation of the fact that language is productive and allows at least infinitely[10] many new sentences. Such rules (or rule sets) are recursive. That is, you can always embed well-formed sequences in other well-formed sequences using a set of phrase structure rules that include recursive patterns. An abstract example of such a set of such rules is given in (33):

(33)   (a) A → a B
       (b) B → b A

The application of each of these rules feeds the application of the other. In other words, we have an infinite loop. The application of rule (33a) replaces an A with an a and the symbol B, whereas the rule (33b) can

---

[10] I use the term "infinitely" here in the imprecise sense as understood by lay people. That is I (and most other authors) use the term to mean "not finite". This is a different from the mathematician's view of what it is to be countably infinite: you can apply a function that puts each sentence in a one-to-one correspondence with a member of the set of positive integers (a set which is by definition countably infinite). The intuitive idea behind the lay person's meaning is that you have a productive system you can produce lots and lots of sentences that have never been heard before, more so than have ever been uttered and more so than we are likely ever to utter. So, more precisely, the claim is that the syntax of languages is *at least* countably infinite. Pullum and Scholz (2005: 496–7) argue against the "infinity" of human language, but their argument seems to be based on a very narrow, and perhaps misleading, interpretation of the claim. They seem to have confused the intended meaning of infinite with the mathematical sense of countably infinite. Langendoen and Postal (1984) show that the set of grammatical sentences is greater than countably infinite. (From this, they conclude that generative grammars can not be correct, but this is largely besides the point.) The point that most syntacticians are trying to make about recursive systems is that they generate a set that is not finite. Whether the set is countably infinite and something larger is largely irrelevant to that specific point. (Although in the long run it may bear on the larger question of whether generative rule systems are plausible models of grammar or not—a question about which I will remain agnostic.)

replace that B with a *b* and another A, and so on. Infinitely looping these rules (or nesting their applications) will result, presumably, in the possibility of (at least) infinitely long sentences, sentences that presumably have never been heard before.[11] For example, if we have the

[11] As noted in n. 10, Pullum and Scholz (2005) argue against the idea that language is (countably) infinite noting that their formalism of this claim (which they call the "master argument for language infinity") is circular. The master argument is based on the number of words in any given member of the set of well-formed sentences. Roughly, given the premise that there is a well-formed sentence with a length greater than zero, and the premise that for any well-formed sentence you can find another with more words in it (due to embedding rules) such that *that* sentence will also be a member of the set of well-formed sentences, we can conclude that for any *n*, *n* = the length of some sentence, there is another sentence that has a length greater than *n*. If we assume that the set of well-formed sentences described in the first premise is finite, that is a direct contradiction to the second premise. That leaves us with the only possible interpretation of the first premise such that the set of grammatical sentences is infinite. The intended conclusion of the proof that the set of sentences is infinite, then, is circular since it is assumed in the second premise. This, alas, is nothing more than a straw-man version of the argument.

It is not difficult to get around this problem by casting the proof differently, thus eliminating the premise that there is an initial (infinite) set of grammatical sentences. For example, we could assert the grammaticality of only one very long sentence—that is we do not have to assert membership in a set of grammatical sentences, only the existence of one such sentence. Further, we assert that this sentence is the longest possible sentence. We can then show that this very long sentence can be embedded in another (say embedded under *I think that . . .*), and we have a proof by contradiction. Alternately, we need only prove that a subset of some language's sentences is at least infinite, and it follows that the entire language is at least infinite as well. We can do this by asserting that there is some string which is grammatical (by native speaker intuition), say *Susan loves peanuts*, and assert that it is possible to embed this string under any number of sequences of *I think that . . .* (that is, by native speaker intuition, we know that *I think that Susan loves peanuts, I think that I think that Susan loves peanuts* and *I think that I think that I think that Susan loves peanuts*, etc. are all grammatical). The set that these two assumptions give us is the one given by the function (*I think that*)* + *Susan* + *likes* + *peanuts*. If we assert a closure on this based on the embedding operation (given a function $f: A \rightarrow A$, A is said to be "closed under" an operation iff $a \in A$ implies $f(a) \in A$), such that the initial sentence and its embeddings are the only grammatical sentences of English, we have proven that a subset of English is at least infinite, so it follows that English is at least infinite. Pullum and Scholz seem to dismiss this kind of argument since it involves an artificial closure of the set of English sentences:

"The authors quoted above apparently think that given any productive expression-lengthening operation it follows immediately that the set of well-formed sentences is countably infinite. It does indeed follow that the set formed by closing a set of expressions under a lengthening operation will be infinite. But the argument is supposed to be about natural languages such as English. What needs to be supported is the claim that (for example) English actually contains all the members of the closure of some set of English expressions under certain lengthening operations."

(Pullum and Scholz 2005: 496)

This misses an important assumption common in generative grammar. Pullum and Scholz seem not to distinguish between i-language (linguistic knowledge) and the set of

PSRs in (34) (ignoring the rules that introduce lexical items), we can generate a tree such as (35), where the triangle and "..." represent an infinite continuation of the structure.

(34) (a) NP → D N PP
      (b) PP → P NP

(35)

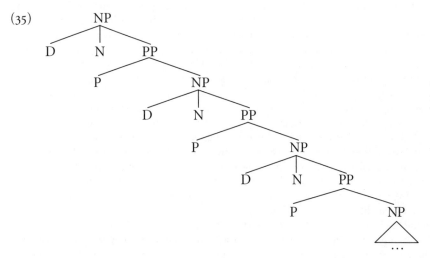

5.6 The ontology of PSRs and trees

Up to this point, we have been assuming the oldest view of what phrase structure rules and trees represent. We've been assuming that phrase structure rules are rewrite rules that proceed in a derivation stepwise from the root node to the terminal string. This derivation can be represented formally as a P-marker or as an RPM, informally as a conflated derivation tree. This particular view of what it means to be a PSG is rarely found in most recent versions of our understanding of PSRs. It seems to be limited in the modern literature to formal language theorists and computer scientists. There are two competing visions of what a phrase structure grammar (and its near-relations to be

productions (e-language). If we make this common assumption, we need close only a set of e-language productions, and assert that native speaker judgments about productive embedding systems (for example, the judgments are compatible with a set of recursive PSRs) tell us that a closed set of infinite e-productions of the form (*I think that*) * + *Susan* + *likes* + *peanuts* is a subset of the i-language-possible sentences of English. (Every production in the subset is compatible with our knowledge about what those productions may be.)

discussed in later chapters) really *is*, linguistically speaking. One view common to the derivational models of generative grammar from the late 1970s and early 1980s holds that PSRs are projection rules that work from the terminal string *up* to the root, and that trees (not P-markers) are the structures that syntactic operations apply to. The other view, most prevalent in the GPSG, HPSG, and LFG traditions, is that tree structures aren't "derived" per se. Instead, we view trees as structures that are subject to filtering constraints. Phrase structure rules are one kind of constraint, known as "node admissibility conditions". I will describe each of these alternatives in turn.

The projection-rules view of PSRs relies on an insight borrowed from the dependency grammar tradition: the idea that it is no accident that NPs always have a noun in them and VPs, a verb. The obligatory element that gives its category to the phrase is the *head* of the phrase. The adoption of the notion of headedness (see Ch. 7 on X-bar theory for a more explicit discussion of this) coincided with the emergence of the idea that it is the properties of the terminals themselves that drives whether they can be combined with other elements in the sentence. The most straightforward implementation of these two trends is one in which phrase structure rules are read backwards. That is, instead of construing the rule NP → D N as "replace an NP symbol with a D followed by an N symbol," we interpret it as "whenever you find a D and an N sequence, build an NP node on top of it." This might be more perspicuously written as NP ← D N, but no one to my knowledge has ever used this reversed arrow notation (McCawley 1968 attributes the earliest version of this hypothesis to Stockwell, Bowen, and Martin 1965). This approach is called "projection" because the head of the phrase is seen to "project" its parent into the tree, rather than replacing it in the derivation.

This change in point of view had several implications for our understanding of phrase structure. First, it is incompatible with the set-theoretic[12] P-marker approach to syntactic description. Trees thus became our primary (perhaps only) mechanism for describing syntactic structure. This in turn gave us the insight that geometric relations over tree structures (such as c-command and government) were primary in defining constraints over the grammar and operations applied

---

[12] Trees *are* describable in terms of set theory, of course, since they are graphs. What I mean here is that the sets we call P-markers are not compatible with the projection-rule view.

to the grammar (for example, the geometric restrictions on binding theory). Indeed at the same time that this insight was revolutionizing how we view phrase structure, we see a shift in the way that transformations were defined: instead of being defined over strings of symbols, transformations in the 1970s and 1980s start to be defined in tree-geometric terms (see Emonds 1976, among other sources). Another important change is that, instead of root to terminal derivations, sentences came to be constructed from the terminal string up to the root. This has been the standard view within Chomskyan generative grammar from the Revised Extended Standard Theory right through GB and Minimalist versions of the Principles-and-Parameters Framework. This in turn was part of the motivation (although by no means the only motivation) for distinguishing between competence and performance in syntax. Bottom-to-top trees for a left-headed language such as English pretty much have to be constructed from right to left, which is of course the reverse order to the order that the words are pronounced. A terminal-to-root grammar is thus easier to describe in a competence model than in a model that also tries to capture actual productions.

Around the same time as the projection model was gaining strength in Chomskyan syntax, the view of phrase structure rules as node-admissibility conditions gained currency among approaches that rejected derivationalism in syntax, in particular GPSG and LFG, although the earliest instantiation of it is found in the transformationalist analysis of McCawley (1968) (who attributes the idea to a personal communication with Richard Stanley). McCawley observes that there are ways in which two or more trees might correspond to the same syntactic derivation. For example, assume the PSG fragment in (36):

(36) $\mathbb{N} = \{A, B, C, S\}$, $\mathbb{S} = \{S\}$, $\mathbb{T} = \{\dots\}$,
$\quad \mathbb{P} = \quad$ (i) S → A B
$\qquad\quad$ (ii) A → A C
$\qquad\quad$ (iii) B → C B
$\qquad\qquad$ etc.

Such a grammar could produce the following derivation:

(37) (a) S
$\quad$ (b) A   B$\qquad$ i
$\quad$ (c) A   C   B$\qquad$??? ii or iii ???

The problem is that in step (37c) the line could have been created either by applying rule ii or by applying rule iii. This means that this derivation is compatible with either of the following trees (representing rule applications, or constituency, rather than p-markers).

(38)   (a)   (b)

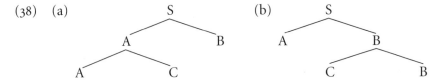

It is possible, then, for the derivational root-to-terminal approach to fail to distinguish among possible ambiguities in constituency (compare the example given in section 5.2). McCawley suggests that instead of rewrite rules, we have declarative node-admissibility conditions that recursively specify the range of possible trees. McCawley argues that instead of the A → A C notation, that such rules be stated as a pair of a dominator with its dominatees: <A; A C>.[13] Most practitioners of node-admissibility phrase structure style syntax (e.g. Gazdar, Klein, Pullum, and Sag 1985), however, keep the traditional arrow notation.

As with the projection approach, the node-admissibility view abandons the traditional rewrite view of trees as secondary, and places trees in the forefront as devices over which conditions are stated (known as "constraints over local trees" or "local constraints").[14]

The PSG format, while apparently straightforward, frequently means quite different things in different theoretical traditions. It can be a root-to-terminal rewrite rule, as in early generative grammar; it can represent a structure creating projection rule that builds a tree from the terminals to the root as in later Chomskyan approaches; or, it can be a set of node-admissibility conditions that serve to filter out possible trees. In later chapters we will see a fourth possibility where the tree has the status of a formal proof that the meaning/feature structure of a

[13] Interestingly, but almost certainly coincidentally, this notation is similar to that used by Langendoen (2003)'s version of Bare Phrase Structure Theory.

[14] In the descendent of GPSG: Head-driven Phrase Structure Grammar (which, ironically, at least in its most recent incarnations is not a phrase structure grammar in any recognizable form at all), this arboreal-centric view is abandoned in favor of constraints over combinations of complex feature structures. Trees, to the extent that they have any formal status in HPSG at all, amount to little more than proof structures that show the resultant root feature structure can be constructed compositionally out of the feature structures of the words themselves. The complex, hierarchically organized, root feature structure, however, serves the purpose of the "representation" of the description of the sentence rather than the proof-tree.

sentence can be composed from the meanings/feature structures of the individual words.

5.7 The information contained in PSRs

Our survey of simple PSGs would not be complete without a look at precisely the kinds of information that phrase structure rules and their resultant constituent trees or P-markers represent. In the next chapter, we will look at the various ways these kinds of information are either restricted or embellished upon by extending PSGs in various ways.

Starting with the obvious, simple PSGs and the trees they generate capture basic constituency facts, representing at least the set of dominance relations. Such relations are marked by the arrows in the PSRs themselves. Equally obviously (although frequently rejected later), PSGs represent the linear order in which the words are pronounced. For example, given a rule NP → D N, the word that instantiates the determiner node precedes the word that instantiates the N node; this is represented by their left-to-right organization in the rule. In versions of PSG that are primarily tree-geometric rather than being based on P-markers or RPMs, the tree also encodes c-command and government relations.

Less obviously, but no less importantly, phrase structure rules contain implicit restrictions on which elements can combine with what other elements (Heny 1979). First, they make reference to (primitive) non-complex syntactic categories such as N, V, P, Adj, and D, and the phrasal categories associated with these, NP, VP, AdjP, etc. Next they stipulate which categories can combine with which other categories. For example, in the sample grammar given much earlier in (14), there is no rule that rewrites some category as a D followed by a V. We can conclude then that in the fragment of the language that this grammar describes there are no constituents that consist of a determiner followed by a verb. Phrase structure rules also at least partly capture subcategorization relations; for example, the category "verb" has many subcategories: intransitive (which take a single NP as their subject), transitive (which take two arguments), double-object ditransitive (which take three NP arguments), prepositional ditransitive (which take two NPs and a PP). These classes correspond to three distinct phrase structure rules: VP → V; VP → V NP; VP → V NP NP; and V → V NP PP. The subcategories of verb are thus represented by the four different VP rules. However, there is nothing in these rules, as stated, that prevents a verb of one class being introduced by a rule of a different class. Without further restrictions (of the kind we will introduce in Ch. 6), PSGs cannot stop the verb *put*, for example, being used intransitively (**I put*). PSGs, then, contain some, but not all of the subcategorization information necessary for describing human language.

In summary, PSGs encode at least the following organizational properties:

(39) (a) hierarchical organization (constituency and dominance rela-
           tions);
      (b) linear organization (precedence relations);
      (c) c-command and government relations or local constraints (in
           tree-dominant forms of PSGs only);
      (d) categorial information;
      (e) subcategorization (in a very limited way).

There are many kinds of other information that PSGs do *not* directly encode, but which we might want to include in our syntactic descriptions. Take the grammatical relations (Subject, Object, Indirect object, etc.) or thematic relations (such as Agent, Patient, and Goal). Neither of these are directly encoded into the PSRs; however, in later chapters, we will see examples of theories like Lexical-Functional Grammar, in which grammatical relations are notated directly on PSRs. Within the Chomskyan tradition, however, grammatical relations can be read off of syntactic trees (for example, the subject is the NP daughter of S), but they are not directly encoded into the rule.

Similarly, semantic selectional restrictions are not encoded in simple PSGs. Selectional restrictions govern co-occurrence of words in a sentence beyond (sub)categorial restrictions. For example, the verb *die* in its literal sense requires that its subject be animate and alive. Since it is an intransitive verb, it should appear in any context given by the VP → V version of the VP rule. However, its selectional restrictions prevent it from appearing in sentences such as **The stone died*. Unacceptability of this kind does not follow from PSGs themselves.

In all the examples we have considered thus far, with the exception of the sentence (S) rule, the PSRs are always of the form where NPs are always headed N, VPs by V, etc. This is the property of *endocentricity*. This is particularly true of PSRs when they are construed as projection formulas. A formal mechanism for stipulating endocentricity will be discussed in Chapter 7, when we turn to X-bar theory (see also Ch. 8, where we discuss head-based dependency grammars). In simple PSGs, however, nothing forces this result. Indeed, within the tradition of generative semantics, as well as in LFG, one can find unheaded phrase structure rules where NPs dominated S categories without an N head, or VPs dominated only an adjective, etc.

Finally, consider non-local relationships (that is, relationships other than immediate precedence and immediate dominance) among elements in the tree. While we can define notions such as c-command over trees, there is nothing inherent to PSGs that defines them. As such, in order to indicate such relationships we need to extend PSGs with notational devices such as indices or features. The same holds true for long-distance filler–gap relations (also known as "displacement operations"). For example, in the sentence *What did Norton say that Nancy bought ___?* we want to mark the relationship between the *wh-*word and the empty embedded object position with which it is associated. This kind of information just is not available in a simple PSG.

In the next two chapters (and to a lesser degree other chapters later in the book), we will look at how information already present in PSGs is either limited or shown to follow from other devices (or slightly different formalizations). We will also look at the ways in which information that is not part of simple PSGs has been accommodated into the PSG system. In Chapter 6, we will look at such devices as the lexicon, complex symbols (i.e. feature structures), indices, abbreviatory conventions, a different format for rules (the ID/LP format), and transformations of various kinds which have all been proposed as additions to simple PSGs so that the information they contain is either restricted and expanded. Chapter 6 focuses on extended PSGs in early Chomskyan theory, in GPSG (and to a lesser degree in HPSG), and in LFG. In Chapter 7, we turn to the influential X-bar theory in its various incarnations. The X-bar approach started off as a series of statements that restricts the form of phrase structure rules, but eventually developed into an independent system which allows us to capture generalizations not available with simple PSRs.

6

Extended Phrase Structure Grammars

6.1 Introduction

In the last chapter, we looked at a narrow version of a phrase structure grammar. Here we consider various proposals for extending PSGs. We are interested in things that PSRs do not do well and therefore require extending mechanisms, and things that PSRs can do but would be better handled by other components of the grammar.

We start with some minor abbreviatory conventions that allow expression of iteration and optionality within PSGs. These conventions are commonly found in most versions of PSGs.

Next we consider Chomsky's first extensions to PSGs: two kinds of transformational rule: structure-changing transformations (SCTs) and structure-building "generalized transformations" (GTs). These account for a range of data that simple PSGs appear to fail on. After this we look at the alternatives first proposed within the Generalized Phrase Structure Grammar (GPSG) framework: feature structures for stating generalizations across categories, and metarules, which offer an alternative to transformations and state generalizations across rule types. We will also look at the immediate dominance/linear precedence (ID/LP) rule format common to GPSG and Lexical-Functional Grammar (LFG) that allows us to distinguish between rules that determine linear order and those that determine hierarchical structure as well as other extensions that make use of a distinct semantic structure.

Chomsky (1965) recognized the power of the lexicon, the mental dictionary, in limiting the power of the rule component. Early versions of this insight included mechanisms for reducing the redundancy between lexical restrictions on co-occurrence and those stated in the PSGs. Some of this was encoded in the feature structures found in GPSG mentioned above. But the true advance came in the late 1970s and early 1980s, when LFG, GB (Principles and Parameters), and HPSG adopted generative lexicons, where certain generalizations are best stated as principles that hold across words rather than over trees (as was the case for transformations) or rules (as was the case for metarules). This shift in computational power to the lexicon had a great stripping effect on the PSG component in all of these frameworks, and was at least partly the cause of the development of X-bar theory—the topic of Chapter 7.

6.2 Some minor abbreviatory conventions in PSGs

The "pure" PSGs described in Chapter 5, by their very nature, have a certain clumsy quality to them. It has become common practice in most theories (except GPSG, which uses a different mechanism for abbreviating grammars; see the section on metarules below) to abbreviate similar rules. Consider the rules that generate a variety of types of noun phrases (NPs). NPs can consist of at least the following types: a bare noun; a noun with a determiner; a noun with an adjectival modifier (AdjP); a noun with a determiner and an adjectival modifier; a noun with a prepositional phrase (PP) modifier; a noun with a determiner and a PP; a noun with an AdjP and a PP; and the grand slam with D, AdjP, and PP. Each of these requires a different PSR:

(1) (a) people   NP → N
     (b) the people   NP → D N
     (c) big people   NP → AdjP N
     (d) the big people   NP → D AdjP N
     (e) people from New York   NP → N PP
     (f) big people from New York   NP → AdjP N PP
     (g) the big people from New York   NP → D Adj N PP

In classical top-down PSGs, these have to be distinct rules. The derivation of a sentence with an NP like that in (g), but with the application of the rule in (d), will fail to generate the correct structure. Replacing NP with AdjP and N (using d) will fail to provide the input necessary for inserting a determiner or a PP (which are present in g). Each type of NP requires its own rule. Needless to say, this kind of grammar quickly becomes very large and unwieldy.[1] It is not uncommon to abbreviate large rule sets that all offer alternative replacements for a single category. What is clear from all the rules in (1) is that they require an N; everything else is an optional replacement category (where "optional" refers to the overall pattern of NPs rather than to the rule for any particular NP). Optional constituents in an abbreviated rule are represented in parentheses (). The rules in (1) thus can be abbreviated as:

(2)   NP → (D) (AdjP) N (PP)

Although it is commonly the practice, particularly in introductory textbooks, to refer to rules like (2) as "the NP rule", in fact this is an abbreviation for a set of rules.

There are situations where one has a choice of two or more categories, but where only one of the choice set may appear. For example, the verb *ask* allows a variety of categories to appear following it. Leaving aside PPs, *ask* allows one NP, one CP (embedded clause), two NPs, or an NP and a CP. However, it does not allow two NPs and a CP in any order (3).

(3)   (a) I asked a question.   VP → V NP
      (b) I asked if Bill likes peanuts.   VP → V CP
      (c) I asked Frank a question.   VP → V NP NP
      (d) I asked Frank if Bill likes peanuts.   VP → V NP CP
      (e) *I asked Frank a question if Bill likes peanuts.
      (f) *I asked Frank if Bill likes peanuts a question.

Note that it appears as if the second NP after the verb (*a question*) has the same function as the embedded clause (*if Bill likes peanuts*) and you can only have one or the other of them, not both. We can represent this using curly brackets { }:

(4)   VP →   V   (NP)$\left\{ {NP \atop CP} \right\}$

The traditional notation is to stack the choices one on top of one another as in (4). This is fairly cumbersome from a typographic perspective, so most authors generally separate the elements that can be chosen from with a comma or a slash:

(5)   VP → V (NP) {NP, CP}   *or*   VP → V (NP) {NP/CP}

---

[1] Practitioners of GPSG (see, for example, Bennett 1995), who often have very large rule sets like this, claim that this is not really a problem provided that the rules are precise and make the correct empirical predictions. See Matthews (1967) for the contrasting view.

In addition to being optional, many elements in a rule can be repeated, presumably an infinite number of times. In the next chapter we will attribute this property to simple recursion in the rule set. But it is also commonly notated within a single rule. For example, it appears as if we can have a very large number, possibly infinite, of PP modifiers of an N:

(6) (a) I bought a basket.   NP → N
     (b) I bought a basket of flowers.   NP → N PP
     (c) I bought a basket of flowers with   NP → N PP PP
          an Azalea in it.
     (d) I bought a basket of flowers with   NP → N PP PP PP
          an Azalea in it with a large handle.
          etc.

There are two notations that can be used to indicate this. The most common notation is to use a Kleene star (*) as in (7). Here, the Kleene star means 0 or more iterations of the item. Alternatively one can use the Kleene plus ($^+$), which means 1 or more iterations. Usually $^+$ is used in combination with a set of parentheses which indicate the optionality of the constituent. So the two rules in (7) are equivalent:

(7) (a) NP → N PP*
     (b) NP → N (PP$^+$)

These abbreviations are not clearly limitations on or extensions to PSGs, but do serve to make the rule sets more perspicuous and elegant.

6.3 Transformations

6.3.1 Structure-changing transformations

Chomsky (1957) noticed that there were a range of phenomena involving the apparent displacement of constituents, such as the topicalization seen in (8a), the subject–auxiliary inversion in (8b), and the *wh*-question in (8c).

(8) (a) Structure-changing transformations, I do not think *t* are found
          in any current theory.
     (b) Are you *t* sure?
     (c) Which rules did Chomsky posit *t*?

These constructions all involve some constituent (*structure-changing transformations, are*, and *which rules*, respectively) that is displaced from the place it would be found in a simple declarative. Instead, a gap or trace[2] appears in that position (indicated by the *t*). Chomsky claimed that these constructions could not be handled by a simple phrase structure grammar. On this point, he was later proven wrong by Gazdar (1982), but only when we appeal to an "enriched" phrase structure system (we return to this below). Chomsky's original account of constructions like those in (8) was to posit a new rule type: the structure changing transformation. These rules took phrase markers (called deep structure) and outputted a different phrase marker (the surface structure). For example, we can describe the process seen in (8b) as a rule that inverts the auxiliary and the subject NP:

(9)   X   NP   Aux   Y $\Rightarrow$ 1324
      1   2   3   4

The string on the left side of the arrow is the structural description and expresses the conditions for the rule; the string on the right side of the arrow represents the surface order of constituents.

Transformations are a very powerful device. In principle, you could do anything you like to a tree with a transformation. So their predictive power was overly strong and their discriminatory power is quite weak. Emonds (1976), building on Chomsky (1973), argued that transformations had to be constrained so that they were "structure preserving". This started a trend in Chomskyan grammar towards limiting the power of transformations. In other theories, transformations were largely abandoned either for metarules or lexical rules or multiple structures, which will all be discussed later in this book. In the latest versions of Chomskyan grammar (Minimalism, Phase Theory), there are no structure-changing transformations at all. The movement operations in minimalism are actually instances of a different kind of transformation, which we briefly introduce in the next section and consider in more detail in Chapter 8.

6.3.2 Generalized transformations

In Chomsky's original formulation of PSGs, there was no recursion. That is, there were no rule sets of the form S → NP VP and VP → V S, where the rules create a loop. In Chomsky's original system, recursion

---

[2] I am speaking anachronistically here. Traces were not part of Chomsky's original transformational theory, although there appear to be hints of them in LSLT (Piatelli Palmarini, pc).

and phenomena like it were handled by a different kind of rule, the Generalized Transformation (GT). This kind of rule was transformational in the sense that it took as its input an extant phrase marker and outputted a different phrase marker. But this is where its similarities to structure-changing transformations end. GTs are structure-building operations. They take two phrase markers (called "kernels") and join them together, building new structure. For example, an embedded clause is formed by taking the simple clause *I think* (where stands for some element that will be inserted) and the simple clause *Generalized transformations are a different kettle of fish*, and outputs the sentence *I think generalized transformations are a different kettle of fish*.

These kind of transformations were largely abandoned in Transformational Grammar in the mid 1960s (see the discussion in Fillmore 1963, Chomsky 1965, and the more recent discussion in Lasnik 2000), but they re-emerged in the framework known as Tree-Adjoining Grammar (TAG) (Joshi, Levy, and Takahashi 1975; Kroch and Joshi 1985, 1987), and have become the main form of phrase structure composition in the Minimalist Program (ch. 8).

6.4 Features and feature structures

Drawing on the insights of generative phonology, and building upon a proposal by Yngve (1958), Chomsky (1965) introduced a set of subcategorial features for capturing generalizations across categories. Take, for example, the fact that both adjectives and nouns require that their complements take the case marker *of*, but verbs and other prepositions do not.

(10) (a) the pile of papers   cf. *the pile papers
      (b) He is afraid of tigers.   cf. *He is afraid bears.
      (c) *I kissed of Heidi.
      (d) *I gave the book to of Heidi.

This fact can be captured by making reference to a feature that values across larger categories. For example, we might capture the difference of verbs and prepositions on one hand and nouns and adjectives on the other by making reference to a feature [+N]. The complement to a [+N] category must be marked with *of* (10a, b). The complement to a [−N] category does not allow *of* (10c, d).

The other original use of features allows us to make distinctions within categories. For example, the quantifier *many* can appear with count nouns, and the quantifier *much* with mass nouns:

(11) (a)   I saw too many people.
      (b)   *I saw too much people.
      (c)   *I ate too many sugar.
      (d)   I ate too much sugar.

The distinction between mass and count nouns can be captured with a feature: [± count].

There are at least three standard conventions for expressing features and their values. The oldest tradition, found mainly with binary (±) features, and the tradition in early generative phonology is to write the features as a matrix, with the value preceding the feature:

(12)
$$\begin{bmatrix} he \\ +N \\ -V \\ +\text{pronoun} \\ +\text{3person} \\ -\text{plural} \\ +\text{masculine} \\ \dots \end{bmatrix}$$

The traditions of LFG and HPSG use a different notation: the Attribute Value Matrix (AVM). AVMs put the feature (also known as an attribute or function) first and then the value of that feature after it. AVMs typically allow both simply valued features (e.g. [DEFINITE +] or [NUM sg]) and features that take other features within them:

(13)
$$\begin{bmatrix} he \\ \text{CATEGORY} & \text{noun} \\ \text{AGREEMENT} & \begin{bmatrix} \text{NUM} & \text{sg} \\ \text{GEND} & \text{masc} \\ \text{PERSON} & \text{3rd} \end{bmatrix} \end{bmatrix}$$

In (13), the AGREEMENT feature takes another AVM as its value. This embedded AVM has its own internal feature structure consisting of the NUM(ber), GEND(er), and PERSON features and their values.

The complex AVM structure can also be represented as a feature geometry, the notation common in distributed morphology[3] (see also Gazdar and Pullum 1982). The feature geometric representation of (13) is given in (14):

(14)

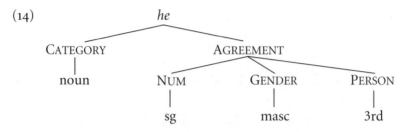

In the feature-geometric representation the attribute or feature is seen to dominate its value. If you can imagine (14) as a mobile hanging from the ceiling, then the AVM in (13) is a little like looking at the mobile from the bottom (Sag, pc).

Feature geometries have an interesting property (which is also present in AVMs but less obvious); they express implicational hierarchies of features. If you look at (14) you will see that if a noun is specified for [PERSON 3rd] then it follows that it must also have a specification for AGREEMENT.

The first of these three notations can still be found in the literature today, but usually in a fairly informal way. The AVM and feature geometry notations are generally more accepted, and as far as I can tell, they are simple notational variants of each other.

6.4.1 The use of features in Generalized Phrase Structure Grammar

Features are one of the main ways that Generalized Phrase Structure Grammar[4] (Gazdar 1982; Gazdar, Klein, Pullum, and Sag 1985; henceforth GKPS, and citations therein) extended (and constrained) the power of phrase structure grammars in a non-transformational way.

An underlying theme in GPSG (and HPSG,[5] LFG, and other approaches) is unification. The basic idea behind unification is that when two elements come together in a constituency relationship, they must be

---

[3] The feature geometry notation is also used in HPSG but usually not for expressing featural descriptions of categories; instead it is used for indicating implicational hierarchies (type or inheritance hierarchies). This usage is also implicit in the Distributed Morphology approach, but descriptions are not formally distinguished from the implicational hierarchies.

[4] See Bennett (1995) for an excellent textbook treatment of GPSG.

[5] Technically speaking, HPSG is not a unification grammar, since unification entails a procedural/generative/enumerative approach to constituency. HPSG is a constraint based,

compatible with each other, and the resultant unified or satisfied features are passed up to the next higher level of constituency where they can be further compared and unified with material even higher up in the tree. We will not formalize unification here because GPSG's formalization is fairly complex, and the formalization varies significantly in other theories. I hope that the intuitive notion of "compatibility" will suffice and that readers who require a more technical definition will refer to GKPS.

In GPSG, features are the primary means for representing subcategorization. For example, a verb like *die* could be specified for taking a subcategorization feature [SUBCAT 1], a verb like *tend* would take the feature [SUBCAT 13]. The numbers here are the ones used in GKPS. These features correspond to specific phrase structure rules:

(15)   (a) VP → V$_{[SUBCAT 1]}$
     (b) VP → V$_{[SUBCAT 13]}$ VP$_{[INF]}$

Rule (15b) will only be used with verbs that bear the [SUBCAT 13] feature like *tend*. This significantly restricts the power of a PSG, since the rules will be tied to the particular words that appear in the sentence.

While constraining the power in one way, features also allow GPSG to capture generalizations not possible in simple phrase structure grammars. Certain combinations of features are impossible, so it is possible to predict that certain combinations will always arise—this is similar to the implicational hierarchy effect of feature geometries mentioned above. In GPSG, the fact that an auxiliary is inverted with its subject is marked with the feature [+INV]. Only finite auxiliaries may appear in this position, so we can conclude that the conditional statement [+INV] ⊃ [+AUX, FIN] is true. That is, if the feature [+INV] appears on a word, then it must also be a finite auxiliary. Such restrictions are called Feature Co-occurrence Restrictions (FCR). Tightly linked to this concept are features that appear in the default or elsewhere situation. This is captured by Feature Specification Defaults (FSD). For example, all other things being equal, unless so specified, verbs in English are not inverted with their subject; they are thus [−INV]. FSDs allow us to underspecify the content of featural representations in the phrase structure rules. These features get filled in separately from the PSRs.

Features in GPSG are not merely the domain of words, all elements in the syntactic representation—including phrases—have features associated

model-theoretic, approach, and as such we might, following the common practice in the HPSG literature, refer to unification as feature satisfaction or feature resolution.

with them. A phrase is distinguished from a (pre-) terminal by virtue of the BAR feature (the significance of this name will become clear when we look at X-bar theory in the next chapter). A phrase takes the value [BAR 2], the head of the phrase takes the value [BAR 0], any intermediate structure, [BAR 1]. Features like these are licensed by (the GPSG equivalent of 'introduced by') the PSRs; the [BAR 2] on a phrase comes from the rule V[BAR 2] → V[BAR 0].

Other features are passed up the tree according to a series of licensing principles. These principles constrain the nature of the phrase structure tree since they control how the features are distributed. They add an extra layer of restriction on co-occurrence among constituents (beyond that imposed by the PSRs). Features in GPSG belong to two[6] types: head features and foot features. Head features are those elements associated with the word that are passed up from the head to the phrase; they typically include agreement features, categorial features, etc. Foot features are features that are associated with the non-head material of the phrase that get passed up to the phrase. Two principles govern the passing of these features up the tree; they are, unsurprisingly, the Head-Feature Convention (HFC) and the Foot-Feature Principle (FFP). Again, precise formalization is not relevant at this point, but they both encode the idea that the relevant features get passed up to the next level of constituency unless the PSR or a FCR tells you otherwise. As an example, consider a verb like *ask*, which requires its complement clause to be a question [+Q]. Let us assume that S is a projection of the V head. In a sentence like (16) the only indicator of questionhood of the embedded clause is in the non-head daughter of the S (i.e. the NP *who*). The [+Q] feature of the NP is passed up to the S where it is in a local relationship (i.e. sisterhood) with *ask*.

(16)   I asked who did it.

(17)

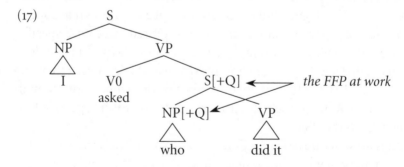

Features are also one of the main mechanisms (in combination with metarules and meaning postulates to be discussed separately, below) by which GPSG generates the effects of movement transformations without an actual transformational rule. The version presented here obscures some important technical details, but will give the reader the flavor of how long-distance dependencies (as are expressed through movement in Chomskyan syntax) are dealt with in GPSG. In GPSG there is a special feature [SLASH], which means roughly "there is a something missing".[7] The SLASH feature is initially licensed in the structure by a metarule (see below) and an FSD—I will leave the details of this aside and just introduce it into the tree at the right place. The tree structure for an NP with a relative clause is given in (18):

(18)

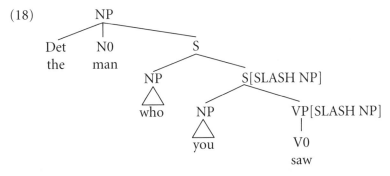

The verb *saw* requires an NP object. In (18) this object is missing, but there is a displaced NP, *who*, which would appear to be the object of this verb. The [SLASH NP] feature on the VP indicates that something is missing. This feature is propagated up the tree by the feature passing principles until a PSR[8] licenses an NP that satisfies this missing NP requirement. The technicalities behind this are actually quite complex; see GKPS for a discussion within GPSG and Sag, Wasow, and Bender (2003) for the related mechanisms in HPSG.

6.5 Metarules

One of the most salient properties of Chomskyan structure-changing transformations[9] is that they serve as a mechanism for capturing the

---

[7] The name is borrowed from the categorial grammar tradition, where a VP that needs a subject NP is written VP\NP and the slash indicates what is missing.

[8] In HPSG this is accomplished by the GAP principle and the Filler rule. See Pollard and Sag (1994) and Sag, Wasow, and Bender (2003) for discussion.

[9] This is not true of the construction-independent movement rules of later Chomskyan grammar such as GB and Minimalism.

relatedness of constructions. For example, for every yes/no question indicated by subject–aux inversion, there is a declarative clause without the subject–aux inversion. Similarly, for (almost) every passive construction there is an active equivalent. The problem with this approach, as shown by Peters and Ritchie (1973), is that the resulting grammar is far more powerful than seems to be exhibited in human languages. The power of transformational grammars is significantly beyond that of a context free grammar. There are many things you can do with a transformation that are not found in human language. GKPS address this problem by creating a new type of rule that does not affect the structural descriptions of sentences, only the rule sets that generate those structures. This allows a restriction on the power of the grammar while maintaining the idea of construction relatedness. These new rules are called metarules. On the surface they look very much like transformations, which has lead many researchers to incorrectly dismiss them as notational variants (in fact they seem to be identical to Harris's 1957 notion of transformation, that is, co-occurence statements stated over PSRs). However, in fact they are statements expressing generalizations across rules—that is, they express limited regularities within the rule set rather than expressing changes in trees. For example, for any rule that introduces an object NP, there is an equivalent phrase structure rule whereby there is a missing object and a slash category is introduced into the phrasal category:

(19)   VP → X NP Y   ⇒   VP[SLASH NP] → X Y

Similarly, for any sentence rule with an auxiliary in it, there is an equivalent rule with an inverted auxiliary.

(20)   S → NP AUX VP   ⇒   S → AUX NP VP

The rules in (19) and (20) are oversimplifications of how the system works and are presented here in a format that, while pedagogically simple, obscures many of the details of the metarule system (mainly having to do with the principles underlying linear order and feature structures; see GKPS or any other major work on GPSG for more details.)

   Although metarules result in a far less powerful grammatical system than transformations (one that is essentially context free), they still are quite a powerful device and it is still possible to write a metarule that will arbitrarily construct an unattested phrase structure rule, just as it is possible to write a crazy transformation that will radically change the structure of a tree. Head-Driven Phrase Structure Grammar (HPSG), a descendant theory of GPSG, abandoned metarules in favor of lexical rules, which are the subject of section 6.8; see Shieber, Stucky, Uszkoreit, and Robinson (1983) for critical evaluation of the notion of metarules and Pollard (1985) for a discussion of the relative merits of metarules versus lexical rules.

6.6 Linear precedence vs. immediate dominance rules

Simple PSGs encode both information about immediate dominance and the linear order of the dominated constituents. Take VP → V NP PP. VP by virtue of being on the left of the arrow immediately dominates all the material to the right of it. The material to the right of the arrow must appear in the linear left-to-right order it appears in the rule. If we adopt the idea that PSRs license trees as node-admissibility conditions (McCawley 1968) rather than create them, then it is actually possible to separate out the dominance relations from the linear ordering. This allows for stating generalizations that are true of all rules. For example, in English, heads usually precede required non-head material. This generalization is missed when we have a set of distinct phrase structure rules, one for each head. By contrast, if we can state the requirement that VPs dominate V (and for example NPs), NPs dominate N and PP, PP dominates P and NP, etc., as in the immediate dominance rules in (21a–c) (where the comma indicates that there is no linear ordering among the elements to the right of the arrow), we can state a single generalization about the ordering of these elements using the linear precedence[10] statement in (21d), (where H is a variable holding over heads and XP is a variable ranging over obligatory phrasal non-head material; ≺ represents precedence).

(21)   (a) VP → V, NP
       (b) NP → N, PP
       (c) PP → P, NP
       (d) H ≺ XP

The distinction between immediate dominance rules (also called ID rules or c-rules) and linear precedence rules (also called LP statements or o-rules) seems to have been simultaneously, but independently, developed in both the GPSG and LFG traditions. The LFG references are Falk

---

[10] See Zwicky (1986b) for an argument from the placement of Finnish Adverbs that ID/LP grammars should represent immediate precedence, not simple precedence.

(1983) and Falk's unpublished Harvard B.A. thesis, in which the rules are called c-rules and o-rules, respectively. The first GPSG reference is Gazdar and Pullum (1981) who invent the more common ID/LP nomenclature. Both sources acknowledge that they came up with the idea independently at around the same time (Falk p.c., GKPS p. 55, n. 4.)

6.7 Meaning postulates (GPSG), f-structures, and metavariables (LFG)

Another common approach to extending the power of a phrase structure grammar is to appeal to a special semantic structure distinct from the syntactic rules that generate the syntactic form. In GPSG, this semantic structure is at least partly homomorphous to the syntactic form; in LFG, the semantic structure (called the f-structure) is related to the syntax through a series of mapping functions.

By appealing to semantics, this type of approach actually moves the burden of explanation of certain syntactico-semantic phenomena from the phrase structure to the interpretive component rather than providing an extension to the phrase structure grammar or its output as transformations, features and metarules do.

6.7.1 Meaning postulates in GPSG

In GPSG, the semantics of a sentence are determined by a general semantic "translation" principle, which interprets each local tree (i.e. a mother and its daughters) according to the principles of functional application. We will discuss these kinds of principles in detail in Chapter 9 when we look at categorial grammars, but the basic intuition is that when you take a two-place predicate like *kiss*, which has the semantic representation $kiss'(x)(y)$, where x and y are variables representing the kissee and the kisser, respectively. When you create a VP [*kissed Pat*] via the PSR, this is interpreted as $kiss'(pat')(y)$, and when you apply the S $\rightarrow$ NP VP rule to license the S node, [$_S$ *Chris* [$_{VP}$ *kissed Pat*]] is interpreted as substituting *Chris* for the variable y. However, in addition to these straightforward interpretation rules, there are also principles for giving interpretations that do not map directly from the tree but may be governed by lexical or other factors. These are "meaning postulates".[11] While metarules capture construction relatedness; the

---

[11] The name comes from Carnap (1952), but the GPSG usage refers to a larger set of structures than Carnap intended.

meaning postulates serve to explain the differences among those constructions. For example, in a passive, the NP that is a daughter of the S is
to be interpreted the same way as the NP daughter of VP in an active
verb. Similarly, the PP daughter of VP with a passive verb is to be
interpreted the same way as NP daughter of S with an active verb.

Another example comes from the difference between raising verbs
like *seem* and control verbs *try*. The subject NP of a verb like *try* (as in
22a) is interpreted as being an argument of both the main verb (*try*)
and the embedded verb (*leave*). By contrast, although *Paul* is the
apparent subject of the verb *seem* in (22b), it is only interpreted as
the subject of the embedded verb (*leave*).

(22)   (a) Paul tried to leave.
       (b) Paul seemed to leave.

In early transformational grammar, the difference between these was
expressed via the application of two distinct transformations. Sentence
(22a) was generated via a deletion operation (Equi-NP deletion) of the
second *Paul* from a deep structure like *Paul tried Paul to leave*; sentence
(22b) was generated by a raising operation that took the subject of an
embedded predicate and made it the subject of the main clause (so *John left
seemed* → *John seemed to leave*). In GPSG, these sentences in (22) have
identical constituent structures but are given different argument interpretations by virtue of different meaning postulates that correspond to the
different verbs involved. With verbs like *try*, we have a meaning postulate
that tells us to interpret *Paul* as the argument of both verbs (23a). With
verbs like *seem* the meaning postulate tells us to interpret the apparent NP
argument of *seem* as though it were really the argument of *leave* (23b).

(23)   (a) $(try' \ (leave'))(Paul') \Rightarrow (try' \ (leave' \ (Paul')))(Paul')$
       (b) $(seem' \ (leave'))(Paul') \Rightarrow (seem' \ (leave' \ (Paul')))$

So the mismatch between constituent structure and meaning is dealt
with by semantic rules of this type rather than as a mapping between
two syntactic structures.

6.7.2 Functional equations, f-structures, and metavariables in LFG

Lexical-Functional Grammar uses a similar semantic extension to the
constituent structure (or c-structure as it is called in LFG): the f-structure,
which is similar to the feature structures of GPSG, but without

the arboreal organization. The relationship between c-structure (constituent structure) and f-structure is mediated by a series of functions. Consider the c-structure given in (24). Here each node is marked with a functional variable (f_1, f_2, etc.) These functions are introduced into the structure via the phrase structure rules in a manner to be made explicit in a moment.

(24)

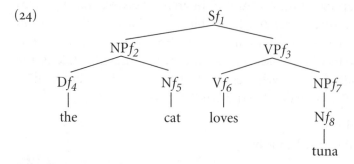

Each terminal node is associated with certain lexical features; for example, the verb *loves* contributes the fact that the predicate of the expression involves "loving", is in the present tense, and has a third-person subject. The noun *cat* contributes the fact that there is a cat involved, etc. These lexical features are organized into the syntactico-semantic structure (known as the f-structure), not by virtue of the tree, but by making reference to the functional variables. This is accomplished by means of a set of equations known as the f-description of the sentence (25). These map the information contributed by each of the nodes in the constituent tree into the information of the final f-structure (26).

(25) $(f_1 \text{ SUBJ}) = f_2$
$f_2 = f_4$
$f_2 = f_5$
$(f_4 \text{ DEF}) = +$
$(f_5 \text{ PRED}) = \text{'cat'}$
$(f_5 \text{ NUM}) = \text{sg}$
$f_1 = f_3$
$f_3 = f_6$
$(f_6 \text{ PRED}) = \text{'love} \langle \dots \rangle\text{'}$
$(f_6 \text{ TENSE}) = \text{present}$
$(f_6 \text{ SUBJ NUM}) = \text{sg}$
$(f_6 \text{ SUBJ PERS}) = \text{3rd}$
$(f_6 \text{ OBJ}) = f_7$
$f_7 = f_8$
$(f_8 \text{ PRED}) = \text{'tuna'}$

(26) f_1, f_3, f_6
$$
\begin{bmatrix}
\text{PRED} & \text{'love <SUBJ, OBJ>'} \\
\text{TENSE} & \textit{present} \\
& \quad f_2, f_4, f_5 \begin{bmatrix} \text{DEF} & + \\ \text{NUM} & \textit{sng} \\ \text{PRED} & \text{'cat'} \end{bmatrix} \\
\text{SUBJ} & \\
\\
\text{OBJ} & \quad f_7, f_8 \begin{bmatrix} \text{PRED} & \text{'tuna'} \end{bmatrix}
\end{bmatrix}
$$

Typically, these functional equations are encoded into the system using a set of "metavariables", which range over the functions as in (23–26). The notation here looks complicated, but is actually very straightforward. Most of the metavariables have two parts, the second of which is typically "$=\downarrow$"; this means "comes from the node I annotate". The first part indicates what role the node plays in the f-structure. For example, "($\uparrow$SUBJ)" means the subject of the dominating node. So "($\uparrow$SUBJ)$=\downarrow$" means "the information associated with the node I annotate maps to the subject feature (function) of the node that dominates me." "$\uparrow=\downarrow$" means that the node is the head of the phrase that dominates it, and all information contained within that head is passed up to the f-structure associated with the dominator. These metavariables are licensed in the representation via annotations on the phrase structure rules as in (27). A metavariable-annotated c-structure corresponding to (24) is given in (28).

(27) S →   NP   VP
              ($\uparrow$SUBJ) $=\downarrow$ $\uparrow=\downarrow$

      VP →   V   NP
             $\uparrow=\downarrow$ ($\uparrow$OBJ)$=\downarrow$

      NP →   (D)   N
             $\uparrow=\downarrow$ $\uparrow=\downarrow$

(28)

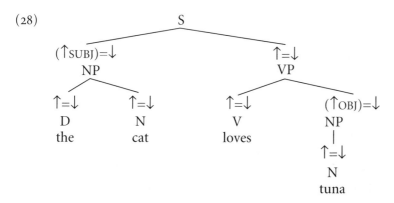

F-equations aren't only licensed by the metavariables; they can also act as statements that correspond almost identically to GPSG's meaning postulates. A raising verb like *seem* has an f-equation in its lexical entry stating that its subject is to be interpreted as the embedded predicate's (↑XCOMP in (29)) subject. This is similar to the meaning postulates in (23).

(29)   *seem* (↑SUBJ) = (↑XCOMP SUBJ)

6.7.3 Summary

The extensions to constituent structure/phrase structure suggested in this section all make reference to mapping the constituent structure onto some kind of enriched semantic structure. The empirical coverage of these extensions, although not the practicalities, correspond in many cases to the kind of phenomena that transformations and metarules were designed to handle. In the next section, we consider extensions that do similar work but instead, shift the added empirical burden to the generative lexicon.

6.8 The lexicon

One of the major problems with structure-changing transformations was their unbounded power. In principle, you could have a transformational rule turn any sentence into any other sentence. This not only extends the constituent structure but makes it nearly limitlessly powerful (Peters and Ritchie 1973). One way to restrict the power of transformation-like rules is to tie them closely to morphological operations. Under such a view, the fact that the argument-reordering principles such as the passive are linked to a particular morphology is explained. If we assume that the lexicon is not a static list, but instead is itself a generative engine, then we can posit certain kinds of operations that hold only over words and the narrow properties of those words. These are known as lexical rules and are found in LFG, HPSG and to a lesser extent in the lexicalist versions of GB and Minimalism.

A typical example common to all three approaches would be a lexical-rule approach to passive. The operation that applies passive morphology to the verb (i.e. changes the verb to its passive participle form) also changes the argument structure of the verb, so that the external (first) NP is either removed or made optional (in a PP). If one assumes HPSG or LFG, the second (internal) argument is promoted to the first position. If one is assuming GB, then the promotion of the internal argument happens via a movement rule in the syntax. Either way, the operation is lexically restricted.

The addition of the generative lexicon thus provides an extension to phrase structure grammars that allows a constrained account of some of the phenomena that a PSG cannot handle.

6.9 Conclusion

Phrase structure grammars and the trees they generate are useful and powerful tools. They can account for a wide range of constituency and related facts. However, they are also simultaneously more and less powerful than is necessary for accounting for human language. In this chapter, we have looked at some of the extensions to PSGs (transformations, features, metarules, lexical rules, ID/LP format, meaning postulates and metavariables) that might allow a greater range of empirical coverage. In the next chapter, we consider X-bar theory, which places restrictions on the form of PSGs and—under some approaches—actually leads to the elimination of PSGs as the primary means of generating constituent structure.

7

X-bar Theory

7.1 Introduction

Phrase structure grammars and their extensions provide us with powerful tools for describing constituent structures, but the range and extent of their adequacy is a matter of debate. There is, however, one particular extension to phrase structure grammars that has been almost universally adopted at one point or another by formal linguists: X-bar theory. X-bar theory serves both as an extension to phrase structure grammars and places a number of restrictions on the form that phrase structure rules (PSRs) can take. We start this discussion by looking at some of the ways in which PSRs are not powerful enough or the ways in which they fail to capture the right level of generalization, and the ways in which they can be too powerful and can over-generate. These will serve as the motivations for some of the central ideas of X-bar theory. Then we turn to the history of X-bar theory and take a look at how it has been variously implemented in grammatical theory.

7.2 Simple PSGs vs. X-bar theoretic PSGs

7.2.1 Headedness

There are a number of ways in which PSGs are overly powerful. Let us start with the relationship between the phrasal element and the categories that rewrite it. Consider the sentences in (1):

(1)   (a) The cat was *running along the fence-posts.*
      (b) *Running along fence-posts* is dangerous for your health.

Let us assume that *was* in (1a) is merely a representation of tense and aspect.[1] This means that, all other things being equal, the gerund participle *running* in (1a) is a verb in the sentence. In (1b) by contrast,

---

[1] This is not an uncontroversial assumption, but we will use it here as a starting position.

a nearly identical phrase to the italicized phrase in (1a) is used as the subject of the sentence and thus has a nominal character. Let us assume that the italicized phrase (in 1a) was partly created by the PSR VP→ V PP; it seems not unreasonable that we could deal with the nearly identical phrase in (1b) with a similar rule NP → V PP. The odd thing about this rule is that there is no noun in this NP. It seems to be compatible with the data and there is nothing in the PSG formulation that prevents rules from not having a clear head. In fact, in many PSGs there is usually at least one rule, S → NP VP, which crucially is non-headed. In early generative grammar[2], one often found examples of other non-headed rules, such as NP → S'. This allows the embedding of tensed clauses in positions otherwise restricted to NPs:

(2) (a) [NP Loud noises] bother Andy.
     (b) [NP [S' That categories are fuzzy]] bothers Andy.

These rules appear then to have empirical motivation. On the other hand, they also seem to significantly overgenerate, as seen in the application of NP → V PP in (3):

(3) *Ran along the fence posts is dangerous for your health.[3]

This sentence is also generated by the unheaded NP rule. Controlling for this type of overgeneration might involve avoiding non-headed rules and generating pairs like (1a, b) by some other means.

The requirement that a phrase bear the same category as its head is known as "endocentricity". Using the variable X to stand for any category, we can schematize this as (4). This is the simple requirement that a phrase (XP) be of the same category as some semantically prominent word (the head) in it. The X here is the "X" in "X-bar theory".

(4) XP → ...X...

As we will see in this chapter, the exact interpretation of what this rule means varies from author to author and from theory to theory, but for now the reader can take this to be simply a metaconstraint

---

[2] In fact, unheaded constituents are still common in Lexical-Functional Grammar (Bresnan 2001).

[3] The ungrammaticality of (3) might be controlled through the judicious use of features (NP → V$_{[-Tense]}$ PP). In addition, the notion of what it means to be a noun or verb or any other category is not at all clear, but the complex discussion over syntactic categories lies well beyond the scope of this book. See Baker (2003) and the references cited therein for a view of this controversial topic.

on the form of phrase structure rules, such that it prohibits rules such as NP → V PP.

7.2.2 Structural refinement[4]

The discussion that follows in this section is not a criticism of the formalism of PSGs nor even of their empirical coverage. Indeed, the distinctions we make here may be captured easily in a PSG. Instead, what is at stake is a question of whether or not a simple PSG properly captures the right generalizations at the right level of abstraction of syntactic structure.

One of the innovations of the 1970s (see in particular Jackendoff 1977) was the realization that syntactic structure is significantly more refined than the PSGs of the 1950s and 1960s might suggest. Consider, for example, the NP *the big bag of groceries with the plastic handles* and take the constituency test of replacement. There is a particular variety of this process, *one*-replacement, that seems to target a constituent that is smaller than the whole phrase and larger than the head word:

(5)   I bought the big [bag of groceries with the plastic handle] not the small [one].

One-replacement seems to be able to target other subgroups intermediate in size between the phrase and the head:

(6)   I bought the big [bag of groceries] with the plastic handle, not the small [one] with the ugly logo.

These facts seem to point to a more refined structure for the NP:

(7)

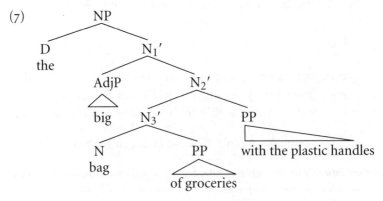

---

[4] Parts of the discussion in this section, including examples, is based on Carnie (2006c).

One-replacement in (6) targets the node labeled N_3', in (5) it targets the node labeled N_2'. We have to change the NP slightly to get evidence for N_1'. If we change the determiner *the* to *that*, we can use *one*-replacement to target N_1'.

(8) I want [$_{NP}$ this [$_{N'}$ big bag of groceries with the plastic handle]] not [$_{NP}$ that [$_{N'}$ one]].

The conjunction test gives us evidence for similar smaller than NP, larger than N, categories.

(9) (a) Calvin is [the [dean of humanities] and [director of social sciences]].

  (b) Give me [the [blue book] and [red binder]].

In each of these sentences the conjoined elements exclude the determiner but include more than the head.

We find similar evidence when we look at other categories. There is a similar process to *one*-replacement found in the syntax of VPs. This is the process of *do-so*[5]- (or *did-so*-) replacement. Consider the VP bracketed in (10a). We find replacement of the whole VP is fine (10b), but so is the replacement of smaller units (10c):

(10) (a) I [ate beans with a fork].
    (b) I [ate beans with a fork] and Geordi [did so] too.
    (c) I [ate beans] with a fork but Janet [did (so)] with a spoon.

This points to a structure at least as refined as (11).[6]

(11)

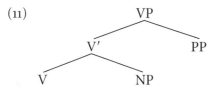

Similarly, conjunction seems to show an intermediate V′ projection:

(12) The chef [eats beans] and [tosses salads] with forks.

The structure of (12) involves the conjunction of two V′ nodes:

---

[5] Depending on which dialect of English you speak, you may prefer *did too* over *did so too* or *did so*. If the VPs below sound odd, try substituting *did* or *did too* for *did so*.

[6] We will in fact argue later that there may be more structure than this in this phrase.

(13)

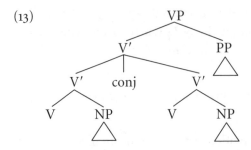

The arguments for intermediate structure in AdjPs are a little trickier, as English seems to limit the amount of material that can appear in an AdjP in any case. However, we do see such structure in phrases like (14):

(14)   the [very [[bright blue] and [dull green]]] gown

In this NP, *bright* clearly modifies *blue*, and *dull* clearly modifies *green*. One possible interpretation of this phrase (although not the only one) allows *very* to modify both *bright blue* and *dull green*. If this is the case then the structure must minimally look like (15).

(15)

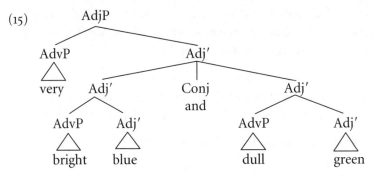

This must be the structure so that the AdvP can modify both *bright blue* and *dull green*.

Under certain circumstances, some adjectives appear to allow prepositional modifiers to follow them:

(16)   (a) I am afraid/frightened of tigers.
       (b) I am fond of circus performers.

These post-adjectival PPs parallel the direct object of related verbs:

(17)   (a) I fear tigers.
       (b) I like circus performers.

Consider now:

(18)   I am [[afraid/frightened of tigers] and [fond of clowns] without exception].

Under one reading of this sentence, *without exception* modifies both *afraid of tigers* and *fond of circus performers*. Again this would seem to suggest that the sentence has the constituency represented by the above bracketing, which points towards intermediate structure in AdjPs too. There is also a replacement phenomenon that seems to target Adj's. This is *so*-replacement:

(19)   Bob is [very [serious about Mary]], but [less [so]] than Paul.

The adjective phrase here is *very serious about Mary*, but *so*-replacement only targets *serious about Mary*.

The following sentences contain complex PPs:

(20)   Gwen placed it [right [in the middle of the spaghetti sauce]].
(21)   Maurice was [[in love] with his boss].
(22)   Susanna was [utterly [in love]].

In these examples, we have what appear to be prepositional phrases (*in the middle of the spaghetti sauce, in love*) that are modified by some other element: *right, with his boss*, and *utterly* respectively. Note, however, that you can target smaller units within these large PPs with constituency tests:

(23)   Gwen knocked it [right [off the table] and [into the trash]].
(24)   Maurice was [[in love] and [at odds] with his boss].
(25)   Susanna was [utterly [in love]], but Louis was only [partly [so]].

Examples (23) and (24) show conjunction of the two smaller constituents. Example (25) is an example of *so*-replacement.

The fine-grained structures that these constituency tests reveal are *bar-level* categories, typically written as N', V', Adj', etc. The name comes from the original notation for these categories, which involved writing an overbar or macron over the letter ($\bar{N}$). Overbars are typographically hard to produce, so most linguists replace the bar with a prime (') or an apostrophe ('). There are equivalent notations for the phrasal level as well, which can be written with a P, a double apostrophe, a double prime, a double overbar, or a superscript ^{max} (NP = N″ = N" = $\bar{\bar{N}}$ = N^{max}). These are equivalent notations in most modern systems of X-bar theory.[7]

---

[7] However, see the discussion below of Jackendoff's (1977) system, where the double bar, double apostrophe, and double prime notations are not necessarily equivalent to the XP or X^{max} notations.

It is not difficult to write PSRs that capture bar-level structure. The following additional rules would account for all the sentences above. (These rules aren't remotely complete or accurate, but they suffice for expository purposes.)

(26) (a)   NP → (D) N′
      (b)   N′ → (AdjP) N′
      (c)   N′ → N′ (PP)
      (d)   N′ → N (PP)
      (e)   AdjP → (AdvP) Adj′
      (f)   Adj′ → Adj′ (PP)
      (g)   Adj′→ Adj (PP)
      (h)   VP → (AdvP) V′
      (i)   V′ → V′ (PP)
      (j)   V′ → V (NP)
      (k)   PP → (AdvP) P′
      (l)   P′ → P′ (PP)
      (m)   P′ → P NP

Obviously, this greatly increases the complexity of the PSG component. More seriously, it seems to miss some basic generalizations. Let us note two here and save the third and fourth for the next two sections. First, the combination of rules for each syntactic category always leads to a structure that has three levels; that is, there are no rules where the phrasal level (XP) goes directly to the head (X); instead there is always an intervening X′ level. Thus for every head noun we will have at least two rule applications; one that rewrites NP as N′ and one that rewrites N′ as N. There are no rules that rewrite NP directly as N.

The second generalization we can make about these rules is that for every head type there is at least one rule, stated at the single bar level, that is self-recursive. That is, there is a category X′ that rewrites as another X′ (e.g. N′ → N′ (PP)).

The PSG in (26) fails to capture these generalizations. With X-bar theory, which uses variables, it is not difficult to express these generalizations. We can revise (4) into a set of statements about the form of phrase structure rules. We need three statements:[8] one to rewrite the phrase into a bar level (XP→…X′…); one to recursively rewrite the bar level into another bar level (X′→…X′…); and finally one to

---

[8] There are many X-bar grammars that do not use three rules (e.g. Jackendoff 1977). We return to details of these systems below.

rewrite the bar level category into a head/terminal ($X' \to \ldots X \ldots$). Again, for the moment one can think of these statements as meta-theoretical restrictions on the form of PSRs that ensure that only rules of the right type can be part of a PSG.

These rules also account for cross-categorial generalizations about the kinds of elements that co-occur with various heads. Consider the classic example using the fairly uncontroversial verb *destroyed* and the uncontroversially nominal *destruction*:

(27) (a) The barbarians destroyed the city.
      (b) The barbarian's destruction of the city...

Consider the relationship between the verb *destroy* and the two NPs in (27a). Semantically, these relationships appear to be identical to the relationships of the argument NPs to the noun *destruction* in (27b). In both (27a) and (27b), the barbarians are doing the destroying, and the city is the thing destroyed. Here we have a cross-categorial generalization. The treatment of such constructions was at the heart of the so-called Linguistics Wars (see Newmeyer 1980, R. Harris 1993, and Huck and Goldsmith 1996 for surveys of the debates). Chomsky (1970) proposed that the easiest way to capture such generalizations was to abstract away from the syntax, and locate them in lexicon. That is, there is a basic root meaning "destroy", which can realized morphologically either as a noun or a verb. The basic argument relations are associated with this root. The syntax provides a schema (the X-bar statements), which ensures that the argument properties of a root can be realized independently of a category-specific rule (such as VP $\to$ V (NP)). This builds on the semantic notion of *head*. The elements that appear in a phrase, and the internal properties of that phrase, are dependent on the properties of the head category. More technically, the properties of the phrase are said to *project* from the head. This means that the exact content of a phrase is determined by the lexical entry for its head (in whatever manner this information is encoded, such as a subcategorization frame or feature). In order to capture cross-categorial generalizations, then, phrase structure rules must be subject to a restriction that different categories can be realized with the same types of arguments. With the X-bar statements in place as restrictions on the form of PS rules, this is guaranteed.[9]

---

[9] This is a slight oversimplification. Chomsky (1981) argues that an additional constraint, the Projection Principle, is required to guarantee that lexical properties are respected throughout the derivation.

We'll conclude this section with a little extra terminology that goes along with the notion of headedness and projection. Consider the NP in (28).

(28)

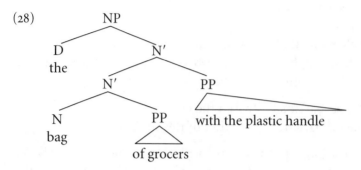

Each of the N's and the NP in (28) are called the projections of the N. The NP is the maximal projection and the N's are intermediate projections. Modification relations are no longer expressed in terms of sisterhood to the head; instead, modifiers of a head are sisters to any projection of that head.

7.2.3 Binarity

The constituency tests we've seen in this chapter and the rules given in (26) reveal another important property that X-bar theory might account for. It appears as if the layers of structure operate in a binary manner.[10] That is, as we add layers of structure, new material is added one element at a time to the existing structure, thus creating a binary branching tree structure. The three X-bar statements mentioned above can be modified to capture this:

(29)   (a) XP → (YP) X'
      (b) X' → (ZP) X'
      (c) X' → X' (ZP)
      (d) X' → X (WP)

Instead of ellipses (...), we use the variable categories YP, WP, and ZP to stand in for the modifiers. These are listed as optional as the phrase can consist of a head without any modifiers at all. They are also all

---

[10] See Chametzky (2000) for a discussion of how this insight is retained in the minimalist non-X-bar-theoretic Bare Phrase Structure system.

listed as phrasal, including the one in (29a), which is typically occupied by a bare determiner. We will return to this contradiction below.

Binarity is a common—but by no means universal—part of X-bar theory.

7.2.4 Distinctions among modifier types

Given our three types of rule, which introduce three distinct layers of structure, we predict that we should have at least three distinct types of head-modifiers. This appears to be true. We find good evidence that we need to distinguish among *specifiers* (the YP in the XP → (YP) X' rule), *adjuncts* (the ZP in the X' → (ZP) X' and X' → X' (ZP) rules) and *complements* (the WP in the X' → X (WP) rule).[11]

Consider the two prepositional phrases that are subconstituents of the following NP:

(30)   the bag [PP of groceries] [PP with the plastic handle]

Using the X-bar schema, we can generate the following tree for this NP:

(31)

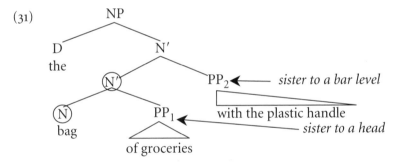

You will note that the two PPs in this tree are at different levels in the tree. The lower PP₁ is a sister to the head N (*bag*), whereas the higher PP₂ is a sister to the N' dominating the head N and PP₁. Notice also that these two PPs were introduced by different rule types. PP₁ is

---

[11] Napoli (1989) argues against this distinction referring to the reverse ordering of adjuncts and complements in Italian NPs such as:

(i) la   distruzione   brutale   de Troia
    the   distruction   brutal   of Troy
    spec *head*   *adjunct* *complement*
    "the brutal destruction of Troy"

See Longobardi (1994) for an alternative analysis that involves movement of the head around the adjunct to its surface position.

introduced by the rule meeting the X′ → X (WP) schema and PP$_2$ is introduced by the higher-level rule type (X′ → X′ (ZP)).

An XP that is a sister to a head is a *complement*. PP$_1$ is a complement. XPs that are sisters to single-bar levels and are daughters of another bar level are *adjuncts*. PP$_2$ in (31) is an adjunct. The third type of modifier is a *specifier*. These are sisters to the bar level and daughter of a maximal category. The determiner in (31) is a specifier. If we abstract away from specific categories we can distinguish among modifiers as seen in (32).

(32)

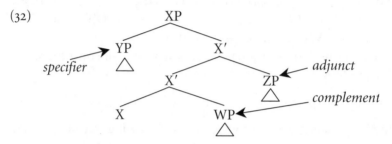

We predict these different kinds of modifier to exhibit different behaviors. We'll concentrate first on the distinction between complements and adjuncts then turn to specifiers.

Take NPs as a prototypical example. Consider the difference in meaning between the two NPs below:

(33) (a) the bag of groceries
      (b) the bag with a plastic handle

Although both these examples seem to have, on the surface, parallel structures (a determiner followed by a noun followed by a prepositional phrase), in reality they have quite different structures. The PP in (33a) is a complement and has the following tree:

(34)

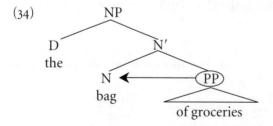

You will note that the circled PP is a sister to N, so it is a complement. By contrast, the structure of (33b) is:

(35)

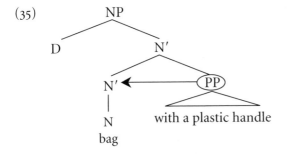

Here the PP *with a plastic handle* is a sister to N', so it is an adjunct.

Observe that rules that introduce complements also introduce the head (X). This means that the complement will be both adjacent to the head and, more importantly, closer to the head than an adjunct.

(36)   the   bag   [of groceries]   [with a plastic handle]
            head   *complement*   *adjunct*

(37)   ??the   bag   [with a plastic handle]   [of groceries]
              head   *adjunct*   *complement*

Since the adjunct rules take an X' level category and rewrite it as an X' category, adjuncts will always be higher in the tree than the output of the complement rule (which takes an X' and rewrites an X). Since lines can not cross, this means that complements will always be lower in the tree than adjuncts, and will always be closer to the head than adjuncts.

The adjunct rules are iterative. This means that the rule can generate infinite strings of X' nodes, since the rule can apply over and over again to its own output:

(38)

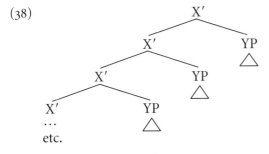

Complement rules do not have this property. On the left side of such rules there is an X', but on the right there is only X. So the rule cannot apply iteratively—that is, it can only apply once within an XP. What this means for complements and adjuncts is that you can have any number of adjuncts (39), but you can only ever have one complement (40):

(39)   the book [of poems] [with a red cover] [from Oxford]
       head   complement   adjunct   adjunct
       [by Robert Burns]
           adjunct

(40)   *the book   [of poems]   [of fiction]   [with a red cover]
             head   complement   complement   adjunct

The tree for (39) is given below; note that since there is only one N, there can only be one complement, but since there are multiple N's, there can be as many adjuncts as desired.

(41)

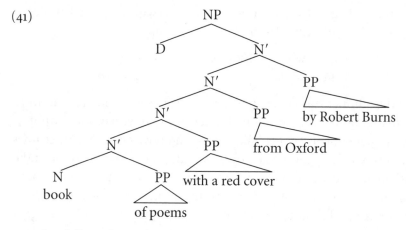

It also follows from the iterative nature of adjunct rules that adjuncts can be reordered with respect to one another, but one can never reorder a complement with the adjuncts:

(42)   (a)   the book of poems with a red cover from Oxford by Robert Burns
       (b)   the book of poems from Oxford with a red cover by Robert Burns
       (c)   the book of poems from Oxford by Robert Burns with a red cover
       (d)   the book of poems by Robert Burns from Oxford with a red cover
       (e)   the book of poems by Robert Burns with a red cover from Oxford

(f) the book of poems with a red cover by Robert Burns from Oxford

(g) *the book with a red cover of poems from Oxford by Robert Burns

(h) *the book with a red cover from Oxford of poems by Robert Burns

(i) *the book with a red cover from Oxford by Robert Burns of poems

etc.

Conjunction also distinguishes these types of modifier. Conjunction is typically restricted to constituents of the same general kind and result in a complex constituent of the same type as its conjuncts. Imagine one were to conjoin a complement with an adjunct, resulting in a contradictory situation: something can not be both a sister to X′ and X at the same time. Adjuncts can conjoin with other adjuncts (other sisters to X′), and complements can conjoin with other complements (other sisters to X), but complements cannot conjoin with adjuncts:

(43) (a)   the book of poems with a red cover and with a blue spine[12]
      (b)   the book of poems and of fiction from Oxford
      (c) *the book of poems and from Oxford

Finally, recall the test of *one*-replacement. This operation replaces an N′ node with the word *one*. Look at the tree in (44):

(44)

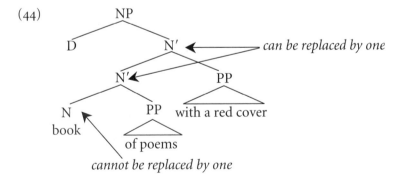

Two possibilities for *one*-replacement exist. It can target the highest N′, and produce (45):

(45)   the one

It can target the lower N′ and produce (46):

---

[12] If this NP sounds odd to you, try putting emphasis on *and*.

(46)   the one with a red cover

For many speakers—but not all—the N head may not be targeted. This means that *one* followed by a complement is ill-formed:

(47)   *the one of poems with a red cover[13]

Since complements are sisters to X and not X′, they cannot stand next to the word *one*. Adjuncts, by definition, can.

   The distinction between complements and adjuncts is not limited to NPs; we find it holds in all the major syntactic categories. The best example is seen in VPs: the direct object of a verb is a complement of the verb, while prepositional and adverbial modifiers are adjuncts:

(48)   I loved   [the policeman]   [intensely]   [with all my heart].
                        complement   *adjunct*   *adjunct*

(49)

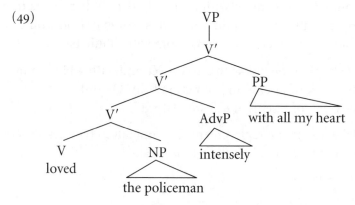

Direct objects must be adjacent to the verb, and there can only be one of them.

(50)   (a) *I loved intensely the policeman with all my heart.
         (b) *I loved the policeman the baker intensely with all my heart.

Did-so (*did-too*) replacement targets V′. Like one-replacement, this means that it can only apply before an adjunct and not before a complement:

(51)   Mika loved the policemen intensely and
         (a)   Susan did so half-heartedly.
         (b)   *Susan did so the baker.

---

[13] Not everyone finds this NP ill-formed. There is at least one major US dialect where sentence (47) is entirely acceptable.

The evidence for the adjunct–complement distinction in adjective phrases and prepositional phrases is considerably weaker than that of nouns and verbs. Adverbs that modify adjectives have an adjunct flair—they can be stacked and reordered. Other than this, however, the evidence for the distinction between PPs and AdjPs comes mainly as a parallel to the NPs and VPs. This may be less than satisfying, but is balanced by the formal simplicity of having the same system apply to all categories.

Specifiers are the third type of modifier. Thus far we've only seen one, the determiner in the NP:

(52)   [the]   [book]   [of poems]   [with a red cover]
         specifier head   complement   adjunct

(53)

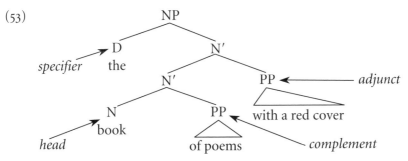

The specifier is defined as the daughter of XP and sister to X′:

(54)   *Specifier*: An element that is a sister to an X′ level, and a daughter of an XP.

Specifiers are different from adjuncts and complements. Since the specifier rule is not recursive, there can only be one specifier:[14]

(55)   *the these red books

The specifier rule has to apply at the top of the structure, which means that the specifier will always be the left-most element (in English):

(56)   *boring the book

This example also shows that specifiers cannot be reordered with respect to other adjuncts or complements. As the final difference between specifiers and other types of modifier, specifiers can only be conjoined with other specifiers:

---

[14] It is not hard to find exceptions to this claim, as in *all the books*. If determiners are heads rather than specifiers (Abney 1987), then this problem disappears.

(57) (a)   two or three books
      (b)   *two or boring books

In the late 1980s, with the advent of X-bar theoretic functional categories (IP, TP, etc.) instead of S (see ch. 11), determiners and other categories that had been assumed to be specifiers shifted in their phrase structure position. Abney (1987) proposed that determiners headed their own phrase, which dominated the NP. What then became of the specifier? Around the same time, it was suggested that specifiers have a special role, serving as the identifiers of subjects of various kinds of phrase (Stowell 1981; for a critique see Borsley 1996). For example, Koopman and Sportiche (1991) propose that subject arguments start as the specifier of the VP (the VP internal subject hypothesis), and then move to the specifier of some higher functional projection (e.g. IP). See also Fukui and Speas (1986) and Fukui (1995). This kind of approach is widely adopted in Chomskyan P&P theory and in the Minimalist Program, but not elsewhere.

7.2.5 Cross-linguistic variation

Consider the position of direct objects (complements) in Turkish. In Turkish, the complement precedes the head:

(58) Hasan   kitab-i   oku-du.
      Hasan-SUBJ   book-OBJ   read-PAST
      "Hasan read the book."

Interestingly, X-bar theory provides an avenue for exploring the differences and similarities among languages. Travis (1989) proposed that a certain amount of cross-linguistic variation in word order could be explained by allowing languages to parameterize the direction of headedness in the X-bar schema. Take, for example, the complement rule. In English, complements of verbs follow the verbal head. In Turkish, they precede it. There are two options in the rule:

(59) (a) $X' \rightarrow X$ (WP)
      (b) $X' \rightarrow$ (WP) X

The child learning English will adopt option (a), the child learning Turkish will adopt option (b). I am obscuring some of the details here, but this provides a relatively elegant account of cross-linguistic variation. X-bar theory allows individual languages to select among a finite set of phrase structure options:

(60) (a) XP → (YP) X' *or* XP → X' (YP)
      (b) X' → X' (ZP) *or* X' → (ZP) X'
      (c) X' → X (WP) *or* X' → (WP) X

For a contrasting analysis in the GPSG framework, see Fodor and Crain (1990).

7.2.6 Summary

In this section, we have surveyed some of the motivations for X-bar theory as well as one particular formulation of the X-bar schema itself. Phrase structure rules can be overly powerful, thus motivating an endocentricity requirement. Evidence for intermediate structure (X') takes us to the point where we see similarities across categories in terms of the kinds of phrase structure rule that are allowed. Cross-categorial generalizations about structure tie up the knot, showing that a variable-based notation is motivated. Next, we saw that the distinct modifier types of complement, specifier and adjunct, predicted by the X-bar schema, seem to be well motivated. Finally, we saw how the X-bar schema at least partly allows for a straightforward and constrained theory of cross-linguistic variation.

In the next section, we survey the history of X-bar theory, including an ontological discussion of what the X-bar formalism represents.

7.3 A short history of X-bar theory[15]

7.3.1 The origins: Harris (1946) and Chomsky (1970)

The bar notation (actually the numerical N^1, N^2, etc. equivalents) is first found in a work on the substitution task for identifying constituency within the word in Harris (1946). This work emphasizes the differences among types of hierarchical modifier, but it does not focus on the syntax, nor does it use the variable notation prevalent in modern X-bar theory. The point of Harris's notation was to limit overgeneration of recursive structures within words.

Chomsky (1970) adapted this part of the notation but developed it into the beginnings of X-bar theory. At the time, one of the driving issues in the theory was to explain the relations between constructions that appeared to have similar semantics but differed in the categorial

---

[15] For excellent histories of the X-bar theory, see Stuurman (1985), Leffel and Bouchard (1991), and Fukui (2001).

realization of the semantic relations. For example, there appears to be a restriction on the animacy of arguments with both the verb *kill* and its nominalization *killing*.

(61)   (a) #Sincerity killed the stone
      (b) #Sincerity's killing of the stone

In the prevailing theoretical paradigm of the time—Generative Semantics—this was captured by a transformational rule of nominalization. However, Chomsky (1970) noted that not all nominalizations behave as if they were transformationally related. He distinguishes between "gerundive nominals" (e.g. *criticizing*), which he claims are transformationally related, and "derived nominals" (e.g. *criticism*), whose categories are syntactically primitive (appear as such at D-structure). For example, he observes among other properties that gerundive nominals can take an adverb but (most) derived nominals can not:

(62)   (a) Marie's constantly criticizing the president was a shock.
      (b) Marie's constant(*ly) criticism of the president was a shock.

Chomsky proposed X-bar theory as an explanation for why derived nominals still express other cross-categorial generalizations (such as those in (61)) even though they are not transformationally related.

7.3.2 Early controversies: Emonds (1976), Jackendoff (1977), Stuurman (1984)

One of the most rigorous early elaborations of X-bar theory is found in Jackendoff (1977). The precise proposals there, along with proposals in Emonds (1973), Siegal (1974), Bresnan (1976), Halitzky (1975), Hornstein (1977) and Muysken (1982) gave rise to a number of interrelated questions about the exact form of X-bar theory. At issue were the number of bar levels (X', X'', X''', etc.), the nature of specifiers (were they auxiliaries, subjects, determiners, etc.?), the number of specifiers, the nature of the S category (is it V'', V''', or something entirely different?). Newmeyer (1986) and Stuurman (1985) both have excellent summaries of the debates.

Although some practitioners of LFG, GPSG, and HPSG still equate the S category with a projection of V, the current thinking within most versions of Principles and Parameters theory holds that the S category is a projection of a functional category (Infl or T). This came with the arguments from verb movement that functional elements were heads in their own right instead of specifiers (as had previously been thought, see for example Emonds 1985). More discussion of this can be found in

Chapter 11. This in turn opened up the possibility that specifiers were uniquely linked to subjecthood (Stowell 1981).

The nature and number of projection types (X', X'', X''') was also an early source of controversy. Chomsky's original proposal did not allow for recursion at the X' level. Jackendoff's version[16] simply allowed an additional prime for each additional layer of structure. Emonds (1976, 1973) and the extensions in Stuurman (1986) had a fairly complicated system that allowed for constituents to rewrite as a bar level equal to or lower than the constituent's own.[17] The consensus in the more recent literature (see e.g. Haegeman 2001) seems to roughly follow the proposal of Muysken (1982)[18] that there are only really three projection types: $X°$ (heads), whose sister is the complement; iterative X' categories, whose sisters are usually adjuncts; and the XP whose sole non-head daughter is the specifier. Although there are many scholars who allow an exception, namely, "Chomsky Adjunction" (see Chametzky 2000 for extensive discussion), where XP or $X°$ categories targeted by a movement operation can iterate, thus creating additional specifiers (or head or adjunct) positions.

7.3.3 A major conceptual shift: metagrammar vs. grammar: Stowell (1981)

Stowell's (1981) dissertation caused an important conceptual shift in the interpretation of what X-bar theory does. Prior to Stowell, the X-bar principles were viewed metagrammatically; that is, X-bar theory was a set of constraints on the formal properties of rules rather than on linguistic forms (see e.g. Lightfoot 1979). Stowell proposed that instead of constraining the form of phrase structure rules, X-bar theory should be viewed directly as a constraint on structure.[19] Other properties of phrase structure rules (selectional requirements, etc.) are part of the

---

[16] "$X^n \rightarrow (C_1) \ldots (C) X^{n-1} (C_{j+1}) \ldots (C_k)$ where $1 \leq n \leq 3$ and for all C_j, either $C_i = Y'''$ for some lexical category Y or C_i is a specified grammatical formative" (Jackendoff 1977).

[17] This has the interesting result that it allows for multiple specifiers, a proposal widely adopted in the minimalism of the late 1990s in slightly different guise.

[18] Muysken's actual proposal is that heads bear the features [$-$proj, $-$max], intermediate projections are [$+$proj, $-$max], and phrases are [$+$proj, $+$max]. There is a single rule: $X[+proj] \rightarrow \ldots X[-max] \ldots$

[19] With the following properties:

  (i) every phrase is endocentric;
 (ii) specifiers appear at X'' level, subcategorized elements appear within X';
(iii) the head is adjacent to a constituent boundary;
 (iv) the head term is one bar level lower than dominator;
 (v) only maximal projections occur as non-heads.

lexical information of the words participating in the relations. Stowell summarizes his arguments for this conception in the following paragraph:

> The descriptive power of individual categorial rules is so strong that the theory as a whole is unable to provide genuine explanations of the phenomena that it has traditionally been supposed to account for. However, in some domains the categorial formulae turn out to be largely redundant within the overall structure of the grammar. Finally, for some languages, it seems that there are serious problems in explicating how the categorial rules are induced from the primary linguistic data, even given the constraints on X-bar theory.
>
> (Stowell 1981: 61)

Kornai and Pullum (1990)[20] offer a reply to Stowell's account. As noted in Speas (1990), however, they seem to have misunderstood the basic point of Stowell: the explanatory burden of PSGs can be shifted to other parts of the grammar (such as the lexicon or licensing rules), and what remains is the X-bar schema, which directly constrains constituent structure without specific phrase structure rules. This perspective is common only in the Principles and Parameters approach, not in LFG, GPSG, or HPSG.

7.4 Summary

The X-bar theory of phrase structure, whether it is construed as a metagrammatical constraint or the actual mechanism of production of constituency itself, provides us with a uniquely powerful tool for describing the hierarchical structure of sentences. There are reasons to think, however, that X-bar theory is too powerful. In the next chapter, we consider work conducted between the late 1990s and the early 2000s in the Chomskyan GB and Minimalist paradigms that proposes constraints on X-bar theory, resulting in its eventual abandonment.

---

[20] Building on Pullum (1984) and (1985).

Part 3
Controversies

8

Towards Set-Theoretic Constituency Representations

8.1 Introduction

X-bar theory has had significant and fruitful empirical consequences for our understanding of constituency. Indeed, to this day, the vast majority of articles published in major syntax journals still use some form of X-bar theory to express constituency relations. However, X-bar theory also has several not-insignificant negative consequences. Within the Principles and Parameters framework, the empirical problems discussed below paired with the programmatic Minimalist theory-attenuation have led to a derived notion of X-bar structure. This is teamed up with a lean and spare set of combinatorics couched in set-theoretic terms. In this chapter, I examine the developments leading up to Chomsky's (1995b) Bare Theory of Phrase Structure (BPS) and survey many of the important, yet occasionally incompatible, extensions of this approach. This chapter is different from others in this book in that I will largely limit myself to work written directly within the Principles and Parameters framework, except where necessary for expository clarity.

The discussion and debate in recent work in the Minimalist Program (MP) centers around the question of how the bar level of a constituent is defined. In the classic work on X-bar theory, the bar levels are defined by the rule that introduces or licenses the constituent. Take for example the kind of system typically found in GPSG,[1] where the valued feature [BAR] represents the bar level of the constituent ([BAR 2] = XP, [BAR 1] = X', [BAR 0] = X°):

(1)   (a) N[BAR 2] → Det, N[BAR 1]
      (b) N[BAR 1] → N[BAR 0], P[BAR 2]

---

[1] The rules here are mine, they aren't associated with any particular instantiation of GPSG, but are consistent with the basic machinery of that approach.

The bar level of a given category is directly determined by the rule that licenses the structure. So the bar level of an N that is a sister to a PP must be 0 if it is dominated by an N with [BAR 1]. Recent work in MP, by contrast, suggests that the bar level is determined not by making reference to a particular rule or schema that licenses or generates the tree, but by looking at the structural relations the constituent bears to other constituents in the tree. In this sense bar level is not defined by the tree-generating mechanism, but is derived indirectly from the tree itself. This "derived" or "relativized" notion of bar level allows a significant simplification in the mechanisms involved in describing constituent structure, pushing the theoretical mechanisms towards a simple set-based system, which in turn makes some interesting empirical and theoretical predictions.

8.2 Projections and derived X-Bar theory

Two MIT dissertations from 1986, Speas (later expanded and republished as Speas 1990) and Fukui (later published as Fukui 1995), although technically pre-MP, contain the seeds of minimalist phrase structure theory. As in Stowell's (1981) work, both Fukui and Speas rely on the idea that the labor done by the phrase structure generation engine is relatively small. Constraints on constituency follow primarily from other parts of the grammar, such as theta theory, Case, or other licensing mechanisms.

Fukui (1986) distinguishes between the properties of lexical and functional categories: the amount of structure in a lexical category is determined by its thematic properties—there is a direct correspondence between the number of arguments that a lexical category requires and its complement–specifier structure. Functional categories allow a maximum of one specifier, provided they host a licensing feature (such as Case). However, they do not *require* specifiers. Fukui examines a variety of evidence comparing Japanese (without licensing features or specifiers) to English (which has them) to argue for this position. The consequences of this for X-bar theory are important. If this proposal is accepted then "maximal category" cannot be equated to XP; some categories (such as functional categories in Japanese) lack licensing features, and consequently lack both specifiers and the XP that dominates them. Fukui claims that the X-bar level of a constituent is not a primitive (such as a feature or annotation on a category), but is defined in terms of the depth of projection. This is calculated using projection paths (Fukui 1995: 89):[2]

(2) Π is a *projection path* if Π is a sequence of nodes $N = (n_1, \ldots n_n)$
  (a) for all i, n_i immediately dominates n_{i+1};
  (b) all n_i have the same set of features;
  (c) the bar level of n_i is equal to or greater than the bar level of n_{i+1}.

In this definition the variable i and the bar level are not the same thing. The i is a counting mechanism, the bar level represents the feature that determines whether the non-head daughter is a specifier (daughter of X″) or an adjunct (daughter of X′). If we look at a tree, the sequence of Xs up and down the tree is the projection path:

(3)

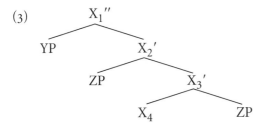

The maximal projection is defined as the topmost member of the projection path (Fukui 1995: 90):

(4) n_i is the *maximal projection node* of a projection path $\Pi = (n_1, \ldots, n_n)$ iff i = 1.

In Fukui's system, the maximal projection can be either X″ or X′ (in the cases where there is no specifier), as long as it is at the top of the path.

(5) (a)   (b)

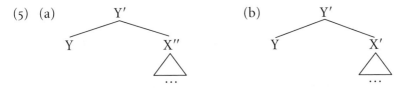

So in (5a) the X″ (=XP) is the "maximal category," in (5b), the X′ is. The difference between the two lies in the nature of the topmost non-head daughter of the X″ and X′ respectively. The topmost non-head

---

[2] Here the idea that a constituency tree is viewed as a projection system rather than a rewrite system is crucial—see Ch. 5.

daughter in (5a) is a specifier, the topmost one in (5b) is an adjunct or complement.

Fukui's analysis dissociates the notion of "specifier" from its structural position in the tree, which seems to me to be a strange move. In previous versions of X-bar theory, the non-head daughter of the highest projection was always the specifier. In Fukui's system such a node can be a specifier (if it is the daughter of X″) or not (if it is the daughter of a maximal X′). In essence, Fukui has replaced a primitive notion of "maximal projection" with a primitive notion of "specifier"; where the specifier is defined as daughter of X″, but not necessarily the "maximal category". This is one step forward, one step back. The definitions in (2) and (4) are also mildly circular, in that in order to figure out which category is the maximal projection, the definition refers to the category which has been labeled as X_1, but X_1 is so labeled because it is in effect the maximal projection. Fukui's system requires not only the notion of bar levels to distinguish among specifiers and other kinds of modifiers, but also a separate and distinct notion of maximal category. The technical details of Fukui seem not to work, but the intuition behind them—that some X-bar theoretic definitions are not primitives—has been widely influential.

Speas's dissertation, written at the same time as Fukui's, takes a slightly different tack, avoiding both of the definitional problems mentioned above. Speas's system provides relativistic definitions of not only maximal categories, but all X-bar theoretic terms. "Maximal projection" and "minimal projection" are defined in terms of trees and intermediate projections are the elsewhere case and undefined. The system is based on a single rule that "projects" structure up from a head to include, like Fukui, all and only the arguments of that head (we return to adjuncts below):

(6) *Project Alpha*: A word of syntactic category X is dominated by an uninterrupted sequence of X nodes.

Speas's equivalent to Fukui's projection path is the projection chain. However, projection chains are not indexed with a numeric value (Speas 1991: 43):

(7) *Projection Chain* of X = an uninterrupted sequence of projections of X.

Maximal and minimal categories are defined solely by looking at the position of the node in question relative to other nodes in the tree.

Essentially, a maximal projection (XP) is the node of some category X that is immediately dominated by some other category. Speas's definition is given in (8):

(8) *Maximal Projection*: X = XP if ∀G, dominating X, G ≠ X.

Speas's definition actually does not work alone, as it would entail that a VP dominated by another VP (say an embedding verb) would not be a maximal category (i.e. in structures such as $[_{VP} \ldots [_{CP} \ldots [_{VP} \ldots]]]$) since it is dominated by some X of the same category. Similarly, it would rule out the now common stacked vP shells. Speas solves related problems by using "lexical indexes" to distinguish between identically categorized yet differently headed phrases. So a projection of V_1 would be distinct from a projection of V_2, even if some of the projections of V_1 dominate V_2. An alternative is to minimally redefine maximal category in terms of immediate domination and the headedness of the constituent:

(9) *Maximal Projection (revised)*: X = XP if ∃G, immediately dominating X, the head of G ≠ the head of X.

I think this definition accurately reflects the spirit behind Speas's intent: maximal categories are the nodes that are not immediately dominated by another projection of themselves (not part of the same projection chain), and does so without reference to "lexical indexes" although it is perhaps merely a matter of notational variation.

The minimal projection (X°) is the element that immediately dominates nothing.[3] The categories between the XP and the X° are undefined for bar level.

The consequences of this proposal center around whether other rules in the grammar can make reference to the various bar levels. Rules that make reference to XPs are many. For example, operations such as *wh*-movement all seem to target XP-level constituents. Similarly, head-movement and morphological operations mostly target individual X° nodes. The relativized definitions of Speas predict that there should be no rules that make explicit reference only to the single bar level. The rules of *one*-replacement and *do-so* replacement that originally motivated the existence of these intermediate categories seem to be good candidates for such rules. *One*-replacement seems to target N′ nodes, not NPs or N°s:

---

[3] Speas actually defines this as "immediately dominates a word". I have changed this so as to be consistent with the claim that preterminals and terminals are instantiations of the same thing (see Ch. 3).

(10) (a) * I wrote on [NP the big pad of paper] not [NP one].
    (b) I wrote on this [N' big pad of paper] not that [N' one].
    (c) I wrote on the big [N' pad of paper] not the small [N' one].
    (d) * 4I wrote on the big [N pad] of sketch paper not the big [N' one] of newsprint.

If these operations do indeed target only N' (rather than say a vaguer notion of "node" or "constituent") then this would be evidence against Speas's proposal. She observes, however, that a more careful probing of the data shows that the apparent X' limiting character of these replacement rules is actually epiphenomenal. Building upon some observations of Travis (1984), she shows that ungrammatical forms such as (10d) follow from case and theta theories, and that the rules of replacement are more liberal than they first appear. *Do-so* replacement fails to apply exactly in the environments where a Case needs to be assigned to the complement:

(11) (a) *I bought a car and Andrew did so a truck.
    (b) I ate at the restaurant and Andrew did so at the museum.

Travis and Speas claim that *do so* is a pro-verb that lacks theta and Case-assigning properties. This explains why it cannot replace a V' in contexts where there is a complement, because complements typically require a theta role and/or Case. A similar analysis can be given to *one*-replacement. Consider the contrast in (12), taken from Speas (1990: 41).

(12) (a) *the student of chemistry and the one of physics
    (b) the picture of Julia and the one of Suzanne

Speas argues that the *of* in (12a) is a case marker, but the one in (12b) is a full preposition. This contrast can be further exemplified by the fact that *of*-phrases like those in (12b) can follow the verb *to be* (13b), but the one in (12a) cannot (13a). The *of* in (13b) parallels the behavior of other full predicative prepositions, which can all follow to be. As such these PPs do not get a theta role (they are predicates), and do not need independent Case licensing (they get their case from the preposition). By contrast, the *of*-PP in (13a) can not function predicatively, suggesting that it needs a theta role, and presumably Case licensing.[5]

---

[4] As noted before, not all speakers of English will find this ungrammatical. However, judgments are fairly uniformly negative for the equivalent form using *do-so* replacement: *I ate the peanuts, John did so the apples.*

[5] For an alternative view of these facts see Harley (2005).

(13)   (a) *This student is of physics.
       (b)   This picture is of Suzanne. (Speas 1990: 42)

If we take the *of* in (12a) to be a Case marker, then the ungrammaticality of (12a) follows from the same mechanism suggested for *do-so* replacement: *one* is a pro-form that cannot assign Case or theta role to its complement. The ungrammaticality of (12a) is not due then to the fact that we are replacing an N° (which we see is allowed in (12b)), but due to the fact that the complement of *one* lacks a theta role and is Caseless.

With this analysis in hand we can see that no rules appear to make direct reference to the single bar level. (Rules like *one*-replacement and *do-so* replacement target a variety of node types, but are constrained by other parts of the grammar, such that in the default situation it appears as if they target only the single bar level.) This lends plausibility to Speas's claim that bar levels are not featural and not marked as primitives on the tree. Instead, constituents are unmarked for any kind of bar level. Rules that make reference to the XP or X° status of a constituent do so to a derived notion that is calculated relative to the rest of the tree.

This approach has important consequences for our understanding of adjuncts. If single-bar levels aren't formally distinguished, then the definition of adjunct as a daughter of a single bar and sister to a single bar level is impossible. Similarly, defining adjuncts in terms of Chomsky adjunction (14) is impossible, since only the topmost projection could get the XP label, the lower one could not.

(14)

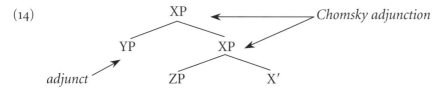

There is evidence to suggest, however, that adjuncts may deserve some alternative treatment in any case. Van Riemsdijk and Williams (1981) observe a set of facts most thoroughly treated in Lebeaux (1988): there appears to be variation in the way the binding theory applies to adjuncts. Consider the noun *John* in the following sentences, and whether or not it is subject to Condition-C effects.

(15)   (a) * He_i believes [the claim that $John_i$ is nice]
       (b) *[Whose claim that $John_i$ is nice]$_k$ did he_i believe t_k?

(c) *He$_i$ likes [the story that John$_i$ wrote].

(d) [Which story that John$_i$ wrote]$_k$ did he$_i$ like t$_k$? (Lebeaux 1988: 146)

(15a and c) exhibit condition C effects. The R-expression *John* is c-commanded and bound by the coindexed pronoun *he*. Sentence (15b) shows that this is true even when the R-expression is contained in a *wh*-phrase that has been moved to the front of the sentence. The usual analysis of (15b) is that either binding condition C holds at D-structure before *wh*-movement applies or the *wh*-phrase "reconstructs" to its D-structure position after the overt component of the grammar. Sentence (15d) is the surprising case, as the R-expression in the fronted *wh*-phrase does not seem to be subject to condition C, in contrast with (15b). These cases are known in the literature as "anti-reconstruction sentences." The difference between the (b) and (d) sentences lies in the nature of the clause containing the R-expression; in (15b) it is a complement to the noun *claim*, but in (15c) the CP is an adjunct[6] on *story*.

(15′) (b)   ...   (d)   ...

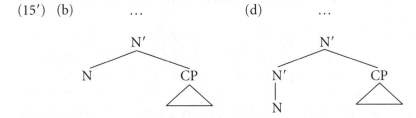

Lebeaux explains these facts by timing operations at different levels. Simple X-bar construction, except for adjuncts, applies at D-structure before any movement. Condition C holds at this level, resulting in the unacceptability of (15a and b). Adjunction is a separate operation, adjuncts are added after D-structure and movement.

(16)   X Bar   ⟶   D-Structure
                              ↓
                       Movement
                              ↓
                 S-Structure (adjunction happens here)

So the derivation of (15d) is such that the adjunct is added after the wh-phrase has moved past the pronoun:

---

6 There is a class of adjuncts that do not exhibit anti-reconstruction effects. Speas (1991) shows that these seem to have semi-argument status, and thus will be present at D-structure in order to meet the theta criterion. We leave this class aside for the discussion here.

(17) (a) He liked [which story]   D-structure
      (b) [which story] did he like   *wh*-movement
      (c) [which story that John wrote] did he like   Adjunction

The sentence is predicted to be well-formed since there is never a point
in the derivation where *John* is c-commanded by *he*. The adjunct in
(15c) is presumably added after D-structure as well, so the ungrammaticality of (15c) requires one further assumption: condition C also
holds at S-structure. Sentence (15d) is not ruled out by this extra
assumption since the R-expression, being inserted directly into the
surface position of the *wh*-phrase, is never c-commanded by the
pronoun, even at S-structure. This suggests that adjuncts are not part
of the X-bar schema, at least at D-structure. See Chametzky (1995) for
further discussion of these facts.

Bobaljik (1994) makes a related observation, although he accounts
for it in a very different way. His focus is on the old observation that
negation and subject arguments that occur between Infl/T and the verb
trigger *do*-insertion, but adjuncts do not:

(18) (a) Andrew (Infl) pai̱d his rent.
      (b) Andrew di̱d *not* pay his rent.
      (c) Di̱d *Andrew* pay his rent?
      (d) Andrew (Infl) *frequently* pai̱d his rent.

In Bobaljik's system, English verb inflection attaches rightwards to the
verb through "merger under adjacency". This is a morphological operation that looks at the linear string. In (18a), the past tense features on Infl
are adjacent to the verb, so undergo merger, showing up as the suffix *-ed*.
In (18b and c) this adjacency is blocked by the intervening negation and
the intervening subject respectively, so *do* is inserted to support the
inflection. What is surprising is the behavior of adverbs in (18d), which
do not appear to block adjacency, and no *do*-support is found. Bobaljik is
one of many to suggest that this follows from a multi-tiered or three
dimensional tree structure, where adjuncts are not immediately part of
the same hierarchy as the arguments and heads, and stand off from the
relationships that count for "adjacency". We return in some detail to
multi-tiered and three dimensional trees in Chapter 10. Bobaljik's analysis
is consistent with Speas's claim that adjuncts are not distinguished by
virtue of where they stand relative to any given bar level. For related
arguments see Lasnik (1998), Nissenbaum (1998), Bošković and Lasnik
(1999), Ochi (1999), and Stepanov (2001).

Speas's system makes a number of other interesting predictions about the nature of constituent structures. Among other things, vacuous projections (i.e. those with no branching) are ruled out. So bare Ns (and other non-branching nodes) have a simple single-node structure:

(19)   (a)   X-bar theory   (b)   relativized approach

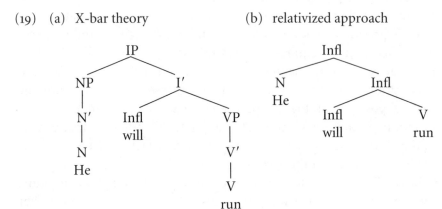

As we will see below in section 8.4, when we look at Chomsky (1995b), this makes some interesting predictions about clitics and other structures with ambiguous phrasality.

Bouchard (1995) and Chametzky (1995) make some claims about constituency that are similar to Speas's but with different motivations. Bouchard claims that all properties of phrase structure should follow from the argument structure/semantics of heads. This proposal is a small step away from a dependency grammar (see Ch. 9), a trend that we will see repeated below several times.

8.3 Antisymmetry

The next major revision to X-bar theory is found in Kayne's (1994) book *The Antisymmetry of Syntax*. Kayne's main concern is the relation of linear precedence. Precedence (and linear order in general) is obviously an important part of syntax. However, rules that make reference exclusively to precedence (without also making reference to some kind of hierarchical relation) are extremely rare (the case of *do* support discussed by Bobaljik being an exception). If you will recall from Chapter 3, the definition of precedence is quite convoluted and complicated. This suggests that precedence relations might also be secondary and derived notions. One such proposal is found in Travis (1984), where she argued that precedence relations were really a matter of the interaction of a set of parameter settings (including headedness, case and thematic directionality). Kayne offers a very different approach. He claims that, universally, precedence can be determined by asymmetric c-command. The essence of his proposal is that if some constituent asymmetrically c-commands another, then it also precedes that element.[7]

8.3.1 The LCA and linear ordering

Let us consider the informal version of this claim first, and then look at the formalization. In all of the following (equivalent) trees, A asymmetrically c-commands G, and G asymmetrically c-commands H. So it follows that all these trees would be expressed with the linear order A G H, despite the printed order expressed in each.[8]

(20)

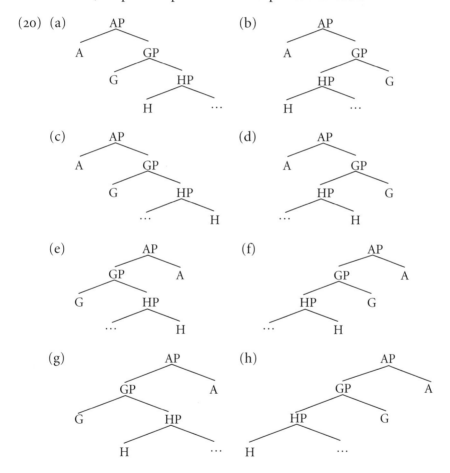

[7] See Chametzky (2000) for a detailed philosophical analysis of Kayne's Antisymmetry analysis.

[8] However, the position of the material in the ellipsis (...) is not uniquely determined in these trees relative to H, since H would symmetrically c-command its sister.

In every one of these cases, A asymmetrically c-commands G, and G asymmetrically c-commands H, translating to an AGH linear ordering.

The technicalities of this intuitive idea are rather more complex. First we need some basic definitions. It is crucial for Kayne's story to work that he distinguishes between the words (which are terminals) and their categories and projections (which are pre-terminals or non-terminals). This is contra to our discussion in Chapters 3 and 5, where we argued that terminals and their categories form single nodes. This assumption is crucial to ensure that the right kinds of c-command relations are established. As a matter of convention we will mark terminal nodes (words) with lower case letters. Their categories (and the nodes that dominate them) are written with uppercase letters. Linear ordering holds only of terminals.

(21)

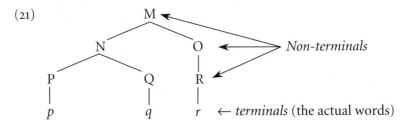

Second, Kayne is operating under an "immediately dominating node" version of c-command (see Chapter 4 in this volume and Barker and Pullum 1990), where c-command relations are made by looking for a minimal upper bound that is defined in terms of immediate dominance. Some node A only c-commands B if the node immediately dominating A, dominates (not necessarily immediately) B. Under the most usual definition of c-command (i.e. *a* c-commands *b* if the first branching node dominating *a* also dominates *b*), *n* c-commands both O and *o* in the following tree. With IDC-command, *n* and *o* do not c-command anything, but N c-commands O and *o*, and O c-commands N and *n*.

(22)

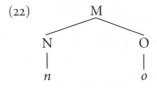

Finally, we must define a number of sets of nodes. First we have *T*, the set of terminals in the tree. Next we have *A*, which is a set of pairs of non-terminals, such that the first member of each pair asymmetrically c-commands the second.[9] Finally, we have $d(A)$, which is the image of A: the set of pairs of terminals dominated by the pairs in A. These sets are easiest to identify if we look at an example. Consider the VP *ate at school*:

(23)

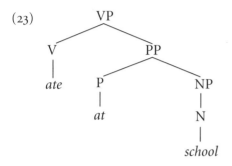

The set T is defined as $T = \{ate, at, school\}$. The set A is based upon the asymmetric c-command relations among *non*-terminals (we will return to the rationale for this below). Notice that symmetric c-command relations are not included. So $A=\{\langle V, P\rangle, \langle P, N\rangle, \langle V, N\rangle, \langle V, NP\rangle\}$. Finally, we take each of the pairs in A and find the terminal nodes they dominate. So the pair $\langle V, P\rangle$ translates to $\langle ate, at\rangle$ in $d(A)$. $\langle P, N\rangle$ translates to $\langle at, school\rangle$. Both $\langle V, N\rangle$ and $\langle V, NP\rangle$ translate to the same set of terminals, since there is nothing that NP dominates that N does not: $\langle ate, school\rangle$. This gives us: $d(A) = \{\langle ate, at\rangle, \langle at, school\rangle, \langle ate, school\rangle\}$. Informally, we can see that this derives the correct order of terminals in terms of precedence relations: *ate* $\prec$ *at* $\prec$ *school*. The constraint or rule that enforces this is called the Linear Correspondence Axiom, or LCA.

(24)   *Linear Correspondence Axiom*: $d(A)$ is a linear ordering of T.

This can be thought of either as an output constraint on the phonetic form (PF) of a sentence or as principle guiding an operation of linearization. Any structure not meeting the LCA cannot be ordered. Consider an example—a possible tree for a grammatical string—that is ruled out by the LCA:

[9] This relation is antisymmetric (rather than asymmetric), because the only situation in which mutual c-command could occur is the case where an element c-commands itself. Hence the title *The Antisymmetry of Syntax*.

(25)

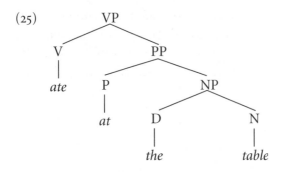

$T = \{ate, at, the, table\}$
$A = \{\langle V, P \rangle, \langle P, D \rangle, \langle P, N \rangle, \langle V, D \rangle, \langle V, NP \rangle, \langle V, N \rangle\}$
$d(A) = \{\langle ate, at \rangle, \langle at, the \rangle, \langle at, table \rangle, \langle ate, the \rangle, \langle ate, table \rangle\}$

D and N symmetrically c-command one another. This means that there is no pairing between these nodes in A. It follows then that this tree would be ruled out by the LCA, since the pair $\langle the, table \rangle$ is missing from $d(A)$. We can conclude $ate \prec at$, $at \prec the$, and $at \prec table$, but the ordering of *the* and *table* is unspecified. Of course this is a grammatical VP of English, so if the LCA is right, then the tree in (25) cannot be the right analysis of this string. Indeed, the LCA can correctly order a tree like this if it is analyzed with a determiner phrase (DP).

(26)

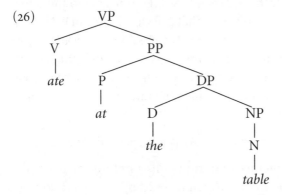

$T = \{ate, at, the, table\}$
$A = \{\langle V, P \rangle, \langle P, D \rangle, \langle P, N \rangle, \langle V, D \rangle, \langle V, NP \rangle, \langle V, DP \rangle, \langle V, N \rangle, \langle D, N \rangle, \langle P, NP \rangle\}$
$d(A) = \{\langle ate, at \rangle, \langle at, the \rangle, \langle at, table \rangle, \langle ate, the \rangle, \langle ate, table \rangle, \langle the, table \rangle\}$

The trees in (25) and (26) also reveal why immediate-dominance-based c-command is crucial to the definitions. The addition of the extra node shifts where the c-command relations are defined, such that N does not symmetrically c-command D in (26). This is only true under an immediate dominance definition; under a branching nodes definition N would still c-command D.

8.3.2 Deriving some X-bar theoretic properties from the LCA

Consider two properties of X-bar theory: complements must be maximal categories and phrases have only one head.[10] These two properties follow directly from the LCA. Consider the following abstract tree,[11] where the phrasal category L could be interpreted either as a structure where both M and P are heads or as a structure where M is a head and P is a non-maximal complement.

(27)

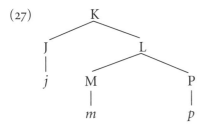

$$T = \{j,\ m,\ p\},$$
$$A = \{\langle J, M \rangle,\ \langle J, P \rangle\},$$
$$d(A) = \{\langle j,\ m \rangle,\ \langle j,\ p \rangle\}$$

Because M and P symmetrically c-command one another, there is no ordering specified for m and p. So any such structure will be ruled out by the LCA. We can imagine such a structure for the VP given in (28).

(28) *

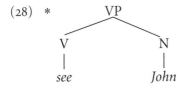

Notice that that the prohibition on trees like this is in direct contradiction to the kind of analysis that Speas gives in (19) above. In Speas's system, vacuous projections are prohibited; in Kayne's system, they are crucial to ensuring the correct command relations hold. We will resolve this contradiction when we look at Chomsky's Bare Phrase Structure system below in section 8.4.

---

[10] See Collins (1997), who argues the single root condition also falls out from the LCA.
[11] All the trees in this section are lifted from Kayne (1994).

A third property of X-bar theory is that structures are endocentric. The LCA derives this effect as well. Consider the trees in (29):

(29) (a)   (b)

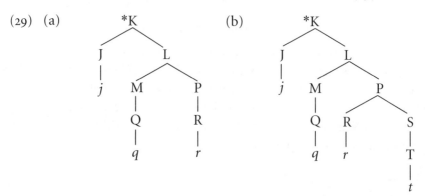

Assume that L, M, and P are all maximal categories. L is unheaded in both cases. Regardless of whether P (or M for that matter) is complex (29b) or not (29a), M asymmetrically c-commands R, and P asymmetrically c-command Q, so both $\langle q, r \rangle$ and $\langle r, q \rangle$ are in $d(A)$. Unheaded structures will necessarily result in cases where a conflicting ordering results. This rules out traditional categories like the unheaded S node, and the kind of unheaded structures found commonly in LFG with verb displacement. It also rules out ternary branching structures.

8.3.3 Adjunction

The discussion in the last section shows that several basic properties of X-bar theory appear to follow from the LCA, although they are at least inconsistent with the Speas–Fukui derived notions. But the LCA also has a surprising property that appears to be undesirable. A careful look at (29b) also reveals that if we were to interpret L as a maximal category headed by R (e.g. R=C, P=C′ and L=CP), then such a structure prevents any element (M), even when phrasal, from appearing in the specifier of another phrase. Kayne resolves this by claiming that the things we currently think of as specifiers are better understood, structurally, as adjunctions, which he claims differ in their c-command properties.

A word on terminology is in order here. we need to distinguish between adjuncts and adjunctions, and among types of adjunct. Many syntacticians use these terms as rough synonyms, but I think there are some trends in usage where differences emerge. The term "adjunction" often refers to the output of an operation. For example, for many years

Chomskyan grammarians have treated topicalization or heavy NP shifts as a type of adjunction. Conversely, "adjunct" seems to be reserved for those situations where base generation is in effect. Adjunct, itself, has several distinct usages (which sometimes converge on the same set of syntactic objects). It has a semantic/functional usage, referring to some category that is not required by the predicate. It also has the X-bar theoretic meaning, referring to the sister of X′ and daughter of X′. To make matters even more confusing, some scholars typically treat adjuncts as adjunctions. Let us distinguish the terms the following way: We will reserve the term "adjunct" to its X-bar theoretic usage; that is, a modifier that is attached between a head, its complement, and the XP projected from that head. We'll use the term "adjunction" to refer to the particular structural configuration case of so-called Chomsky Adjunction.

Chomsky Adjunction involves taking an extant phrasal category as the landing site for a movement, splitting it into two parts called "segments". Neither segment alone counts as a category. The category is the two segments taken together. This can be seen in the abstract tree in (30). Each of the XPs is taken as a segment of the larger XP category. Individually the segments do not count as categories for the purposes of calculating c-command in binding and scope interactions (May 1985).

(30)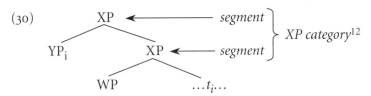

With this structure in place we can explain how specifiers and adjuncts are allowed in Kayne's system. First we require an extra stipulation on c-command as given in (31) and (32). (These definitions are in the spirit of May's 1985 proposal):

(31) A c-commands B iff
      (a) A and B are categories;
      (b) A excludes B;
      (c) every category that dominates A dominates B.

---

[12] Notice again that this kind of structure is impossible in a Speas-style analysis, as there is no primitive XP to be split into two segments. Only the topmost element would count as an XP. For a critical look at Chomsky Adjunction, see Chametzky (1994).

(32)   X excludes Y iff no segment of X dominates Y.

The idea here is that segments do not c-command elements which are dominated by a distinct segment of the category they belong to. So consider the tree in (33), where M (a phrasal level category is in an adjunction relation to P. M is dominated by the higher segment of P, but not by the lower one. The lower segment of P does not c-command M (nor its daughter Q), because the category P does not exclude M.

(33)

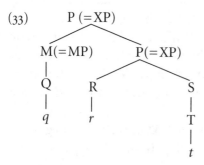

This in turn means that P does not c-command Q. Therefore M asymmetrically c-commands R and P does not asymmetrically c-command Q, so the pair $\langle q, r \rangle$ is in $d(A)$, but the pair $\langle r, q \rangle$ is not. So in order to escape the requirements of the LCA, specifiers are Chomsky-Adjunction structures.

A similar fact explains part of the head-movement constraint (Travis 1984) (heads move into other heads cyclically). In particular, it rules out the adjunction of a phrase to a head. Consider the abstract tree in (34) where U is a phrase adjoined to the head M.

(34)

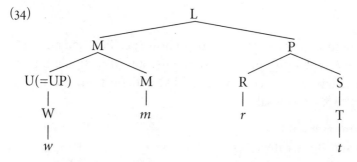

Because M does not exclude U, M is irrelevant for calculating the c-command relations of U. This means that, somewhat counter-intuitively, U asymmetrically c-commands R. More intuitively, P also asymmetrically c-commands W. This means that the pairs $\langle w, r \rangle$, $\langle w, t \rangle$ and $\langle r, w \rangle$, $\langle t, w \rangle$ are in $d(A)$.[13] So a phrase adjoined to a head is unlinearizable. By contast, consider the tree in (35), where a head is adjoined to a head:

(35)

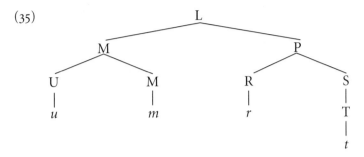

In this tree, U (surprisingly) c-commands P *and* P c-commands U, so the relation is symmetric. This means that the Antisymmetry relations are:

(36) $A = \{\langle U, M\rangle, \langle U, R\rangle, \langle U, S\rangle, \langle U, T\rangle, \langle M, R\rangle, \langle M, T\rangle, \langle R, S\rangle, \langle R, T\rangle\}$
       $d(A) = \{\langle u, m\rangle, \langle u, r\rangle, \langle u, t\rangle, \langle m, r\rangle, \langle m, t\rangle, \langle r, t\rangle\}$

Neither $\langle P, U\rangle$ nor $\langle U, P\rangle$ is in A, so it is not ruled out the same way as (34); there is no contradictory ordering between u and r or t.

Kayne's Antisymmetric approach also predicts that neither multiple adjunctions nor multiple specifiers will exist (cf. Ura 1994). In the following tree M and L should be taken either as multiple specifiers or multiple adjunctions:

(37)

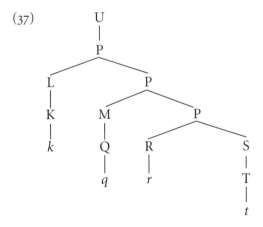

Because the node not excluding all of L, M, R is U, it follows that M asymmetrically c-commands K, and L asymmetrically c-commands Q.

---

[13] $A = \{\langle U, M\rangle, \langle U, R\rangle, \langle U, S\rangle, \langle U, T\rangle, \langle M, R\rangle, \langle M, S\rangle, \langle M, T\rangle, \langle R, T\rangle, \langle P, W\rangle\},$
$d(A) = \{\langle w, m\rangle, \langle w, r\rangle, \langle w, t\rangle, \langle m, r\rangle, \langle m, t\rangle, \langle r, t\rangle, \langle r, w\rangle, \langle t, w\rangle\}$

Therefore both $\langle k, q \rangle$ and $\langle q, k \rangle$ are in $d(A)$—resulting in a violation of the LCA.

One of the most intriguing predictions of the LCA is the claim that underlyingly all sentences in all languages must be ordered as SVO (or more precisely specifier–head–object).

(38)

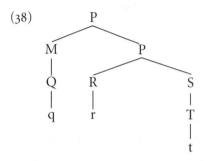

The specifier of any tree (M) asymmetrically c-commands the head (R) and R asymmetrically c-commands the head of the complement (T). This means that the image of A in any such arbitrary tree will include $\langle q, r \rangle$, and $\langle r, t \rangle$ and not their inverses.[14] This results in universal SVO order. This of course has been controversial among linguists working on languages with a non-SVO order! The claim of Antisymmetry is that any non-SVO order must be a derived order. Charges of anglocentrism aside, this claim has generated an important research program involving subtle word-order variations that are analyzed through massive movement of material leftwards in the tree. See, for example, work on Hungarian, German, and Dutch word orders in Koopman and Szabolci (2000). For more information about recent developments on the LCA see Chapter 12.

8.4 Bare Phrase Structure

Both Speas's relativized phrase structure system and Kayne's Antisymmetric system attempt to derive the properties of X-bar theory and phrase structure in general. But they are largely mutually incompatible.

---

[14] Lasnik, Uriagereka, and Boeckx (2005) point out that this aspect of the LCA does seem to make at least one wrong prediction. Observe that the ordering of prehead modifiers and post-head modifiers is a mirror image when it comes to scope relations.

(i) The theory of syntax which is suspect = the suspect syntactic theory. ($\neq$ the syntactic suspect theory)

If we take scope to be an effect of c-command, then we accept that the right-most post-head modifier must c-command elements to its left in violation of the LCA. One can construct a derivation that gets around this by doing massive leftwards movements, but this does seem very suspect.

For example, the notion of a segmented XP adjunction structure is incoherent in Speas's system, as an XP is simply the category immediately dominated by a distinct projection. Conversely, Kayne's system relies on vacuous projections to ensure that the correct c-command relations are established; this is incompatible with Speas, where vacuous projections are not allowed.

Chomsky's (1995b) Bare Theory of Phrase Structure (henceforth BPS), brings together elements of Speas's[15] relativized phrase structure system with Kayne's LCA, along with a largely set theoretic notation for expressing constituent structure.

8.4.1 The basics of BPS

As with other work within the Minimalist Program, the motivations of BPS are conceptual rather than empirical. MP asks the question what the least amount of theoretical mechanisms that is required to capture the appropriate relations and generalizations is. Linear order (as in the LCA) and notions like XP and X′ can be derived from other parts of the grammar, so they are not part of the basic mechanism of constituent construction. However, the notions of constituency as well as modification, labeling, and the distinction between complements and adjuncts (and perhaps specifiers) need to be captured in the system.

Like Speas, Chomsky observes that in terms of phrasality, only maximal categories and minimal categories (X° categories or heads) are referenced by the grammar (see also Baltin 1989). The slightly less formal BPS version of Speas's relativized phrase structure is given as follows:

(39)   Given a P-marker, a category that does not project any further is a maximal projection XP and one that is not a projection at all is a minimal projection X°.   (Chomsky 1995b: 396)

The main mechanism for generating constituency representations, however, is different from Speas's Project Alpha. This version reduces constituency to simple set membership. The primary operation in BPS is a generalized transformation (see Ch. 6) known as Merge (in later versions of BPS this is called External Merge):

[15] Somewhat strangely, Chomsky does not cite Speas for many of these ideas even though they appear in her dissertation and Chomsky was on her dissertation committee.

(40) *Merge*:
      Applied to two objects α & β, Merge forms a new object δ.
      Example: δ = {γ {α, β}}

The γ in this representation is the label of the constituent δ. Chomsky debates a number of options for determining the content of this label including an intersection of the features of the two component parts, a union of those properties or simply choosing one or other of the elements and marking it as the head of the phrase.[16] He rejects the union possibility because it might result in incompatible features (e.g. if one were to merge a noun with a verb, one would have a constituent that was simultaneously +V and −V). If one were to adopt the intersective possibility, then one would end up with constituents without specifications for particular features. As such the label that projects is the one of the element that is the head. So given a verb *loves* and its complement noun *John*, one ends up with the VP {loves, {loves, John}}.

There is an alternative view of labeling that Chomsky does not consider. This is the idea, common in HPSG, that a non-head contributes to the label in terms of valuing features in the head. That is, imagine the verb *loves* comes with the feature COMPS,[17] standing for "complement", which is unvalued. The object *John* values this feature, so that the label of the combined set contains the valued feature [COMPS *John*]. This seems to be a plausible alternative to projecting the head—one which captures the basic notion of compositionality.

BPS-style representations can be loosely translated into trees, but such representations are meant to be informal user-friendly versions. Like Speas's trees, there are no bar-level diacritics:

(41) (a) {loves, {loves, John}}

      (b)

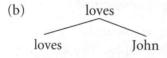

The BPS set notation is particularly difficult to read. Even a simple sentence such as *John will eat the peanuts* shows up as {will, {John, {will, {will, {eat, {eat, {the, {the, peanuts}}}}}}}}. Langendoen

---

[16] See also Lasnik, Uriagereka, and Boeckx (2005).
[17] This feature is roughly the combination of parts of the Arg-Str and DTRS (or COMPS) features in HPSG.

(2003)[18] has observed that set-theoretically, the sequence {x, {x, y}} is equivalent to the ordered pair ⟨x, y⟩ (following Enderton 1972: 6), as such an easier notation might use ordered pairs, where the first member in each pair is both merged with the other, and serves as the label. So the sentence above would be ⟨⟨will, ⟨eat, ⟨the, peanuts⟩⟩⟩, John⟩. An interesting consequence of Langendoen's notation is that one might interpret these sets as a kind of edge set in graph theory. This results in a tree such as (42):

(42)

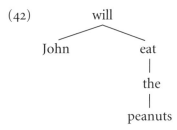

While such edge-defined trees will be unfamiliar to most generative grammarians and do not represent constituency directly, the tree in (42) is very similar to a dependency grammar tree (see Ch. 9). Indeed, some unpublished work by Zwart (2003), Collins and Ura (2004) and Seely (2004), while not drawing this exact conclusion, suggests that BPS, when taken to its logical end, leads to a dependency-style analysis. See chapter 12 for more discussion.

Merge by its very nature induces binarity in trees (Chametzky 2000 refers to this as the "noahistic property" of the operation). This provides a very different explanation for binarity than Kayne's (1984) unambiguous paths.

BPS has a second generalized transformation, known as Move or Internal Merge. Move takes an element that is already present in the phrase marker, copies it, and then remerges the copy with a higher set. For example, we might merge a noun *John* as the complement to the passive verb *eaten*, then copy and remerge it later as the subject of the clause. The lower copy is silent.

Linear order in BPS is determined by the LCA,[19] but without any vacuous projections, and not calculated with the image of non-terminals

[18] See Langendoen (2003) for other revisions to the Merge operation, including the addition of an operation known as "list-merge." It should also be noted that Langendoen, in fact, reserves the ordered-pair notation for adjunction structures only.

[19] See also the discussion in Collins (1997) and Nuñes (1998). For a contrasting view to Chomsky's see Saito and Fukui (1998), who argue, using evidence from scrambling, that linear order is fixed by the Merge operation and that labeling is determined by a headedness parameter. A slightly more sophisticated version of this is found in Fukui and Takano (1998), who derive linear order from an unpacking of the Merge operation. Zepter (2000) presents an optimality-theoretic derivation of linearization. See also Kural (2005)

(as the notions of X° and non-terminal are derived notions). Instead, simple asymmetric command is used. There is at least one problem with this recasting of the LCA. This arises where two minimal categories are merged. In such a situation there is no asymmetric c-command between the two nodes.

(43)

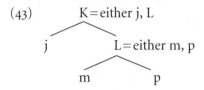

Chomsky's solution to this problem is to appeal to the idea that conditions on linearization are conditions solely on the phonetic representation (PF) of a sentence. If it should be the case that one of the terminal nodes (e.g. *m* and *p* in (43)) is null, then no ordering between them need apply. So he proposes that in all such circumstances, the operation Move applies so that one of the elements is a silent trace. This, he claims, is the motivation for movement of object clitics in Romance languages: they must move to adjoin to a head higher in the tree so that they leave an empty category that need not be ordered with its sister. Both Yang (1999) and Moro (2000) independently take this argument to the next level and argue linearization concerns (based on the LCA) motivate all movement, not just the movement of terminals.

8.4.2 *Adjunction in BPS*

With no X-bar distinctions, it becomes difficult to formally distinguish adjuncts from other modifiers in BPS. Chomsky extends the Chomsky adjunction, multisegmented, analysis of adjunction. This is represented in BPS as a paired label. So an *a* adjoined to a *k* is {⟨k, k⟩{a, k}}. What exactly this is intended to mean is one of the more obscure parts of this work. In Chomsky (2001), adjunction is recast as "pair merge".[20]

---

where cross-linguistic variation in order is due to a parametric variation in how the linearization procedure "traverses" the nodes in the hierarchical tree.

[20] One important criticism of pair merge is that it is unclear what determines when a modifier is treated as an argument of a head (and thus set merged) and when it is an adjunct (and is pair merged). Rubin (2003) provides an important clarification on this point, whereby pair merge occurs only in environments where there is a special functional head (MOD) acting as a predicate that introduces adjunct modifiers. When MOD is present, it is pair merged into the structure, otherwise only set merge applies.

> But it is an empirical fact that there is also an asymmetric operation of adjunction, which takes two objects b and a and forms the ordered pair $\langle a, b \rangle$, a adjoined to b. [...] Given the basic properties of adjunction, we might intuitively think of a as attached to b on a separate plane, with b retaining all its properties on the "primary plane," the simple structure.   (Chomsky 2001: 18)

The clear point of this quote is that constituent structures containing adjunction must be construed three-dimensionally. We hinted at this earlier, and we will return to similar arguments in Chapter 10. It is worth, however, recounting Uriagereka's (1998, 1999) BPS-based account of the Lebeaux anti-reconstruction facts discussed in section 8.3.

Recall the basic facts of anti-reconstruction: some modifiers show condition C effects even when they have moved, but others do not. Those that do are said to exhibit reconstruction. Those that do not show "anti-reconstruction":

(44) (a) *Which portrait of Rivera$_i$ does he$_i$ like the most.
      (b) *He$_i$ likes which portrait of Rivera$_i$.
      (c) Which portrait that Rivera$_i$ painted does he$_i$ like the most.
      (d) *He$_i$ likes which portrait that Rivera$_i$ painted.

The analysis given by Lebeaux of these facts relies on the idea that condition C can hold at either D- or S-structure. In sentences (a) and (b), *Rivera* is c-commanded by *he* at D-structure, so we have a condition-C violation. The adjunct is inserted between D- and S-structure. In (d), *Rivera* is c-commanded by *he* at S-structure, so again we have a condition-C violation. However, in (c), *Rivera* is never c-commanded by *he*, it is inserted after the wh-phrase moves.[21] This is a clever analysis, but the basic organizational principles of MP disallow such a treatment. There are no levels of D-structure and S-structure in MP,[22] so we can not account for the phenomena using level ordering. Uriagereka (1999) presents a clever alternative making use of the three-dimensionality of BPS representations. It is clear that the adjunct modifies the head noun, so it must be attached to it, but it doesn't necessarily form a part of the same sets as those that define the c-command relationships that govern binding. There is no particular reason in BPS that the sets that constitute a representation necessarily bear the properties of single motherhood, in other words, exhibit connectedness. Sets may freely overlap in membership. If this is indeed

---

[21] For other arguments for "late" adjunction see Nissenbaum (1998), Bošković and Lasnik (1999), Ochi (1999) and Stepanov (2001).

[22] See also Lasnik (1998).

a property of constituent structures then it is one that cannot be expressed easily in a simple tree diagram. To see how this might work, consider the following diagram that represents the application of the simple merge and the pair merge operations derivationally. The representations start at the bottom with the first merge operation, and then progresses upwards. ("a" stands for *a*, "p" stands for *portrait*, "s" stands for *of someone*, and "t" stands for the relative clause *that Rivera painted*.

(45)   {a, {{p, {p, s}}, a}} $\boxed{4}$

$\uparrow$

{⟨p, p⟩, {{p, {p, s}}, t}} $\boxed{5}$

$\uparrow$

a → Merge ←{p, {p, s}} $\longrightarrow$ Pair Merge ← t

$\boxed{3}$ $\uparrow$ $\boxed{2}$

p → Merge ← s

$\boxed{1}$

Simple merge combines *p* and *s* (*portrait of someone*) into the set {p, {p, s}} in step $\boxed{1}$. This set is the input into two distinct operations which are not ordered with respect to each other, nor interact with each other. In $\boxed{2}$, the adjunct *that Rivera painted* (t) is merged with {p, {p, s}} resulting in {⟨p, p⟩, {{p, {p, s}}, t}} *portrait of someone that Rivera painted*. Simultaneously, {p, {p, s}} is identified in $\boxed{3}$ as a member of the set {a, {{p {p, s}}, a}} *a portrait of someone*. It is this later set that merges into the derivation with the potential c-commander that should trigger (but fails to trigger) a condition-C effect. The set containing t (*that Rivera painted*) $\boxed{5}$ intersects with $\boxed{4}$, accounting for the compositional meaning, but is not part of it—explaining the Lebeaux effects. The set-theoretic notation then amounts to a tiered three-dimensional representation, much like that found in autosegmental phonology, except that the tiers are not linked geometrically but through set intersection. We return to multidimensional representations in Chapter 10, but it is worth noting that this explanation fails in one crucial regard—it does not explain why sentences such as (44d) are ungrammatical. If adjuncts are on a different dimension and do not interact with the c-command relationships in the non-adjunct portions of the representation, then (44d) is predicted to be fully grammatical. One possible solution, which lies beyond the scope of this book, can be found in Stepanov (2001).

8.4.3 Bottom-to-top and top-to-bottom derivations

Another consequence of the BPS system is the strictly upwardly cyclic nature of the phrase structure derivation. The merge operation works from the terminals to the root. This is of course true of all projection-based theories of phrase structure, but is particularly acute in BPS where there is no plausible top-to-bottom or purely representational equivalent. This is even more the case in the latest "phase-theoretic" versions of BPS, where the bottom-to-top derivation is crucial to the mechanics of the Move operation.

8.4.3.1 Bottom-to-top derivations   It has long been observed that both syntactic and syntactico-phonological operations are frequently limited in their scope by the hierarchical structure of the sentence (see for example the notion of a "kernel sentence" found in Chomsky 1955, 1957; and the notion of cycle found throughout the 1960s and 1970s, Fillmore 1963; the notion of Government Domain in the 1980s; the notion of minimality in the 1990; and phases in the 2000s). In particular, various phenomena from stress placement to binding theory to displacement operations seem to function as if they work on the smallest, most embedded structure outwards to the largest least embedded structure. If BPS is a strictly bottom-to-top model, we can see syntactic cycles as a natural consequence of the derivation procedure. This was first pointed out by Epstein (1999) and Epstein *et al.* (1998), who argue that all locality constraints, especially those based on c-command relationships, follow from this basic organizational principle (as you will recall from our discussion in Ch. 3, section 3.5.4).[23]

8.4.3.2 Top-to-bottom derivations   A consequence of bottom-to-top derivations—especially ones that are subject to the LCA—is that they are also typically right to left (or more saliently, from the end of the sentence to the beginning). There is something singularly counter-intuitive about this, especially since sentences are obviously spoken (and processed) from the beginning to the end. We might use the old competence–performance distinction to get out of this, but it still feels like a cop-out in the end.

  Phillips (2003) presents some evidence that a top-to-bottom tree derivation[24] elegantly explains why some constituency tests appear to

---

[23] Uriagereka (1999) converges on a similar view, but suggests further that units formed by merge (command units) are spelled out cyclically. This in turn leads to the Chomskyan Phase Theory (Chomsky 2001) and the Minimalist/Tree Adjoining Grammar fusion of Frank (2002). Interestingly, Uriagereka's command unit hypothesis also explains why structures like [$_A$ [$_B$ D E] [$_C$ F G]] are not violations of the LCA, since B and C would be independently spelled out.

[24] Richards (1999) has also argued for a top-to-bottom derivation using data from island effects (and the occasional lack thereof). Baltin (2006) provides an alternative analysis of some of Phillips facts using VP-remnant movement.

be contradictory. Consider the following sentences taken from Phillips, which show straightforward evidence for a rightward-branching structure. Coordination (46a), ellipsis/replacement (46b), movement (46c), binding/c-command (46d, e) all seem to point to a Verb + Object constituent (all examples taken from Phillips).

(46)   (a)   Gromit [likes cheese] and [hates cats].   VO constituent
       (b)   Gromit [likes cheese] and   VO constituent
             Wallace does too.
       (c)   [Like cheese] though Gromit does *t*, he   VO
             can not stand Brie.
       (d)   Wallace and Gromit like each other.
       (e)   *Each other like Wallace and Gromit.

But when we look at more complex constructions like ditransitve verbs, the results seem mixed. We see behaviors where strings that we normally identify as non-constituents obey some constituency tests (47a–c), but the same strings do not obey others (47d–e).

(47)   (a)   Wallace gave [Gromit a biscuit] and [Shawn some cheese]
             for breakfast.
       (b)   [Wallace designed] and [Gromit built] an enormous tin
             moon rocket.
       (c)   Alice [knew that Fred wanted to talk] and [hoped that he
             wanted to argue] with the president.
       (d)   *[Gromit a biscuit] Wallace gave t for Breakfast.
       (e)   *Wallace gave t at breakfast [his favorite pet beagle an enor-
             mous chewy dog biscuit].

Phillips claims that an explanation for these kinds of phenomenon follow if we build trees incrementally from left to right (and consequently in a right-branching language, top to bottom.) The basic rule of tree construction is given in (48).

(48)

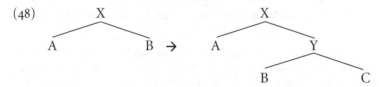

The behaviors seen in (47) follow if constituency tests apply to those strings that are constituents at the point in the incremental derivation the phenomenon is exhibited. This can be seen in the various applications of coordination at various left to right portions in the following sentences.

(49) (a) [Wallace will]
           [Wallace will] and [Wedonlene probably won't]
           [Wallace will] and [Wedonlene probably won't] give Grommit crackers.

      (b) [Wallace will give]
           [Wallace will give] and [Wendolene will send]
           [Wallace will give] and [Wendolene will send] some crackers.

      (c) [Wallace will give Gromit]
           [Wallace will give Gromit] and [Wendolene will give Preston]
           [Wallace will give Gromit] and [Wendolene will give Preston] a new collar.

      (d) [Wallace will give Gromit crackers]
           [Wallace will give Gromit crackers] and [Wendoline will give Preston dog food]
           [Wallace will give Gromit crackers] and [Wendoline will give Preston dog food] before breakfast.

      (e) [Wallace will give Gromit crackers before]
           [Wallace will give Gromit crackers before] and [Wendoline will give Preston dog food after]
           [Wallace will give Gromit crackers before] and [Wendoline will give Preston dog food after] breakfast.

8.4.4 Derived X-bar theory

The particular version of derived X-bar theory found in BPS has some interesting empirical and theoretical consequences. Consider the case of a head that does not project. Such an element is simultaneously an X° and an XP (as it is dominated by the projection of another category). Interestingly, such animals appear to exist. Clitics have the behavior of elements that are simultaneously X°s and XPs. They are theta-marked and allow violations of the head-movement constraint, yet they adjoin to other X°s; such behavior is expected of elements that are ambiguous in their phrasality.

Chomsky limits the range of such ambiguity by proposing that morphology (or its LF analog "word interpretation") gives no output to an element that has complex internal structure (cf. Nuñes 1998). So we expect to find cases like the clitic case above, where a simplex element is simultaneously an XP and an X°, but complex elements are not allowed in this position.

In Carnie (1995) and (2000), I argue that a more liberal definition of phrasality is in order. In particular, I suggest that the phrasal status of a constituent is not determined by its position in the projection structure in the tree. Further, I claim that phrasal status does not predict outward behavior with respect to interface conditions and constraints (such as the morphology, thematic relations, case marking, and head-movement rules). Rather, the syntax can operate freely on any node in the tree, applying operations as needed. The output conditions, in particular the morphology, then determine what nodes are to be spelled out as words and which are to be spelled out as phrases. The cases that show this to be true are those where we have either an apparently X° functioning like a phrase (as in the clitic case mentioned above) or more interestingly, an apparent XP functioning like an X°. We can identify such cases with the following criteria: if a particular p-marker behaves differently in terms of its phrasality with respect to two different output conditions or two different components of the grammar, then it must be the case that its phrasality is not determining its behavior, but rather the behavior determines the phrasality relative to the particular output condition or component of the grammar.

The first case I consider are copular constructions in Irish. Irish is a VSO language, and I assume that this order is derived via movement of the V around the subject into some functional head via head movement. There is a privileged position occupied by predicates in the language, which is between sentence initial complementizer particles and agreement (Particle < Predicate < Agreement < Subject <...). Following standard practice (Sproat 1985 and many others), I identify this position as being derived through head movement. In predicative copular constructions ($\lambda x[NP'(x)]$) nominal and other non-verbal predicates appear in this position (a), even when they are phrasal (b):

(50) (a) Is ollamh   (é) Aindriú.
           C professor   (AGR) Andrew
           "Andrew is a professor."

      (b) Is amhrán   a^L bhuailfidh an píobaire "Yellow Submarine."
           C song   C play.FUT   the piper
           " 'Yellow Submarine' is a song which the piper is going to play."

Here we have a surprise. If indeed the predicate initial order is derived through head movement then we do not expect phrases to appear in this position. Nevertheless there is evidence to suggest that these phrases function like X°s with respect to other parts of the grammar. I'm going to contrast the predicative cases to equative constructions (λxλy [COP' (x, y)]) in the language, which do not have head movement to the privileged position.

(52) Is é Aindriú   an t-ollamh.
      C AGR Andrew the professor
      "Andrew is the Professor."

Irish does not, in general, seem to have the usual brand of islands. In particular, no nominal or wh-islands are observed as long as a special complementizer type and resumptive pronoun are used (53). The exception to this appears to be precisely in the head-moved XP in predicatives (54), where an island emerges. Contrast this with the equative construction where there is no predicate movement (55).[25]

(53) (a) Bíonn   fios   agat i gconaí [$_{cp}$ caidé$_i$ a^L bhuailfidh
          be.HAB know   at.2.s always   what$_i$ C   play.FUT
          an píobaire t$_i$].
          the piper t$_i$
          "You always know what the piper will play."

     (b) Cén Píobaire$_j$ [$_{cp}$a^N mbíonn fios   agat i gconaí
          which piper   C be.HAB know at. 2.s always

          [$_{cp}$caidé$_i$ a^L bhuailfidh sé$_j$ t$_i$]]?
          what$_i$ C   play.FUT. him
          "Which piper do you always know what he will play?"

(54) *Cén Píobaire$_j$ arb [$_{np}$ amhrán$_i$ [$_{cp}$ a^L bhuailfeadh sé$_j$ t$_i$]] (é)
       Which piper REL   song   C play.COND him   AGR
       "Yellow Submarine?"
       "*Which Piper is 'Yellow Submarine' a song which he/t$_i$ is going to play?"

(55) Cén Píobaire$_j$ arb é "Yellow Submarine" [$_{np}$ an t-amhrán$_i$ [$_{cp}$
      Which piper RE AGR   the song

      a^L bhuailfeadh sé$_j$ t$_i$]]?
      C play.COND him
      "Which Piper is 'Yellow Submarine' the song which he/t$_i$ is going to play?"

---

[25] These facts are similar to the facts of canonical and reverse constructions in Italian discussed in Moro (1997). However, as discussed in Carnie (1995), these require a different analysis.

Relatedly, *wh*-in-situ is usually not allowed in Irish, but is required when the question word is inside a complex predicate (56b).

(56)　(a)　Is　[dochtúir　ainmhí]　　Daibhí.
　　　　　　C　doctor　　animals.GEN　Davey
　　　　　"Davey is a doctor of animals."

　　　(b)　Ø [Cen　sort　dochtúra]　Daibhí?
　　　　　　　what kind　doctor.GEN　Davey
　　　　　"What is Davey a doctor of?" (lit. "Davey is what kind of doctor?")

Other evidence comes from the responsive system of Irish. Standard Irish lacks words for *yes* and *no*. Instead, the verb is typically repeated in either positive or negative form.

(57)　(a)　An　bhfaca　tú　　an　teangeolaí?
　　　　　　Q　saw　　you　the　linguist
　　　　　"Did you see the linguist?"

　　　(b)　Ní fhaca.　　　　　　　(c)　Chonaic.
　　　　　　NEG saw　　　　　　　　　saw
　　　　　"No." (lit. "not saw")　　　"Yes." (lit. "saw")

McCloskey (1991) analyzes this as a kind of ellipsis, where everything but the verb in Infl and any complementizer particle (i.e. the Infl head and its adjoined C) is elided. It follows that anything predicated in Infl, even complex ones, should remain in response to a yes/no question. This appears to be the case (although the complex cases show up as a pronoun).

(58)　Q:　An　le　　Seán　an　Subaru?　　A:　Is leis.　　　"Yes."
　　　　　　Q　with　John　the　Subaru　　　　C+INFL
　　　　　"Does John own the Subaru?"　　　　　C with.him

(59)　Q:　An　ceart mo　chuimhne?　A:　Is ceart.
　　　　　　Q　right my　memory　　　　C+INFL
　　　　　"Is my memory is right?"　　　　"yes" (from Doherty 1992)

(60)　Q:　An　dochtúir　tú?　　　　A:　Is ea.
　　　　　　Q　doctor　you　　　　　　C it
　　　　　"Are you a doctor?"　　　　"Yes."

I presented other arguments from the construct state in Irish vs. Arabic, the *Ezafe* construction in Persian, and from CP-inside-N nouns in English.

This analysis has been strongly criticized. Among other arguments, it has been claimed that ambiguous phrasality should show greater exponence in grammar. Many others have suggested that an alternative analysis should be given to the predicate initial orders exhibited in Irish and other VSO languages. In particular, several scholars have suggested that such orders arise through VP remnant movement and full NP movement. For discussion see Adger and Ramchand (2003), and many of the papers in Carnie and Guilfoyle (2000) and Carnie, Harley, and Dooley (2005), especially McCloskey (2005) and Massam (2005).

8.4.5 Label-free and projection-free structures

In an influential but controversial paper, Collins (2002) also suggests that the BPS representation contains too much information. He suggests that labeling in general (including feature structure) can be dispensed with and reduced to mechanisms motivated elsewhere in the grammar. So a phrase {V, {V, X}} is actually {V, X}. In Collins's system, instead of categories, operations target the featural properties of the heads of phrases. Without labels, the principles of phrase structure composition must target elements that are complete. For example, a verb such as *see* takes a DP as a complement, targeting the relevant features in a D head. But for reasons of compositionality, it is crucial that it not target a determiner such as *the* by itself. In versions of BPS that have labels, this is trivial since the verb looks for a DP. In label-free BPS this is accomplished by placing a restriction on the grammar (known as the Locus Principle), whereby two elements can only be merged if the non-head element is complete in terms of its featural requirements. So *the* must combine with an N before it can be merged with a head with unchecked requirements. Again a consequence of this is that constituency representations must be derived strictly bottom to top. As observed by Collins himself in later work, this proposal also naturally leads to the view that syntactic structure shouldn't take constituency as the primary relation, but instead leads to a view where semantic dependencies lie at the heart of the matter. We turn to this claim in the next chapter.

9

Dependency and Constituency

9.1 Introduction[1]

Up to this point in the book we've been assuming that constituency representations—usually trees or sets—are primitives of syntactic representation and the primary means of representing syntactic structure. Semantic relations (such as thematic relations) and semantico-syntactic relations (such as subjecthood, or even predicate–argument relations) can be viewed as derived from, or at least dependent on, constituent hierarchies. For example, in many of versions of Chomskyan generative syntax (Extended Standard Theory, Government and Binding, Minimalism), grammatical relations such as subject are arboreally defined. In the EST, the "subject" of the sentence is the non-VP daughter of the S node. In GB and MP, the notion of subject is at least partly synonymous with specifier (and in particular the specifier of IP/TP/AgrSP and NP/DP). Objects are also defined in terms of trees with a variety of definitions. Hale and Keyser (1991) argue that it is not only grammatical relations that are defined by argument position in a tree; for them, thematic relations (agent, theme, etc.) are defined by the base position of the argument in the tree. In particular, the phenomenon whereby certain thematic relations such as agent are more prominent than others (such as theme or goal) corresponds to the position of those arguments in the tree in their base positions. Even such rich notions as quantifier-variable scope relations can be viewed as dependent upon the hierarchy of the constituent structure (May 1985; Diesing 1992). Diesing and Jelinek (1995) and Jelinek and Carnie (2003) take this idea and propose that in fact almost all hierarchy effects (such as person rankings, definiteness effects, ergative splits, and animacy effects) are in effect side effects of hierarchical constituent structure.

---

[1] For excellent in-depth and textbook treatments of many of the questions touched on in this chapter, see Van Valin (2001) and Moravcsik (2006).

However, such a constituent-centric view is by no means universal. The idea where the relationships are reversed (that is, constituent structure is dependent upon semantic relations[2]) is much older (dating at least to Pāṇini or Aristotle) and is fairly pervasive outside the Chomskyan tradition.

There are various approaches to non-constituency-based syntax (perhaps better referred to as "derived constituency" approaches). These vary along the following dimensions:

(1) (a) The degree to which relational structure determines constituent structure or vice versa.

(b) Whether the relational structure is based on syntactic category, grammatical relations, or more traditional semantic relations (such as predication or thematic relations).

(c) The mechanism by which constituent structures are derived: by dependency grammars, type-logical proofs, mapping rules, or construction schemata/templates.

The variation in (1a) concerns the degree to which constituency is dependent on semantic or semantico-syntactic relations and to what degree it is independent. On one extreme we have the view articulated above and in previous chapters, where syntactic constituency is primary and semantic relations are dependent on these. On the other extreme, we have views like those of Dependency Grammar in its various guises, including Word Grammar, Functional Grammar, Construction Grammar, Cognitive Grammar, and, surprisingly, some recent versions of the Minimalist Program, where constituent structure is entirely or mostly derived from semantic relations. In between these two extremes, we have views where we have simultaneous and equal semantic and syntactic representations. This is represented in the views of Lexical-Functional Grammar and Role and Reference Grammar.

The variation in (1b) refers to the type of semantic or syntacticosemantic relationship serving as the primitive from which constituent structure is derived. Theories such as Lexical-Functional Grammar, Relational Grammar and to a lesser degree Construction Grammar rely on primitive grammatical relations or functions such as "subject" and

---

[2] Miller (1999) provides formal proofs that dependency grammars and (some) constituent-grammar types are equivalent in terms of their expressive power (strong and weak generative capacity).

"object". Some approaches, such as Dependency Grammar, Role and Reference Grammar, and Case Grammar, use basic semantic or thematic relations (such as agent, theme etc.) to a greater or lesser degree. A more refined view is found in the type-logical theories such as Categorial Grammar and HPSG. In these approaches the driving force is the notion of a functional application or predication. Essentially this boils down to the idea that many individual syntactic objects are "incomplete" and require an argument to flesh out their syntactic and semantic requirements. Take for example an intransitive verb like *leave*. Such a verb has simultaneously the semantic requirement that it needs a entity to serve as the subject, and the syntactic requirement that that entity be represented by an NP. Other syntactic objects (such as the NP *John*, which presumably represents an entity), serve to complete these requirements. The operations involved here are variously referred to as unification, feature satisfaction, functional application, or feature checking.

The last type of variation lies in the means of syntactic representation of the dependency or relation; that is, the nature of the representation that is formed by the semantic or semantico-syntactic relationships. A wide variety of accounts of word order and constituency can be found. As we will see below, Relational Grammar (and to a degree its successor, Arc-Pair Grammar) mapped grammatical relations onto syntactic templates. Closely related are the constructions or schemas found in Construction Grammar, Cognitive Grammar, and, to a lesser degree, some versions of HPSG. HPSG and Categorial Grammar use tree or tree-like structures. But in fact, as we will see these are meant as proofs that the semantics/syntactic structure of the whole can be derived from the parts, rather than direct syntactic constituent representations. As mentioned briefly in Chapter 6, LFG uses a series of mapping principles encoded into "metavariables" that allow a correspondence between the constituent structure and the semantic form. A similar, although distinct, approach is found in RRG. Finally, we have theories such as Dependency Grammar and Word Grammar that use dependency trees (stemma) and related notations (such as networks).

This chapter is devoted to looking at these alternatives to strict constituency-based approaches to syntactic structure. Needless to say, these different topics are tightly interconnected, so I will attempt to provide the relevant parts of each theoretical approach as a whole in turn. I start out with Lexical-Functional Grammar and Relational

Grammar which are to a greater and lesser degree based on the primitive notions of subject and object. Next I turn to the more liberal class of dependency grammars, where semantic relations are viewed to determine constituent structure. Next we return to the more formal categorial grammars, which express dependencies through categorial requirements. We extend this approach to survey Tree-Adjoining Grammar (TAG), which, although arboreal, builds upon the basic insights of categorial grammar. Then we consider two functionalist frameworks of grammar (Dik's functionalist grammar and Van Valin's Role and Reference Grammar (RRG)). Finally, we turn to construction- and cognitive-grammar approaches, where instead of constituent trees we simply have templatic constructions or schemata, into which words are mapped.

There are so many interrelated and intertwined questions here that teasing out the empirical arguments that favor one approach over another is very difficult. To a large extent I will remain agnostic about these approaches, but will try to point out their particular advantages or disadvantages as we go along. The reader is warned that the discussion in this chapter may be inconsistent both with other parts of this book and internally to this chapter itself. They should also be aware that the surveys presented here are largely based on the single question of the nature of phrase structure representations in these approaches, so the reader shouldn't judge these frameworks on that criteria alone, there is much more to each of them than is presented in a couple of paragraphs in this chapter.

9.2 Systems based primarily on grammatical relations

A number of approaches to grammar consider the primacy of grammatical relations, such as subject and object (see Farrell 2005 for an introduction to these relations and their representation in various grammatical frameworks).

9.2.1 A semi-arboreal system: Lexical-Functional Grammar

Strictly speaking, Lexical-Functional Grammar does not belong in this chapter, because it posits separate constituent and relational structures (c- and f-structures); but I include it here because of the primacy it places on grammatical functions (relations). As discussed in Chapter 6, LFG makes use of a structured representation of grammatical functions, as shown in (2). These f-structures are mapped to the constituent structure (c-structure) using metafunctions and functional equations.

(2)

$$
\begin{bmatrix}
\text{PRED} & \text{'love} <\text{SUBJ, OBJ}>\text{'} \\
\text{TENSE} & \text{present} \\
\text{SUBJ} & \begin{bmatrix} \text{DEF} & + \\ \text{NUM} & \text{sng} \\ \text{PRED} & \text{'professor'} \end{bmatrix} \\
\text{OBJ} & [\text{PRED} \quad \text{'phonology'}]
\end{bmatrix}
$$

Among the arguments for an independent functional structure is the idea that different elements in the constituent structure can contribute to a single f-structure unit. Take the following example, which is taken directly from Falk (2001). The plurality of the subject in the following sentences is realized in the auxiliary, whereas the definiteness and the semantic content come from the NP element. There is no single constituent contributing all the information about the nature of the subject.

(3) (a) The deer are dancing.
     (b) The deer is dancing.

This suggests that a separate component is required for semantico-syntactic relations, which, although mapped to the c-structure, is independent of it. See Baker (2001a, b) for an attempt to show that a structurally derived notion of relation is more explanatory for non-configurational languages.

9.2.2 Relational Grammar

We begin our survey of purely derived-constituency or dependent-constituency approaches by looking at a theory that was at its height in the late 1970s and early 1980s: Relational Grammar (RG). Later versions of this theory are known as Arc-Pair Grammar. The basic premise of RG is that grammatical relations such as subject (notated as 1), object (2), indirect object (3), predicate (P) and a special kind of adjunct known as a "chômeur" (chô) are the primitives of the grammar. Various kinds of grammatical operation apply to these primitive relations. For example, passive is seen as the promotion of an object to the subject role and the demotion of the subject role to the chômeur role. This is represented by one of two different styles of relational diagram—the most common of which is shown in (4). This is a representation of the passive *The puppy was kissed by the policeman*. The first line represents the underlying roles in the sentence, the second line represents the final form. Word order is irrelevant in these diagrams.

(4)   initial stratum

final stratum

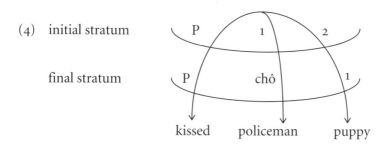

kissed   policeman   puppy

Word order is handled by mapping the roles to templates. The declarative template for English is *1 P 2 3 chô*, the final stratum is mapped to this order so that the subject comes first, then the predicate, then in order the object, indirect object, and any chômeurs.

Templates are a kind of construction grammar. That is, there is a set of templates associated with particular types of construction. For example, a *wh*-object question would be associated with a *2 aux 1 P 3* template.

Many of the insights of RG have been subsequently adapted by other theoretical approaches. For example, the discovery of the unaccusative class of verbs has been particularly influential. GB theory borrowed the results of Relational Grammar, coding the effects into the Case module. The significant difference between RG and GB is that GB associates the particular relations with particular positions in the tree rather than using a template (e.g. Nominative case corresponds to the 1 relation, and it is tied to the specifier of IP or TP; promotion is viewed as movement).

Baker (2001a) addresses the question of whether relational notions are best represented as primitives or as part of the phrase structure. He suggests that RG and LFG distinguish at least two kinds of prominence: relational and embedding. Relational prominence is reflected in the number of Relational Grammar: 1 is more prominent than 2, etc. These relations are clause bound. Embedding prominence expresses the idea that some phrases are higher in the tree or complex relational diagram than others and includes relationships between argument structures in different clauses. RG and LFG distinguish these types of prominence; Chomskyan grammar does not: it subsumes them under the c-command relation. In a constituency-based theory, subjects naturally c-command objects, deriving the argument hierarchy. To see a case where grammar treats two different argument positions differently, consider the case of objects and embedded subjects. As Baker argues, RG distinguishes between these two. The embedded subject is a 1 in a structurally embedded relational network, the other is a 2 in the same set of arcs as the main subject:

(5) (a)

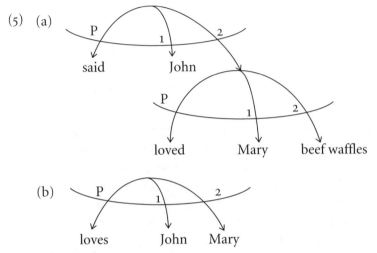

(b)

By contrast, in Chomskyan grammar the two have at least one identical property, they are both related to the matrix subject by the c-command relation. *Mary* in both sentences is c-commanded by *John*. RG predicts then that these two positions should not be targeted uniformly by grammatical rules. Baker convincingly shows that this is not true. The subject of an embedded clause (the c and d examples) and the object of a main clause (the a and b examples) are subject to the same restrictions on bound variable anaphora (6) and Condition C effects (7) (all data taken from Baker (2001a: 37–8). Baker gives related evidence from Reciprocal binding, Superiority effects, Negative Polarity licensing, including cross-linguistic evidence. Facts like these point away from distinguishing between clause-internal relational prominence and cross-clausal embedding prominence:

(6) (a) *Every boy* persuaded *his* mother that video games are good for you.
     (b) *Her son persuaded *every woman* that video games are good for you.
     (c) *Every boy* persuaded the principal that *his* mother sang professionally.
     (d) *Her son persuaded the principal that *every woman* sang professionally.

(7) (a) *He persuaded *John's* mother that video game are good for you.

(b) *Her* son persuaded *Martha* that video games were good for you.

(c) *He persuaded the principal that *John's* mother sang professionally.

(d) *Her* son persuaded the principal that *Martha* sang professionally.

It should be noticed that this argument, while a valid criticism of RG, does not necessarily mean that a constituency grammar is correct; it means only that grammars must have some mechanism for treating relational and embedding prominence in a unified way.

9.3 Dependency grammars[3]

RG and LFG are breakaways from the American generativist movement. A distinct but related tradition comes to us from Europe. In particular, the work of the Prague and London schools of linguistics developed into a group of approaches known as dependency grammars.

Although they also make reference to relational concepts, the notion of dependency extends to other kinds of semantic relations. Semantic relations are mediated through a broader notion of the head–dependent relation. The types of things that appear in head–dependent relations include a wide variety of notions including extractee, focus, and adjunct thematic relations.[4] The types of relation are determined by the lexical entry of the words at hand. The notion of head should be familiar from X-bar theory—indeed, it appears as if X-bar theory lifted the notion directly from Dependency Grammar (Stuurman 1985). A head is a word that licenses (or from the other view point, requires) the dependent.

There are at least three major mechanisms for representing head–dependent relations: two types of Stemma, and word-grammar

---

[3] Many thanks to Dick Hudson, who provided much helpful advice and materials for the writing of this section.

[4] The meaning of notion "head" is controversial. The first references to it appear in Sweet (1891) and are largely based on syntactic category; Zwicky (1985) offers a syntactic definition; Speas (1985) suggests the notion should be construed semantically as the element that is unsaturated in terms of its argument structure; Hudson (1987) also argues for a semantic definition; Croft (1996) suggests an intermediate position, where the head is the element in the structure that is both the semantic head (i.e. X is the head of X+Y if X describes the kind of thing that X+Y describes), and the primary information-bearing unit—a syntactic notion.

dependency structures. Tesnière (1959) introduced tree-like "stemmas" where heads dominate their dependents (8):

(8)
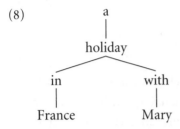

In this diagram, the word *holiday* licenses two modifiers (*in France* and *with Mary*). *With* licenses *Mary* and *in* licenses *France.* The linear order is not expressed in this diagram. Linear order falls out from basic headedness properties of the language. English, being right-headed, linearizes the structure starting at the top, putting the head before each of the dependents. The order of multiple dependents is either free (*a holiday with Mary in France*) or depends on some secondary relations.

Word Grammar uses the different notation seen in (9) (taken from Hudson 2007):

(9)
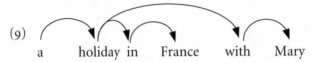

To a certain degree, this is a flattened stemma, as each arrow corresponds to a vertical line in (8), but this diagram expresses linear order as well. The head is represented as the tail of an arrow; the dependent is at the point. To every extent possible, head–dependent relations must be adjacent. More deeply embedded dependent relations (e.g. *in* and *France*) take priority in adjacency over less dependent relations (e.g. *holiday* and *with*). Linear order is provided by headedness require-ments[5] (modulo some lexical restrictions).

The third, most common, notation, based on the work of Hays (1964) and Gaifman (1965) is the dependency tree. This notation also indicates linear order, but retains the stemma structure using categories instead of the words. The words are linked to the stemma by dotted lines.

---

[5] Hudson (2007) uses an alternative method of establishing order, borrowing the notion of landmark from Cognitive Grammar.

(10)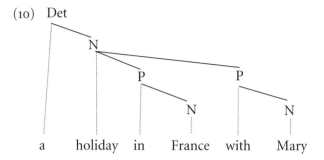

a   holiday   in   France   with   Mary

The words project a category and these categories express the dependency relations in a stemma organization.

A property of all three of these notations, expressed most explicitly in the Word Grammar approach—but present in all of them—is the fact that the number of nodes is in a one-to-one relation with the number of words in the sentence. For example, in the complex NP in (8)–(10), each dependency representation has exactly six nodes. The equivalent representation in a PSG might have eleven; in X-bar theory at least 18. This corresponds to the idea that syntactic structures are tightly connected to the properties of the words that compose them.

Hudson (1984, 1990, 2007, p.c.) has made the case that once one adopts dependency as an integral part of syntactic representation, as for example X-bar theory has done, then constituent structures need not be primitives. Constituent structures can be derived algorithmically from dependency structures, so are at best redundant. If we take each dependency relation and express it as a headed phrase, then we result in a phrase structure tree. For example, if we take the dependency between the preposition *with* and the noun *Mary* and translate this into a PP projection, we have a constituency representation. If a head licenses several dependencies, then the phrase contains them all, so the noun *holidays* heads a phrase dominating both of its PP dependents. The same operation can be applied to each dependency.

Hudson (2007), based on work by Pickering and Barry (1991), suggests that the phenomenon of dependency distance—the number of words that intervene between a head and its dependent—has some effect on the ability of speakers to process sentences. This suggests that dependencies are more important than constituencies. Indeed, even the classic constituency experiments of Garrett (1967)—using the interpretation of click placement—might be interpreted as targeting the edges of dependencies. See Hudson (2007) for other arguments that constituency is at best a derived notion.

Interestingly, a number of generative grammarians working in the Minimalist program have converged on a dependency grammar-like approach. Based on his notion of projection Brody (1998) (which is nearly identical to that of Speas 1990), Brody (2000) proposes the Telescope Principle which reduces constituency representations into dependencies by collapsing projections of categories into a single node which dominates all the elements dominated by elements of the projection chain in the X-bar theoretic structure; see (11).

(11)

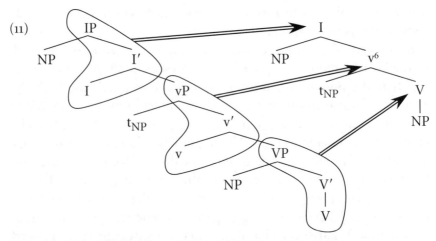

Bury (2003, 2005) builds upon this, combining it with the set theoretic BPS system to explain the fact that languages with left-peripheral verbal structures (VSO and V2 languages) often require an element to the left of the verb (a particle in the case of VSO, a topic in the case of V2 languages). Independently, in largely unpublished work, Collins (2002), Zwart (2003), Collins and Ura (2004), and Seely (2004) all have suggested that the minimalist Merge operation is really an operation that implements a dependency relation. That is, one merges (or remerges) precisely when the non-head element satisfies some requirement of the head. See also chapter 12.

9.4 Categorial grammars

For the most part, the relations expressed by dependency grammars are semantic in nature including, but not limited, to thematic and grammatical relations, but extending to other semantic relations such as topic and focus. In this section, we consider the independently conceived of notion of a categorial grammar (see among other sources Ajdukiewicz

---

[6] The nature of the 'little v' category will be discussed briefly in Ch. 11.

1935; Lambek 1958; Bar-Hillel 1964; and more recent work such as Oehrle, Bach, and Wheelan 1988); Moortgat 1989; Steedman 1989, 1996, 2000; and Wood 1993). For a minimalist critique of Categorial Grammar see Lasnik, Uriagereka, and Boeckx (2005) and Chametzky (2000). For a critique of Categorial Grammar from the perspective of GPSG, see Borsley (1996). For a comparison of dependency grammars to phrase structure grammars see Chomsky (1963), Bar-Hillel (1964), and Miller (1999). For a comparison of dependency grammars to X-bar grammars see Dowty (1989). Pollard has a new framework, called Higher-Order Grammar, which is a development of Categorial Grammar. Details of this approach can be found at http://ling.ohio-state. edu/~hana/hog and Pollard (2004) but I will not describe this approach in detail here.

Categorial grammars are similar to dependency grammars in that they impose restrictions on co-occurrence among words, phrasal composition follows directly from those restrictions and they are non-arboreal. However, they differ in the nature of the co-occurrence requirements. In a categorial grammar, the restrictions come from the category of the head and its dependent rather than their semantic function. For example, an intransitive verb might be characterized as an element (or function) that is missing an NP subject (an entity), and when that requirement is met, it licenses a clause (a truth value). In this section, we will look at, in turn, classical categorial grammars and Montague Grammar, TAG, and at the categorial grammar components of HPSG.

9.4.1 Classic Categorial Grammar and Combinatorial Categorial Grammar

Like dependency grammars, categorial grammars start with the assumption that co-occurrence among words is licensed by the individual properties of the words themselves. These restrictions are encoded in the category of the word instead of, for example, phrase structure rules. To see how this works, it is perhaps easiest to look at a toy version of such a system, which I couch here in a simplified version of Combinatorial Categorial Grammar (Steedman 1996). The main work of the system is defined by the lexical entries:

(12) (a) Mary NP   *Mary*
      (b) apple NP   *apples*

(c) left   S\NP $\lambda x(left'(x))$
(d) ate   (S\NP)/NP $\lambda x\lambda y\,(ate'(x,y))$

The categories of *Mary* and *apple* should be self-evident, but the categories of the predicates *left* and *ate* are less transparent. The category of an intransitive verb, S\NP, indicates that the predicate represents a function that looks to the left (indicated by the back slash \) for an NP, and results in a clause (S). (S\NP)/NP represents a transitive verb that looks to the right (/) for an NP object. Satisfaction of that part of the function outputs another function (S\NP), which represents a verb phrase, which like an intransitive verb, looks to the left for an NP and results in an S. The material to the right of the categories in (12) represents the semantics of the word. (12a and b) represent the entities of *Mary* and *apples* respectively. Examples (12c and d) are functions (the lambdas (λ) indicate this—these indicate that these forms are incomplete or unsaturated and require missing information (x, y)). Application of *left* to some NP, such as *Mary*, will mean that Mary left. Application of *ate* to two NPs indicates that the entity characterized by the first NP ate the second.

The fact that the meaning of an expression such as *Mary left* is in fact *left'(Mary)* can be shown by means of a proof. Such proofs use rules such as the rules of forward and backward application shown in (13).

(13)   (a) X/Y:F Y:a → X:$f(a)$ forward application (>A)
       (b) Y:a X\Y:F → X: $f(a)$ backward application (<A)

It should be noted that although these rules look like phrase structure rules, they are not. They are rules of inference—that is, they are rules that allow one to prove that the meaning of a complete expression can be determined from the categorial combination of the words. They do not create constituent structures, although these might be derived from the proofs if necessary. Because of this, these proofs are more like the derivations of early generative grammar and very unlike the projection rules of current practice.

The rule in (13a) says that given a forward slash category (X/Y), which is a function that is followed by a Y with a semantic value of a, we can deduce a category of X, with a semantic interpretation of the function f being applied to a ($f(a)$). Example (13b) is the same rule but applying backwards, with the argument Y on the left.

To see how this works, consider the proofs in (14) and (15). In (14), on the top line we have the words in the sentence *Mary left*. We want to prove that the categories and their semantic values add up to a sentence with the semantic value of the (backward) application of the open function represented by the predicate to the argument. The application of this rule is indicated by the underscore followed by the <A symbol. This rule, in essence, takes the NP on the left and substitutes it for the NP in the S\NP category, canceling out the NPs, resulting in category S. The entity *Mary* is substituted in for the x in the formula for the open function represented by the predicate, canceling out the lambda, and resulting in the semantic category *left'(Mary)*.

(14)   Mary   left
      NP:*Mary*   S\NP: $\lambda x(left'(x))$
      ————————————————————— < A
          S: *left'(Mary)*

(15) shows a more complicated proof showing a transitive verb.[7]

(15)   Mary   ate   apples
      NP:*Mary*   (S\NP)/NP $\lambda x\lambda y(ate'(x, y))$ NP:*apples*
      ———————————————————————————————————— ->A
          S\NP: $\lambda x(ate'(x, apples))$
      ————————————————————————— < A
          S: *ate'(Mary, apples)*

The individual words and their contributions are on the first line of (15). Using the rule of forward application, we cancel out the outermost NP and substitute its denotation in for the variable y, which results in the open function representing the traditional VP. The next underscore indicates the application of backwards application to the preceding NP, substituting its denotation in for the variable x. The resulting line indicates that these words can compose to form a sentence meaning that *Mary* ate *apples*.

Like the derivations of early phrase structure grammars, it is a relatively trivial matter to translate these proofs into trees. If we take (15) as an example, we need simply turn the derivation upside down so

---

[7] I've slightly simplified how the semantic structure is calculated here for expository purposes. In particular, I've ignored the procedures for ensuring that the object NP is substituted in for the y variable and the subject NP for the x variable.

the last line represents the root node, connected to the each of the elements involved in forming it by branches, and doing the same for the middle and top lines:

(16)

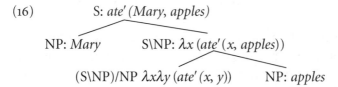

$$\text{S: } ate'\,(Mary,\ apples)$$

$$\text{NP: } Mary \qquad \text{S\textbackslash NP: } \lambda x\,(ate'\,(x,\ apples))$$

$$\text{(S\textbackslash NP)/NP } \lambda x \lambda y\,(ate'\,(x,\ y)) \qquad \text{NP: } apples$$

Such trees are common, for example, in the Montegue Grammar variant of categorial grammar, but they are also present in the work of type-logical semanticists who work in parallel with generative syntacticians (see for example the semantic system described in Heim and Kratzer 1997) and in the proofs and representations in HPSG. However, it should be noted that ontologically speaking the proofs (and any resultant trees) are not a constituency representation per se in traditional categorial grammar. The reason for this lies in the fact that the rules of inference in this system include rules that would create a structure that does not correspond to our usual understanding of the clause. For example we have the rule of swapping (associativity), which allows the system to combine a transitive verb with the subject before the object:

(17) $(X\backslash Y)/Z{:}\lambda v_z \lambda v_x[\,f(v_x, v_z)] \;\rightarrow\; (X/Z)\backslash Y{:}\ \lambda v_z \lambda v_x[f(v_x, v_z)]$

This rule takes a predicate that looks first rightwards for an object then second leftwards for a subject and turns it into a predicate that looks leftwards first for a subject, then rightwards for the object. This rule creates a "structural" ambiguity between the proofs, but because the semantics remain the same on each side of the rule in (17) this does not correspond to a semantic ambiguity. After swapping a valid proof for our sentence would be:

(18) Mary   ate   apples
      NP:*Mary*   (S/NP)\NP $\lambda x \lambda y(ate'\,(x, y))$ NP:*apples*
      _____<A

              S/NP: $\lambda y(ate'\,(Mary, y))$

      _____> A

              S: $ate'(Mary, apples)$

This corresponds to the tree in (19):

(19)

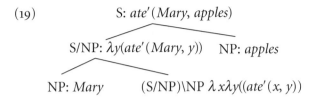

$$S: ate'(Mary, apples)$$
$$S/NP: \lambda y(ate'(Mary, y)) \quad NP: apples$$
$$NP: Mary \quad (S/NP)\backslash NP\ \lambda x\lambda y((ate'(x, y))$$

The reason for positing such rules as swapping is that they allow accounts of, for example, non-constituent conjunction such as the right-node raising example in (20).

(20)   John loves and Mary hates semantics.

With swapped functions, we can combine *loves* and *John*, and *hates* and *Mary* first, conjoin them into a composite function, then satisfy the requirement that the verbs have an object second. Such sentences are largely mysterious under a phrase structure analysis.[8] On the other hand, without additional mechanisms, subject–object asymmetries are unexplained; nor is non-constituent conjunction in languages that put both arguments on the same side of the verb (VOS, SOV), since there is no obvious way in which to compose the verb with the subject before the object in such languages. The net effect of these rules is that the proofs cannot be equated straightforwardly with constituency diagrams.

There are a number of notational variants and versions of categorial grammar. They differ in what rules of inference are allowed in the system and in the meaning of the "slashed" categories and whether these categories should be given in terms of traditional syntactic categories or in terms of semantic types—for instance, $<e>$ is an entity (an NP), $<t>$ is a truth value (an S), $<e,t>$ is a function from an entity to a truth value (an intransitive verb or a verb phrase). For a relatively complete catalog of the various notations, see Wood's (1993) textbook.

9.4.2 Tree-Adjoining Grammar (TAG)

Somewhat ironically, one of the theories that belongs in this chapter about theories without constituent trees is one that is based on the idea that parts of trees are themselves primitives. This is a particular variant on categorial grammar known as Tree-Adjoining Grammar (TAG) (Joshi 1985; for a more detailed description see Joshi and Schabes

---

[8] See, however, the discussion in Phillips (2003).

(1996) or the introductory chapter in Abeillé and Rambow (2000). In the TAG formalism, the categories come along with a tree (treelets), which include information about the co-occurrence restrictions place on words. For example, the CCG category $(S\backslash NP)/NP$ is represented as the lexical entry in (21b). The ↓ arrow means that the category to its left is required.

(21)   (a)   (b)   (c)

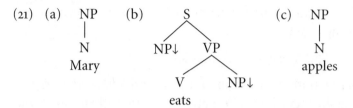

The NP in (21a) substitutes for the first NP↓ in (21b) and the NP in (c) substitutes for the lower one resulting in the familiar:

(22)

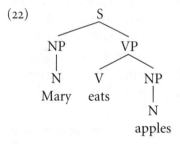

This is the operation of substitution. TAG also has an adjunction operation that targets the middle of trees. Both of these rules are generalized transformations (see Chapters 6 and 8).

Since these tree structures are lexicalized—that is, they represent constituency through a structure that is specified lexically, they provide an interesting hybrid between a categorial grammar[9] and a constituency-based grammar. They also are a step in the direction of a construction grammar: the topic of section 9.5. First, however, we examine the feature-based version of categorial grammar found in HPSG, which also has (under at least one conception) constructional properties.

---

[9] As an aside, a second kind of tree structure can be found in TAG. This is the derivation tree, which indicates which treelets were attached to other treelets by the combinatorial principles. Since TAG is head-oriented, it's not surprising that these derivation trees look very much like Stemma. See Abeillé and Rambow (2000) for more discussion.

9.4.3 Features in HPSG

In Chapter 6, we looked at how phrase structure grammars might be enriched by feature structures. This was a prominent part of GPSG and became a driving force in HPSG, which is a more stringently lexical framework. As part of its name (*Head-driven* Phrase Structure Grammar) implies, there is a dependency grammar and categorial grammar flavor to HPSG. (For discussion see Pollard 1985, 1988.) The features include those that entail co-occurrence among constituents.[10] For example, a verb like *ate* may require that its COMPS feature (complement feature) be satisfied by an NP to its right. The second part of the framework's name (Phrase Structure Grammar) might lead the reader to think that the framework is largely an arboreal feature-rich variant on a phrase structure grammar, and historically this would be accurate. However, it is not at all clear that current conceptions of HPSG are really phrase structure grammars at all, nor are the "trees" of the system clearly constituent structures. The PSG portion of HPSG may well represent rules of inference like a categorial grammar rather than a structure building (or structure licensing) set of rules.

In the summer of 2004, I posted a message to the HPSG listserv (the archive of which can be found on the Linguist List: http://www. linguistlist.org[11]) asking about the ontological status of tree diagrams in HPSG. Interestingly, there was widespread disagreement about what the trees actually represent. Many scholars viewed them as traditional constituency diagrams; others considered them to be more akin to categorial-grammar proofs or trees; there were many who even considered them to be derivational histories in the same way early phrase structure trees represented an abstracted derivational history (see ch. 5) or even nothing more than convenient pedagogical/presentational devices. The heart of the problem is that the feature structure itself for a sentence (i.e. the features associated with an S node) includes all the information about the constituency of the tree. That is, there are features representing complement, specifier (or DTRS, daughters) features for each node, which specify the constituency, or at least the

---

[10] See Karttunen (1989) for a feature-based version of CCG that is not couched in HPSG.

[11] In particular, see the threads with the subject lines "trees", "increasing interest in the HPSG conference", and "Trees, pheno, tectogrammar" in late June and early July 2004, in particular the messages from Ash Asudeh, Georgia Green, Ivan Sag, Carl Pollard, Tibor Kiss, Andrea Dauer, Shalom Lappin, and Stefan Müller. Ivan Sag and Carl Pollard were both particularly helpful in answering some private questions about the discussion and providing insights into the current practice.

combinatorial properties of that structure (see the next chapter when we discuss linear ordering in HPSG which need not correspond to the combinatorial properties). These feature structures can be embedded inside each other. As such, a tree structure is largely redundant or at least can be fully reconstructed from the feature structure (or, more accurately, "sign") associated with the clause. Sag (p.c.) pointed out to me that there is in fact a one-to-one relation between the depth of embedding of features in a feature structure and the structural depth in a tree diagram; and this has meant that practitioners of HPSG use trees even when they intend feature-structure graphs.

Again, like TAG, HPSG appears to be an interesting hybrid between a constituency-based analysis and categorial/dependency based one.

9.5. Functionalist Grammar and Role and Reference Grammar

In this section, I briefly consider two approaches that, while not identical to dependency, relational, or categorial grammars, have a set of basic organizational premises which are largely in the spirit of semantically-derived/driven constituent structures.

Functionalism, oversimplifying wildly, is the idea that language structure follows from language function or use. The grammatical mechanisms of generative grammar, by contrast, are assumed to be largely independent of their function but provide for generalizations across types of language use. In functionalist theories, use determines form to a greater or lesser degree. It is easy, then, to see that in functionalist linguistic frameworks, constituent structures should follow from the semantic and pragmatic properties of the message that is being conveyed. In this sense these approaches derive constituent structures, if they have them from the semantics. This is nearly a definitional property of functionalism.

Functionalism is hardly a homogeneous research paradigm (Newmeyer 1998, Croft 1999; cf. Van Valin 2000). I have chosen to very briefly mention two functionalist approaches here, both of which have significant emphasis on the relationship between semantic interpretation and syntactic form (as opposed to focusing on largely semantic, pragmatic or even sociolinguistic concerns). These are Dik's (1989) Functional Grammar and the more elaborate model of Role and Reference Grammar (RRG) (Van Valin 1993, 2003).

In Dik's Functional Grammar, the meaning of a sentence is represented by a formulation in an enriched variety of formal logic, with the primitives being predicates (including nominals), variables, and various kinds of operator. We will address the precise content of these forms in Chapter 11. These semantic elements are ordered by constructional templates (known as "realization rules"), as in Relational Grammar.

RRG is a more sophisticated framework, but is based on the same basic intuition. The driving forces in the syntax are the semantics of the individual words. Through a series of semantic linking principles these are collocated into a logical structure. This logical structure is then mapped into two different constituent structures, the layered structure of the clause (LCS) and the operator structure, which are representations using constructional templates. The constituency facts are thus just a result of mapping elements in the logical structure into the constituent structures. The procedures involved here are relatively complex and interact with material we will discuss in Chapters 10 and 11.

9.6. Construction Grammar and Cognitive Grammar

Each of the constituent systems—in categorial grammars and dependency grammars that we have described in this chapter and elsewhere in this book—have in common that they are based on a pair-wise matching between words. In the Principles and Parameters framework and unification-based grammars like LFG and GPSG, words that constitute a phrase must be compatible in terms of features. In categorial grammars the matching occurs pair-wise between two categories where one element satisfies the categorial requirements of the other. In dependency grammars, syntactic structures are created by matching pair-wise head–dependent relations. In each case, we have word-to-word composition that follows from some general procedure or licensing mechanism. One way of putting this is that each of these approaches (with the exception of LFG) is to some degree compositional in that the meanings of expressions are calculated pair-wise (or at least locally) by some general, non-construction-specific, combinatorial principles. These might be rules of inference, phrase structure rules, or the application of head–dependent relations. In this section, we consider some approaches which, while they have general procedures for syntactic structure composition, derive the form of the sentence by making reference to phrase level or sentence level "constructions" or "schemata".

Constructions/schemata are larger-than-word memorized (or lexicalized) forms. The templates of Relational Grammar are one such kind of construction. Varieties of Construction Grammar (Goldberg 1995, 2006; Croft 2001) and Cognitive Grammar (Langacker 1987; van Hoek 1997) are closely related frameworks that adopt this position. Similarities between constructions are captured by the notion of an inheritance hierarchy, where constructions and other lexical entries are organized into types and the properties of more general types are inherited by specific cases. For example, we might take the general class of subject–predicate constructions, which have certain properties holding of the subject position. This class is divided into two or three groups including at least intranstives and transitives. These more narrow classes of constructions inherit the general properties of the predicate subject class of constructions. Generalities among sentences, then, come not from the application of general compositional principles, but from among inheritance among constructions. Some recent varieties of HPSG (see, for example, the version described in Sag, Wasow, and Bender 2003) are essentially construction grammars in this sense.

Cognitive Grammar and Construction Grammar concern the general cognitive principles that map between memorized conventionalized expressions and their extensions, but hold that these principles are not rules per se and the representations are not constituent structures. Constructions themselves are unanalyzable wholes. Properties that hold across constructions follow from the hierarchically organized lexicon. Van Hoek (1997) argues that other phenomena that are supposed to derive from a constituent structure (e.g. c-command asymmetries) can be articulated in purely semantic terms by making reference to the speaker's knowledge of the pragmatic context and prominence of arguments within a representation of that knowledge.

10

Multidominated, Multidimensional, and Multiplanar Structures

10.1 Introduction

The "standard" version of phrase structure sketched in the beginning part of this book has the following properties, whether it is defined using a PSG, an X-bar grammar, Merge, or by other means: it graphically represents constituency; it represents word order—even if in a derived manner—and as claimed in Chapter 3 it is subject to restrictions on the interaction of the vertical and horizontal axes of the graph such that vertical relations such as dominance must be represented in the linear order (the horizontal relations). This has two consequences: (1) it means that words that are grouped hierarchically must be contiguous in the linear order (i.e. there is no line crossing in the tree); (2) it also means that a single word can belong to only one hierarchical constituent. We stipulated these effects in Chapter 3 with the non-tangling condition (A9).[1, 2]

A9. *Non-tangling condition*:
    $(\forall wxyz \in N) [((w \prec_s x) \& (w \triangleleft^* y) \& (x \triangleleft^* z)) \rightarrow (y \prec z)]$.

As discussed in chapter (3), this rules out line crossing. It says that if w sister-precedes x, and w dominates y and x dominates z, then y must precede z. Assume that in (1) w and x are sisters, then (1a) is licit by A9, but (1b) is not.

---

[1] I will retain the axiom numbering of Chs. 3 and 4 and continue from it rather than renumbering axioms in this chapter.

[2] See GKPS for a principled account of what they call the ECPO (Exhaustive Constant Partial Ordering) properties of language. Line crossing is ruled out because precedence principles hold only over local trees (i.e. the only relation is a relation of sister precedence).

(1)   (a)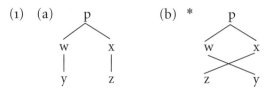

So this constraint rules out crossing lines.[3] It also rules out multiply mothered nodes such (2) when combined with the restriction that nodes cannot precede themselves (T1[4] from Ch. 3).

(2)   *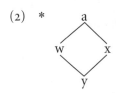

Since y is dominated by w, which sister-precedes x, and y is also dominated by x, it follows that y precedes y; but such situations are ruled out by the independently required restriction that items cannot precede themselves. Given (A9) and (T1), multidominated trees will always result in a contradiction.

This gives constituent structures a measure of explanatory power. It predicts the existence of constituency-based and structure-dependent phenomena. This insight is at the heart of Generative Grammar in most of its guises. Nevertheless, there are a number of attested phenomena which either escape explanation under these premises or are predicted not to occur without additional mechanisms added to the grammar. Chomsky (1957) used this observation to argue for transformations. He claimed that when you had phenomena that lay outside the power of PSGs (and we can extend that to related formalisms), then a higher-order grammatical system, such as one that uses transformational rules, is in order. Take, for example, the phenomenon of *wh*-extraction without pied-piping of the preposition:

(3)   Who did you give the book to?

The preposition *to* is separated from its complement *who* by the rest of the clause. There is no way to draw a tree for this sentence using a

---

[3] The prohibition against crossing lines is also found in autosegmental phonology. See Goldsmith (1976), McCarthy (1979), Pulleyblank (1983), Clements (1985), Sagey (1986, 1988), and Hammond (1988, 2005) for discussion.

[4] T1. *P is irreflexive*: $(\forall x \in N) \, [\neg(x \prec x)]$.

simple PSG, maintaining the complement relation of *to* to *who* without crossing a line and violating (A9).

In addition to traditional examples of movement such as *wh*-movement and raising constructions, McCawley (1982, 1989) observes that parentheticals, such as (4a), Right-Node Raising structures (4b) and other examples of non-constituent conjunction, relative clause extraposition (4c), and scrambling (4d) seem to exhibit discontinuous constituents (all examples from McCawley 1982):

(4)   (a) John [$_{VP}$ talked, <u>of course</u>, about politics].
       (b) Tom may [$_{VP}$ be, <u>and everyone is sure Mary is</u>, a genius].
       (c) [$_{NP}$ A man <u>entered</u> who was wearing a black suit].
       (d) [$_{NP}$ Huic   <u>ego me</u>   bello]   ducem   profiteor. (Latin)
                this   I myself   war   leader   announce
            "For this war, I announce myself leader."

Blevins (1990) adds the case of VSO (verb–subject–object order) languages such as Irish, where the subject appears in the middle of the verb phrase:

(e) [$_{VP}$ Chonaic   <u>Seán</u>   an fear].
        saw   John   the man
     "John saw the man."

In each case the underlined words appear in the middle of a string that otherwise passes tests for constituency (as marked by the brackets). Similar effects were noted in Pike 1943; Wells 1947; Yngve 1960; and Speas 1985. A related but distinct problem are cases of linear order and hierarchical effects, such as the binding conditions and negative polarity licensing, which seem to be in conflict.

In mainstream generative grammar, the solution to these problems is either a transformational rule in the traditional sense or a movement rule in the Principles and Parameters or MP sense (see Ch. 8). An alternative to this approach suggests that we should relax our condition on line crossing and/or multidomination (McCawley 1982, 1987, 1988, 1989; Huck 1985; Speas 1985; Baltin 1987; Blevins 1990; among others). So, for example, we might allow a sentence such as (3) to be represented by a diagram like (5a) or (b), which are alternative representations of the same kind of diagram.

(5) (a)

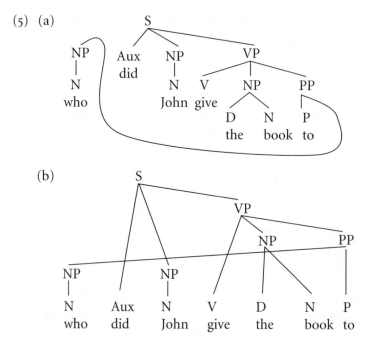

(b)

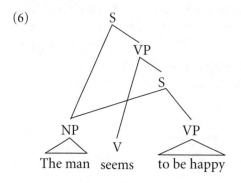

Let us call the views expressed in (5) "line-crossing approaches". Although there are no graphically represented line crossings in (5a), this diagram is equivalent to the line crossing form in (b) as the domination relations and linear orderings inside the two graphs are identical. It should be noted that in fact, structures such as (5) are entirely possible in ID/LP format grammars (Blevins 1990).

A related alternative involves line crossing only in the limited circumstance where a single node is dominated by more than one parent. Let us refer to the class of these proposals as "multidomination" approaches. Multidomination is most useful when an element simultaneously satisfies the requirements of two different positions in the tree. For example, if an NP is simultaneously the subject of both the embedded and the main clause (as in a raising construction), then it might be dominated by both the S nodes (Sampson 1975):

(6)

It should be noticed that line crossing is not a requirement of multi-domination, but merely a common consequence. Take for example a simple analysis of subject-to-object raising:

(7)

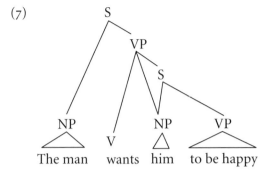

Here *him* is multidominated by VP (explaining the object case), and is simultaneous the logical subject/agent of the predicate *to be happy*.

A constituent-sharing approach also provides a straightforward analysis of non-constituent coordination (see below for citations and discussion). For example, Right-Node Raising could be viewed as the sharing of the second VP's object with the first:

(8)

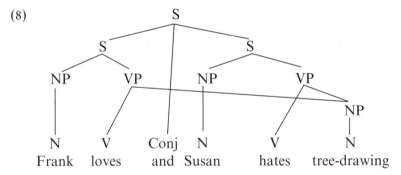

Since the speech stream is linearly ordered in a single dimension (through time), and our written representations of language are typically limited to two dimensions (up and down), linguists rarely consider the possibility that the hierarchical structure of language is not limited to two dimensions and instead branches into at least a third. Approaches with line crossing actually hint at such possibilities. Line crossing might be thought of as extending the structure out into a third dimension. I hinted at such possibilities in the discussion of adjunction in Chapter 8, where the BPS interpretation of adjunction points towards the structures existing on separate planes which explains a wide variety of phenomena including restrictions on do-support and condition C-effects in anti-reconstruction environments. To schematize, we might hypothesize that simple constituent structure is represented on one plane, and the shared NP is in a third dimension:

(9)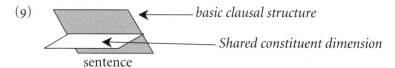

basic clausal structure

Shared constituent dimension

sentence

In this sort of approach, multiple dimensions hang off of the single constituent tree. I will refer to this kind of analysis—a variant of the line-crossing approach—as "multidimensional." I reserve this term for approaches where there is a single constituent-structure representation branching into three dimensions.

There is another, more common, three-dimensional structure found in the literature. This is the view where we have fully formed independent planes of representation for different kinds of information. This is distinguished from multidimensional approaches in that we have more than one representation of constituency. I will call this kind of approach "multiplanar" to distinguish it from the multidimensional approaches. There are two major versions of the multiplaner approach. The first, which I call "wheel and spoke" syntax, involves different constituents (and other relational structures) acting as spokes around a central linearized string of words:

(10) *words in the sentence* 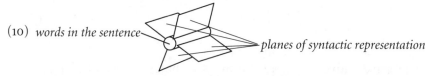 *planes of syntactic representation*

This is the approach taken by Autolexical Syntax (Sadock 1991), Role and Reference Grammar (Van Valin 1993, 2003), Pesetsky's (1995) layers and cascades, and the Simpler Syntax Model (Culicover and Jackendoff 2005).

The other version of this we might call the "parallel-structures model." This view of multiplanar structure has the various planes of syntactic structure, including constituent structure(s), developed in parallel and linked to one another by linking rules or related principles. Usually in such a system one of the planes contains the linear order:

(11) *linking principles*

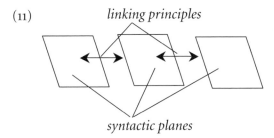

syntactic planes

We might call this the "parallel-planes" approach. Such a system is at least partly representative of traditional transformational grammar, Hale's L-syntax model, Curry's (1961) tecto- and phenogrammatical structures, as well as the Kathol (2000) and Reape's (1994) implementation of Curry's distinction in HPSG, and the phase-theoretic version of MP.

In this chapter, we will look first at line crossing, multidomination, and multidimensional structures, and consider how they have been used to characterize mismatches between expected syntactic form and linear order; then we turn to multiplanar approaches in both their guises and look at the range of data that these account for. This will in turn lead us into the topic of the last chapter of this book—the contentful nature of categories and nodes in a constituent representation.

10.2 Line crossing and multidomination: axiomatic restrictions on form

In Chapter 3, we looked at axiomatization of the basic structural properties of phrase structure trees. In this section, we consider what happens if we relax these axioms or replace them with others.

10.2.1 The non-tangling–exclusivity controversy

Let us start with the arguments that we should allow line crossing, and leave multidomination for further discussion below. Recall the data given in (4):

(4) (a) John [VP talked, of course, about politics].
  (b) Tom may [VP be, and everyone is sure Mary is, a genius].
  (c) [NP A man entered who was wearing a black suit].
  (d) [NP Huic ego me bello] ducem profiteor.
       this I myself war leader announce
    "For this war, I announce myself leader"

(e) [$_{VP}$ Chonaic   Seán   an fear].
　　　　　Saw　　　 John　 the man
　　　　"John saw the man."

McCawley (1982)[5] and Blevins (1990) claim that these kinds of sentences all involve trees like (12):

(12)

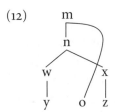

In (12) some constituent crosses into and appears in the middle of its sister (or in the middle of one of the descendents of its sister). It goes without saying that this kind of tree cannot be represented in bracket notation. Recall the exclusivity condition (A8) from Chapter 3.

A8.　*Exclusivity condition:*
　　　$(\forall xy \in N) \ [((x \prec y) \lor (y \prec x)) \leftrightarrow \neg \ ((x \vartriangleleft^* y) \lor (y \vartriangleleft^* x))]$.

This condition states that if two nodes are in a precedence relation with each other then they may not be in a dominance relation as well. Tree (12) violates condition A8: *o* is ordered before *z*, but note that *n* meets all the conditions for being ordered before *o* (*n* sister precedes *o*). Since precedence is transitive, this means that *n* precedes *z*. But this is impossible, since *n* dominates *z*, and domination and precedence are mutually exclusive. McCawley[6] suggests that such trees should be allowed by weakening the exclusivity condition, so that it is possible for two nodes to be unrelated by *either* dominance or precedence:[7]

A8′.　*Exclusivity condition:*
　　　$(\forall xy \in N) \ [(x \vartriangleleft^* y) \rightarrow \neg((y \prec x) \lor (x \prec y))]$.[8]

By doing this, *n* and *o* can be unordered with respect to one another (*n* doesn't dominate *o*, and *n* doesn't precede *o*). Therefore, *n* need not precede its daughter, which was the offending situation. McCawley also

---

[5] See also McCawley (1989).

[6] Blevin's solution is quite different; we return to it below.

[7] McCawley (1982: 93) phrases this as follows: "[these axioms] do not rule out the possibility of a node x_1 dominating nodes x_2 and x_4 without dominating a node x_3, where $x_2 \prec x_3$ and $x_3 \prec x_4$."

[8] I give here a slightly altered version of Huck's (1985) formalization of the axiom, simply because it is more consistent with the notation I use in this chapter.

weakens the non-tangling condition (A9′), so that it simply requires that daughter nodes be ordered relative to their mothers. He also adds a condition that ensures that all terminals are ordered (A10) with respect to one another.

A9′.   *Non-tangling condition (McCawley):*
$$\forall xw\ [w \prec x \leftrightarrow (\forall yz[(w \lhd^* y\ \&\ x \lhd^* z)\ \to y \prec z])].$$

A10. $\forall xy\ [(\neg \exists z\ [x \lhd^+ z \lor y \lhd^+ z])$
$$\to ((x \prec y) \lor (y \prec x) \lor (x = y))].$$

This is an elegant solution to the problem, but I think McCawley is wrong about this. I believe there are at least two problems with this kind of analysis. First, even if we accept that McCawley is correct about the non-tangling constraint allowing structures such as (12), we have the problem that there is nothing in his system which *forces* such an order. That is, while the order $y \prec o \prec z$ is allowed, there is nothing in the axioms that requires it. (A10 stipulates that all terminals be ordered, but it does not require that o be ordered before z.) For McCawley such orders are only ever derived transformationally, but it is not at all clear to me why they can not be base generated—as is argued by Blevins (1990). Second, observe that all[9] of the constructions in (4) except (4e) involve constructions that today we identify as adjuncts (4a) or adjunctions (4b–d). As we discussed in Chapter 8, recent work on binding and reconstruction (Lebeaux 1988 and Speas 1990) has argued that adjuncts and adjunction structures like those in (4) are not present at all levels of representation, so they are not even clearly part of the constituent structure of the sentence[10] or, alternately, exist on a distinct geometric plane. This may, in fact, be the effect of McCawley's proposal, but then a different set of axioms is needed to force or license linearizations between planes. I do not know of any proposals to this effect.

Huck (1985) has also argued, however, that the non-tangling constraint must be relaxed for different kinds of constructions. Consider what happens when o is dominated by another node p which itself is ordered after n, as shown by the presence of r, which follows z:

---

[9] See Van Valin (2001: 118) for examples in Serbian and Croatian that are not easily analyzed as adjunction.

[10] This of course comes with its own set of problems, not the least of which is that at some levels of representation we will have constituent structures that are unconnected.

(13)

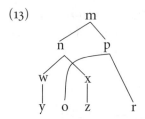

This structure is excluded by McCawley's versions of the axioms as *o* is not the sister of *n* (as it is in 10). However, this appears to be precisely the structure required for cross-serial dependencies such as the Dutch sentence in (14) (Huck 1985: 96) (see also the sentence from Züritüütsh in Ch. 2):

(14) ...dat   Jan   Marie   Piet   zag   helpen   zwemmen.
      ...that J.   M.   P.   saw   help-INF   swim-INF
      ..."that Jan saw Marie help Piet swim."

The structure of this sentence might be something like (15).

(15)

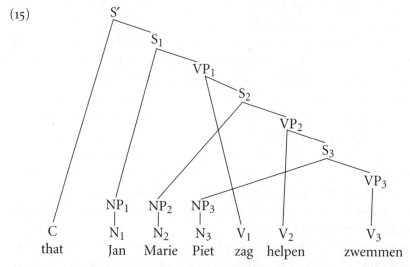

In this sentence, N_1 is correctly linearly ordered with respect to V_1, N_2 with V_2, and N_3 with V_3. However, N_2 is not correctly ordered with respect to V_1, because S_2—which follows V_1 (as shown by the fact that its daughters V_2 and V_3 follow V_1)—dominates NP_2. A similar problem is found with NP_3, but the problem is compounded by the fact that it is ordered before both V_1 and V_2, in double violation of the non-tangling constraint. A similar example from English is seen in (16) (Huck 1985: 95):

(16)   Nancy <u>called</u> <u>the fellow</u> <u>up</u> <u>she met at Jimmy's last night</u>.

There are two interlocked discontinuous constituents here (*call up* and *the fellow she met at Jimmy's last night*). In order to account for these kinds of sentence, Huck replaces the exclusivity condition with (A8″), which he calls the "inclusivity condition". This condition requires that there be either a relation of precedence or dominance or both between any two nodes in the tree.

A8″.   *Inclusivity condition (Huck):*
$$(\forall xy \in N) \; [((x \vartriangleleft^* y) \vee (y \vartriangleleft^* x)) \vee ((y \prec x) \vee (x \prec y))].$$

However, he restricts the precedence relation by a revised version of the non-tangling condition based on the dependency or X-bar theoretic notion of head, where nodes may only be ordered in the same order as their heads.

A9″.   *Non-tangling condition (Huck's Head-Order Condition):*
$$(\forall xw \in N) \; [(w \prec x) \leftrightarrow (Hw \prec Hx)], \text{ where } Hw = \text{head of } w.$$

Chametzky (1995) points out that this condition is of a very different type than the axioms we have previously considered; notice that by referring to heads, it requires reference to syntactic (rather than graph- or set-theoretic) objects. Bunt (1996b) solves this problem by having the condition refer to leftmost daughter instead of head:

A9‴.   *Non-tangling condition* (based on Bunt 1996b[11]):
$$(\forall xw \in N) \; [(w \prec x) \leftrightarrow (Lw \prec Lx)], \text{ where } Lw = \text{the leftmost daughter of } w.$$

Needless to say, there is something vaguely circular in specifying that there is a condition that specifies a fit left to right order of the clause that is defined in terms of a more basic notion of leftness. All of the approaches described above require that we abandon our notion of a precedence relation defined in terms of sister precedence. For example, if we adopt a structure allowed by (A9‴):

---

[11] Bunt's system is actually recursive rather than axiomatic. He uses a variety of Generalized Phrase Structure Grammar (Discontinuous Phrase Structure Grammar)—see Ch. 4 for more on GPSG. The definitions there are sufficiently distinct from those here, so I simply recast Bunt's definition of precedence (Bunt 1996b: 73) in axiomatic form here. See the original for a complete set of definitions; see also Bunt (1996a).

(17)

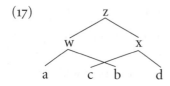

Here the left-most daughter of *w, a,* appears to precede the leftmost daughter of *x, c.* This meets Bunt's definition of the non-tangling condition. However, it also forces us to abandon our sister-precedence-based definition of precedence, as *w* sister precedes *x,* so *b* should precede *c.* While relaxing this condition is the goal of McCawley, Huck, and Bunt, it also means abandoning any clear definition of what it means for some item to be "to the left" of another. If we abandon this, we lose the primitive notion of leftness used in the definition in (A9''') and are forced to intuit the meaning of "left."

Higginbotham (1982/1985), Zwicky (1986a), and Blevins (1990) draw the discussion of discontinuity into the context of grammatical theory. Blevins observes that context-free PSGs are, by their very nature, unable to represent discontinuities[12] (as Chomsky himself observed in 1957), due to the fact that in their original format they were a rewrite system. Switching to a node-admissibility condition or projection system partly solves this problem, particularly when it is in the ID/LP format (Falk 1983; Gazdar, Pullum, Klein, and Sag 1983). Since linear order is specified independently of dominance relations in such a system, the effect of McCawley, Bunt, and Huck's proposals follow directly (Pullum 1982; Higginbotham 1982/1985; Zwicky 1986a).[13]

10.2.2 C-command and the non-tangling condition

If we adopt the notion of c-command, the question of the non-tangling condition discussed takes on a different face. Since c-command does not rely on any notion of precedence, only dominance, and tangled

[12] For a contrasting view see Yngve (1960) and Harman (1963), who claim to have phrase structure grammars that do allow discontinuities by using ellipses (. . .) or slashes in the rules. It may well be the case that such grammars have a different level of generative power than CFGs as they seem to introduce a measure of context-sensitivity into the system. This is not necessarily a bad thing, but it makes the grammatical systems hard to compare. See Postal (1967) for discussion.

[13] Pullum (1982) and Zwicky (1986a) also appeal to "Liberation metarules" (a notion not very distinct from the Union feature of Kathol 2000, discussed below) to account for scrambling and related phenomena. These rules licensed derived PSRs that in turn admitted trees with missing or displaced constituents.

trees involve a permutation of precedence only, we expect that c-command relationships in constituents are maintained whether or not lines cross. By contrast, if crossing lines are not allowed and discontinuous constituents are created by other means (transformations, multiple levels of representation, etc.), then the c-command relationships of continuous constituents will be distinct from those of discontinuous constituents. McCawley (1987) argues that c-command relationships of discontinuous arguments are maintained; I will repeat two of his arguments here. The first one relates to VP modifiers. When a PP modifies a verb, it is c-commanded by the subject, as can be seen in the following condition-C violation (examples from Reinhart 1983). *Rosa* here is not allowed to corefer with *she* as it is c-commanded by *she*:

(18)   *She$_i$ [$_{VP}$ tickles people with Rosa$_i$'s peacock feather].

McCawley notes that fronted VP-modifying PPs appear to retain the c-command relationships of their non-fronted equivalents. That is, (19) still shows a condition-C violation, even though *she* does not seem to c-command the NPs inside the PP.

(19)   *With Rosa$_i$'s peacock feather, she$_i$ tickles people.

(Note that this cannot be a condition-B violation since *Rosa* does not c-command *she* either.) This is explained by McCawley as a case of crossing lines:

(20)

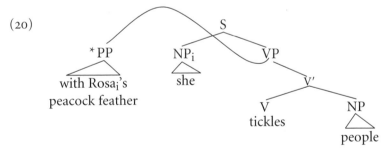

The binding relationship here reflects the fact that *Rosa* is still c-commanded by *she*. This kind of phenomenon is more typically dealt with in more standard approaches by allowing the fronted PP to "reconstruct" to its base position for the purposes of nominal interpretation (just as the phrase *which pictures of himself* reconstructs to object position in sentences such as *Which pictures of himself does John dislike?*).

The second case that McCawley discusses are postposed PPs. Consider the sentences in (21):

(21) (a) Chomsky$_i$'s recantation of his$_i$ 1973 theory has just appeared.
     (b) *His$_i$ recantation of Chomsky$_i$'s 1973 theory has just appeared.

Sentence (b) is a condition-C violation. Now consider what happens when [$_{PP}$ *of Chomsky's 1973 theory*] is postposed (McCawley's judgments).

(22) (a) Chomsky's recantation has just appeared of his 1973 theory.
     (b) *His recantation, has just appeared, of Chomsky's 1973 theory.

Here again, according to McCawley, we have retained the c-command relationships, thus arguing for crossing lines. There are, however, a few things to note about the examples in (22). First—for me at least—neither of the sentences in (22) is remotely grammatical, but for reasons having nothing to do with binding. For many speakers, post-posing of a complement *of*-phrase (see Ch. 5 for a discussion of the difference between complements and adjuncts), is not allowed, whether or not they contain a coindexed element:

(23) (a) *Chomsky's recantation has just appeared of *Syntactic Struc-tures*.
     (b) *His recantation has just appeared of *Syntactic Structures*.

This suggests that the ill-formedness of (22b) may not be as illustrative as McCawley contends. I have checked the grammaticality of (22a) with a number of speakers of Scots English (McCawley's own dialect), but they all agree that (22a and b) are equally ill-formed.

McCawley lists scrambling as one of the phenomena that exhibit line crossing.[14] Much of the literature on scrambling[15] holds that it retains the binding properties of unscrambled sentences—that is, scrambling is essentially an A-bar property that "reconstructs". This is entirely consistent with McCawley's approach, which limits line crossing to constructions where grammatical relations are not altered. However, Mahajan (1990) claims that at least some scrambling in Hindi changes the c-command relationships between the scrambled constituents (i.e.

---

[14] My thanks to Heidi Harley and Simin Karimi for very helpful discussion about this section.

[15] See Karimi (2003) for a survey and a collection of recent papers.

exhibits A-movement). If this were true it would be strong evidence against McCawley's claim. He posits that, for example, the scrambling in (24b) licenses the possessive reflexive by moving the object in front of the subject, thus disrupting the reversing the c-command relations seen in (24a):

(24) (a) *[apne   baccoN-ne] Mohan-ko maaraa.
        self   children-ERG Mohan-ACC beat
        "*Self's children beat Mohan."

    (b) ?Mohan-ko [apne baccoN-ne] maaraa.
       Mohan-ACC self children-ERG beat
       "Self's children beat Mohan."

This evidence is disputed by Dayal (1993). She claims that (24b) is fully ungrammatical for her and all native speakers she has checked with. She argues that scrambling in Hindi is always A-bar movement, and thus always reconstructs. Her judgments are, of course, also compatible with McCawley's crossing-lines approach since the basic unscrambled order's c-command relations are maintained.

However, evidence from other languages has emerged that there are in fact scrambling operations that do not change grammatical relations, but do change binding relationships (and thus by assumption, c-command relationships); see Moltmann (1991) and Déprez (1994) for German; Kim (1992) for Korean; Miyagawa (2001, 2003) for Japanese; and Bailyn (2003) for Russian. For example, in Russian the scrambling can feed binding relationships—the unscrambled sentences (the (a) sentences) are violations of condition A, but the scrambled ones (the (b) sentences) are not (data from Bailyn 2003):

(25) (a) ???$Svoj_i$ dom   byl   u $Petrovyx_i$.
       [self house]$_{NOM}$ was   at Petrovs
       "The Petrovs had their own house."

    (b) U $Petrovyx_i$ byl $svoj_i$ dom.
       at   Petrovs   was   [self   house]$_{NOM}$

(26) (a) ???$Svoja_i$ rabota   nravitsja $Mashe_i$
       [self   work]$_{NOM}$ pleases   Masha$_{DAT}$
       "Masha likes her work."

    (b) $Mashe_i$ nravitsja $svoja_i$ rabota
       Masha$_{DAT}$ pleases   [self's   work]$_{NOM}$

(27) (a) *Starshij brat$_i$ pojavilsja v   ego$_i$ dome
           [older   brother]$_{NOM}$ appeared in his   house
           Intended meaning: "The older brother appeared in his house."

      (b) ? V ego$_i$ dome pojavilsja starshij brat$_i$
           in   his   house appeared   [older   brother]$_{NOM}$
           "In his house appeared the older brother."

(28) (a) * Tol'ko Masha$_i$ est' u   nee$_i$
           only   Masha$_{NOM}$ is   at her
           Intended meaning: "Masha$_i$ is all she$_i$ has."

      (b) ? U   nee$_i$ est' tol'ko Masha$_j$.
           at   her   is   only   Masha$_{NOM}$
           "All she has is Masha."

Scrambling can also bleed c-command relationships (that is, it can destroy a previously licit binding relationship.) This is seen in (29), where the unscrambled (a) sentence is grammatical, but the scrambled (b) one is not (data again from Bailyn 2003).

(29) (a) [Znakomye Ivana$_i$] predstavili ego$_i$ predsedatelju.
           [friends$_{NOM}$ Ivan] introduced   him$_{ACC}$ chairman$_{DAT}$
           "Ivan's friends introduced him to the chairman."

      (b) *Ego$_i$ predstavili [znakomye Ivana$_i$]   predsedatelju.
           him   introduced [friends$_{NOM}$ Ivan]   chairman$_{DAT}$
           Intended meaning: "He was introduced to the chairman by Ivan's friends."

These data, and others like them, suggest that for at least some cases of scrambling, c-command relationships are not maintained. This in turn is an argument against McCawley's crossing lines approach to discontinuous constituency.

10.3 Multidomination and multidimensional trees

In this section, we discuss the related but distinct question of whether a single element can have more than one mother (multidomination). As discussed in the introduction to this chapter, this is often tightly interconnected with the proposal that sentences have a single constituent structure, but that constituent structure branches in multiple dimensions (allowing, but not requiring,[16] multidomination).

---

[16] Multidimensional trees need not involve multidominance, as in the cases of adjuncts and adjunctions discussed in Ch. 8 where a constituent is argued to be on a distinct

Sampson (1975) was one of the first to argue for multidomination.[17] He proposed that raising and control constructions and certain kinds of pronominalization (donkey anaphora) were best construed as multidomination. Donkey anaphora and pronominalization are not formed by a transformational rule in any current theories, so I will ignore that argument here. Raising and control could be construed as argument sharing:

(30)

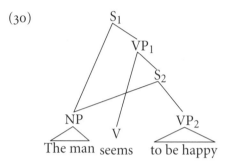

A variant of this is found in the LFG literature, except that in LFG, argument sharing holds in the f-structure rather than the c-structure. Blevins (1990) extends the argument-sharing analysis to other languages, such as Niuean.

Multidomination is also a central tenet of Phrase-Linking Grammar (Peters and Ritchie 1982; Engdahl 1986). Phrase-Linking Grammar is a declarative/axiomatic framework that defines the relations in a syntactic tree set-theoretically. Aside from labeling, it allows three primitive relations: Immediate Domination (D), Precedence (P), and the special Immediate-Link Domination (LD)[18] (also known as "weak" immediate domination; Gärtner 2002). As an illustration consider the tree in (30), pretending for the moment that the triangles represent unanalyz-

---

dimension because it does not participate in the c-command relations (Uriagereka 1999) or block adjacency in *do*-support (Bobaljik 1994). However, the easiest interpretation of multidomination involves at least a third dimension.

[17] See Borsley (1980), who argues against Sampson using evidence from prominalization. Unfortunately, Borsley's arguments rely on the existence of a pronominalization rule, and most modern views of pronouns have them lexically inserted and subject to some version of the binding theory rather than created by a pronominalization rule. This makes Borsley's arguments irrelevant.

[18] It appears as if every author who has worked on phrase-linking grammar has used a slightly different notation and axiomatization. I will not vary from this trend, giving my own interpretation to the notation. I do so, so as to make the notation as maximally consistent with the notation elsewhere in this book.

able wholes. The two domination relations expressed in this tree are given in (31):

(31) $D = \{ \langle S_1, NP \rangle, \langle S_1, VP_1 \rangle, \langle VP_1, V \rangle, \langle VP_1, S_2 \rangle, \langle S_2, NP \rangle, \langle S_2, VP_2 \rangle \}$
       $LD = \{ \langle S_2, NP \rangle \}$

There is also a special algorithm for ordering elements that are in both relations. In very rough-cut terms, the LD pairs are factored out of the D set, then linear-order relations are defined over those pairs. This results in the multidominated element being linearized in the position it would be linearized in if it were dominated only by the higher element in the tree. So in (30), the NP is dominated by both S_1 and S_2, but it will be linearized as if it only were dominated by S_1 (i.e. in the higher position). Gärtner (1999, 2002) presents a derivational version of this couched in terms of the Minimalist Program. He uses phrase linking to express chain formation in BPS. The motivation is a fairly technical one about the distribution and copying of "uninterpretable" features and need not concern us here, however the result is an interesting one. Essentially, taking the head and tail of a chain (i.e. a *wh*-phrase and its trace) to be a single item, "movement" is essentially a kind of multidomination. So *wh*-movement, for example, could be arboreally represented as (32).

(32)

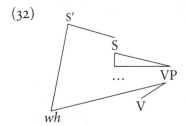

This is possible for Gärtner, as he assumes Aczel's (1988) axiom of extensionality which forces identity in set membership to correspond to simple set identity.

The system in phrase-linking grammar does not, however, account for another kind of multidomination, namely, that found in coordination phenomena where the two parents are equivalent in their depth in the tree. In the phrase-linking system, one of the two parents must be more prominent in the immediate dominance relations. When dealing with, for example, right-node raising (RNR), the two parents are on equivalent depths of embedding:

(33)

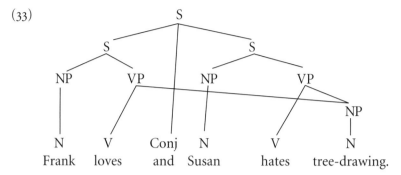

Multidomination accounts of these phenomena and related phenomena such as nominal ellipsis, gapping, and across-the-board raising have been proposed by Goodall (1987),[19] Grootveld (1992), Moltmann (1992), Muadz (1991), Wilder (1999), Uriagereka (1998), de Vries (2003, 2004, 2005),[20] Citko (2005) and Chen-Main (2006) (written in the TAG framework). The last four of these build on the set theoretic nature of BPS, using the fact that sets can overlap in membership to result in multidomination.[21] Osborne (2006) also presents a multidimensional analysis of these phenomena, except that his analysis is based in a three dimensional dependency structure rather than a constituent structure. Collins (1997) argues that Kayne's (1994) Linear-Correspondence Axiom rules out multidomination.

10.4 Multiplanar structures

In this section, we review the various proposals that sentences are best described not in terms of a single constituent structure, but a system where there are multiple planes of constituent representation which are either mapped between each other via linking rules or revolve around the single spoke of syntactic structure.[22] The evidence for

[19] See van Oirsouw (1987) and Haegeman (1988) for a critical evaluation of Goodall's proposals and Fong and Berwick (1985) for a computational implementation.

[20] De Vries coins the term "behindence", which sends shudders down the spine of this native speaker of English. The term is presumably as a parallel to precedence, but personally I would have preferred something like "dimensional prominence".

[21] Recent unpublished work by Seungwan Ha of Boston University has raised arguments against multidomination account of these kinds of phenomenon using data from English and Korean.

[22] Multiplanar approaches amount to a relaxation of the condition that trees have a single root. For the most part, this is not made explicit in approaches that adopt multiplaner approaches. However, see McCawley (1989), where sentences with parentheticals are represented as multiply rooted trees (with crossing lines).

these multiple planes typically comes from cases where one set of
constituency requirements is in conflict with another, or where constituency tests show one structure, but other tests of hierarchical
prominence show a different organization.

10.4.1 Parallel Plane Hypotheses: Classic Transformational Grammar, LFG, Simpler Syntax

The classic theory of transformational grammar (TG or EST) operated
under the hypothesis that basic semantic and thematic relations, including modification relations, held of one constituent structure, the
deep structure. Other relations, such as surface subjecthood and linear
order were represented in a separate constituency diagram, the surface
structure. Structure-changing transformations could then be conceived of as mapping principles that held between these two planes
of representation. Constituency might be represented at either level
and conflicts of constituency result from the mapping between the two
(i.e. the fact that *wh*-words can be separated from the preposition that
they are the logical subjects of). The fact that linguists used a metaphor
of temporal relationship between the levels (i.e. surface structure
followed deep structure) rather than a spatial metaphor (two dimensions of existence), seems to be largely irrelevant. Although admittedly
within the theory the relationship between the two levels was asymmetric, such that the surface structure was largely dependent on the
deep structure.

In the Government and Binding versions of the Principles-and-
Parameters framework, the status of D- and S-structures (as well as
LF and PF) as planes of syntactic representation is more complicated,
as there was a conceptual shift from structure-changing rules to
transformations that took a single constituent tree and moved
items around within that same tree. By the time we reach minimalist
versions of the theory structure-changing rules had been entirely
replaced by generalized transformations (structure-building transformations) and the multiplanar character of mainstream generative
grammar was greatly reduced, at least to the extent that transformations are the mapping principles between levels of representation.
On the other hand, the levels of PF and LF, at least in the early
versions of MP (that is, leaving aside the Phase theory of Chomsky
2001), are clearly multiple planes of syntactic representation, one of
which is largely semantic, the other largely related to morphological

and phonological content. While they are distinct levels of representation, it is not as clear if they can be described as parallel planes as there is no direct mapping between them (only coincidental co-construction for part of the derivation).

Lexical-Functional Grammar also has parallel levels of representation. One directly represents surface constituency (the c-structure), the other, various semantic–syntactic relations such as subjecthood (the f-structure). The parallel levels of representation are linked to each other through the mapping principles known as "functional equations" (see Ch. 6, Falk 2001, or Bresnan 2002 for more discussion). Conflicting evidence for syntactic relations is dealt with by having these two distinct systems of syntactic organization. Surface constituency is represented directly in the c-structure. Syntactic prominence phenomena such as the binding theory are stated as conditions on the depth of embedding of structures in the f-structure.

Most recently, the Simpler Syntax theory of Jackendoff (2002) and Culicover and Jackendoff (2005) uses parallel planes of representation coupled with a TAG-like constructional formulation. Each word comes into the sentence with at least a morphophonological representation, a syntactic treelet, and a semantic structure, which are related to one another using correspondence rules.

10.4.2 Parallel Plane Hypotheses: L- and S-syntax and pheno- and tectogrammatical structures

Hale (1983)[23] was among the first to suggest that surface constituency and the constituency representations motivated by semantic relations need not correspond to each other directly. On the basis of the relatively free word order of the Australian language Warlpiri, he suggests that there are at least two distinct planes of syntactic organization. The first is what he calls "L-syntax" which represents the basic predicational structures of the clause (and determines among other things the case morphology and binding relations); this is mapped to a different level, the S-syntax, which reflects the surface-constituent relations. Scrambling and non-configurational languages differ from stricter-word-order languages parametrically in whether both levels are subject to the projection requirements of X-bar syntax or if only the L-syntax is. The two levels are related through linking rules. The L-syntax encodes hierarchical relations which may not be exhibited in

---

[23] See also Higginbotham's (1985) discussion of Hale (1983).

the S-syntax. For example, while we want to retain a subject–object hierarchical distinction to explain effects like binding phenomena in scrambling/non-configurational languages, we do not necessarily want these to correspond with the word order. L-syntax, then, can represent the semantic and syntactic relations that refer to constituency. The S-syntax may realize the elements differently. Imagine, for example, a sentence with VSO order. The L-syntax would represent the $[_S \text{NP}_{subj}$ $[_{VP} \text{V NP}_{Obj}]]$ constituency consistent with our understanding of argument structure and compositionality. The S-syntax by contrast would represent this as a flat $[_S \text{V NP}_{subj} \text{NP}_{obj}]$ structure, reflecting the actual pronunciation of the sentence. In a configurational language like English, the S-syntax and L-syntax are more tightly linked with both, exhibiting the X-bar theoretic projection properties.

Around the same time, Dowty (1982)[24] reintroduced the distinction between tectogrammatical and phenogrammatical structures in the Montague Grammar version of categorial grammar, based on a proposal by Curry (1961). Tectogrammatical structures represent the means by which a sentence is composed semantically from its component parts. It largely ignores the actual order the words appear in. Phenogrammatical structures by contrast reflect the actual order and morphological composition of the sentence. Tectogrammatical structures are typically hierarchical trees; phenogrammatical ones are strings.

Take the phenomenon of VSO order. On a semantic level we want the subject to be predicated not only of the verb, but of whole verb phrases. For example, in the sentence *John likes apples* the denotation of this sentence is true precisely when John is a member of the set of people who like apples, not just the set of people who like. On the other hand, there appears to be no surface VP constituent (see the next chapter for a discussion of this claim). This can be captured by creating a prototypical hierarchical tree to reflect compositionality, but allowing the linear string to be affected by special ordering functions that apply as each level of structure is created. For VSO languages there are two such functions:

(34) (a) $F_1(\alpha, \beta)$ = the result of inserting β after the first word in α.
      (b) $F_2(\alpha, \beta) = \alpha \wedge \beta$ (the linear concatenation of β after α).

The second rule is the rule that presumably applies in a language like English which constructs the linear order in strict parallel to the hierarchical structure. Rule (8a) is essentially Bach's (1979) "right wrap" rule,

---

[24] See also the discussion in Huck and Ojeda (1987).

which inserts the newly hierarchically attached item inside the already created structure (this amounts to a syntactic infixation operation). So an Irish sentence like (35a) has the proof tree in (35b). The tree represents the tectogrammatical structure created by the lexical properties of the words involved. The strings are the result of the parallel application of the above-mentioned functions to the phenogrammatical string:

(35)   (a) D'ól   Seán   poitín.
             drank   John   homebrew
             "John drank homebrew."

   (b)

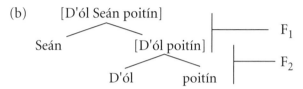

The verb and its object are joined to form a VP, and the words are concatenated in the order they appear in the sentence (VO). At the next level up in the tree the subject is predicated of the VP, the F_1 rule inserts the subject between the verb and the object.

"Free"-word-order languages are dealt with in a similar way; such languages are viewed to have a single word-order function that creates an unordered set (36). Take the Latin sentence in (37) as an example:

(36) $F_1(\alpha, \beta) = a \cup b$

(37)   (a) Marcus Fluvian amat.
             Marcus Fluvian loves
             "Marcus loves Fluvian."

   (b) Marcus amat Fluvian.
   (c) Fluvian Marcus amat.
   (d) Amat Fluvian Marcus.
       etc.

   (e)

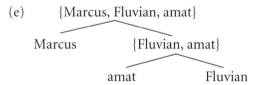

Dowty (1996) presents an updated version of his theory using GPSG-style LP principles and allowing reference to the heads of phrases. Another version of the pheno/tectogrammatical distinction can be found couched within the HPSG framework as described by Kathol

(2000) (see also Kathol and Levine 1993). Kathol draws on Reape's (1994) idea that word order in HPSG should be described in terms of a special word-order domain feature (DOM). Word order is determined by a feature structure that constrains the linear order of elements within that feature. Scrambling is accomplished by virtue of a set theoretic operator that creates "shuffled" sets (subject to restrictions based on the original order of elements within the original ordered sets). See also Langendoen (2003), who pursues a version of Dowty's approach but couched within Minimalist set theoretic Bare Phrase Structure.

10.4.3 Wheel-and-spoke multiplanar approaches

In the parallel multiplanar approaches the link between planes of representation is largely abstract and concerns semantic relationships that do not appear to be represented in the surface word order (for example, in scrambling or VSO contexts). The next group of approaches uses the surface string of the sentence itself as the glue that holds together the multiple planes. The motivations here are not usually a mismatch between semantic/syntactic criteria and surface order, but mismatches in the apparent behavior of linearly ordered strings with respect to different constituency tests, such that all the constituency tests reveal the same linear order, but different hierarchical properties. The evidence for parallel structures, by contrast, came from situations where the linear order did not reflect some predicted syntactic or semantic property. These two approaches thus emphasize different kinds of data and may not be entirely incompatible. Indeed, one finds approaches like RRG, which has aspects of both (mapping from basic predicate and semantic relations to the constituent structure—called the LSC—is done by mapping rules, as is the relationship between the argument structure and the focus structure) but various kinds of constituency relationship are mapped from plane to plane through the surface linear string.

In this subsection, we consider a variety of approaches in a variety of frameworks that take a wheel-and-spoke approach to multiplanar structures. Starting in the mid 1980s, this view was adopted by a variety of scholars and at least some versions of it were influenced by the theory of autosegmental phonology (Goldsmith 1976). I am not in a position to decipher who proposed a multiplanar model for syntax first, so I will simply describe the arguments of the various main players. As elsewhere in this part of the volume, the seas of shifting assumptions make it nearly impossible to fairly compare the various approaches described here with each other or with non-multiplanar accounts. Instead I hope the reader will be able use my brief descriptions as a rudder for negotiating said shifting sea.

Haegeman and van Riemsdijk (1986), working within GB theory, suggest that an analysis of pseudopassives and cross-serial dependencies motivates multiple constituent structures for a single clause. Consider first the case of Zuritüüsch and Dutch cross-serial dependencies that we have mentioned several times in this book. Haegeman and van Riemsdijk propose that these have a normal non-line-crossing representation consistent with the usual understanding of tree structures. However, Dutch (and other languages with crossing dependencies) has a rule of reanalysis that takes the verbal string and reanalyzes it as a single V_r (in effect, unioning all the embedded clauses). This unioned tree is on a separate dimension from the one that is represented basic compositionality. There is then a morphological rule that reorders the verbs (indicated by the arrows in the lower tree).

(38) (a) ... dat hij het   probleem   probeert   te begrijpen.
          that he the   problem   tries   to understand
       "... that he tries to understand the problem."

(b)

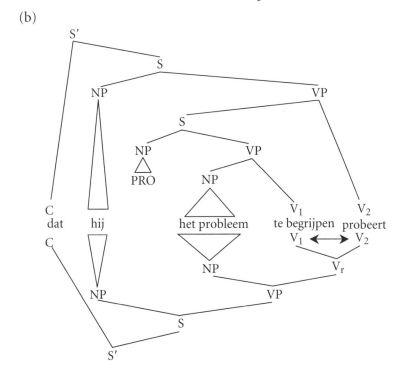

They also propose that trees with reanalysis are the explanation for pseudopassives (39). In such forms the object of a preposition moves to subject position even though it is not the direct object of the verb:

(39)   a) John talked to Mary.
       b) Mary was talked to.

In effect, the verb + preposition sequence behaves as if it were a verb-particle construction (e.g. *blow up*), even though the verb and the preposition never actually form a constituent. Haegeman and van Riemsdijk suggest that this is due to a process of reanalysis which is represented in a second tree structure:

(40)

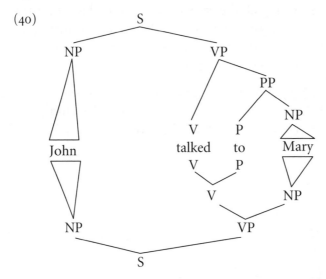

The top constituency structure represents our lexical understanding of the verb *talk* with a full preposition *to*. The bottom tree represents the reanalyzed form where *Mary* is the direct object of the complex verb *talk to*. This bottom tree is the input to the passive operation.

In both of these cases, we have one set of syntactic or semantic information pointing to one constituent structure, but another set of information pointing to a different constituency. These kinds of phenomena we can loosely term "bracketing paradoxes." A different type of bracketing paradox motivated multiple planes of structure in the Autolexical Syntax approach (Sadock 1991):[25]

---

[25] See Zwicky (1986c) for discussion of how Autolexical syntax and Zwicky's version of GPSG achieve similar results.

mismatches between the syntactic form, the morphological form, and the semantic representation. Sadock lists a number of these, including noun-incorporation structures, various kinds of morphologically complex inflectional structure, and clitics. Let us take the last as an example. As is well known, the possessive *'s* in English attaches not to the head of the possessor nominal but to the end of it. However, from a morphophonological perspective, we see that it must be attached to the final word, as it is subject to the typical patterns of assimilation found with other *s* morphemes in English. There is thus a conflict between the morphological properties of the morpheme, which require it to be bound to the final word in the possessor, but structurally and syntactically it behaves as if it were an independent word following the possessor. This can be expressed in terms of multiple planes. (The tree that follows is not identical to that in Sadock, but are consistent with his analysis of possessive *'s*.)

(41)

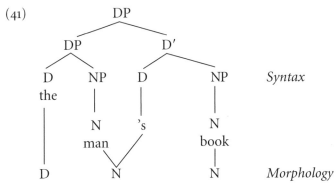

Pesetsky (1996) considers a different kind of bracketing paradox, namely, one where the constituency evidence contradicts c-command prominence in the tree. We have conflicting information about the italicized string in (42a). The evidence from binding shows that the DP *them* must c-command the reciprocal (*each other*) that it binds. This c-command relationship is reflected in the structure in (43a) which Pesetsky calls a "cascade." In the cascade, in order to insure that *them* c-commands *each other*, there is no constituent consisting solely of the V and DP to the exclusion of the PP. However, the data in (42b) shows that such a constituent must exist. The ellipsis of *visit them* excludes the PP. Pesetsky suggests then that the same string has the "layered" structure in (43b) where the lower V' is the target for the ellipsis. These two structures hold simultaneously of the VP.

(42)   a. I visited them₍ᵢ₎ on each other₍ᵢ₎'s birthdays.

b. John said that he would [visit the children] and visit them₍ᵢ₎ he did on each other₍ᵢ₎'s birthdays.

(43)   (a) *Cascade* V′   (b) *Layered* V′

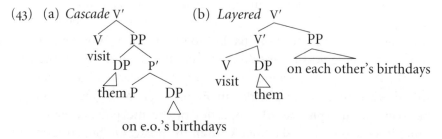

Baltin (2006) offers an alternative analysis of these facts. He suggests that the underlying form of the VP is like that in (43b) (a layered structure), but that there is a more fine-grained functional structure (44), such that the object raises out of the VP to get case in an AgrP, creating the c-command structure necessary for binding the reciprocal. (Surface word order results from subsequent movement of the remnant VP.)

(44)

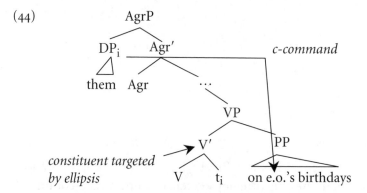

As mentioned briefly above, the theory of Role and Reference Grammar (RRG) (Van Valin 1993, 2003; Van Valin and LaPolla 1997) uses both linking principles (to link between, for example, semantic representations and syntactic ones) and spoke-and-wheel links between multiple planes of constituent structure (which are typically semantically or pragmatically motivated). One plane of representation is the layered structure of the clause (LSC), which represents the non-endocentric predicate (the nucleus) and its arguments (together with the nucleus forming the core) along with various modifiers (including the "periphery" and two positions to the left of the clause for left detached items like sentential adverbials and things like *wh*-phrases). At the same time, grammatical items such as aspect, modality, negation, tense, and illocutionary-force markers are represented on a separate plane for operators. Finally, there is a third dimension that represents focus (as we will discuss in Ch. 11) which is one way in which VP-like (verb–object) constituencies are represented in RRG.

(45)

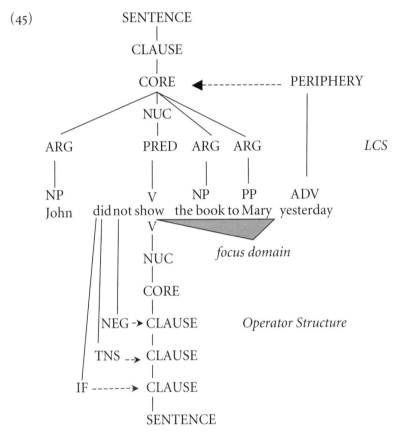

These three constituent structures are motivated by the semantics or discourse and licensed by mapping principles (including those that map to argument structure and other semantic structures), but all pivot around the linear string of words. In the next chapter, we will address exactly what is meant by categories like "predicate", "NP", "VP" and Tense in some detail.

10.5 Conclusions

In this third part of this book, we are looking at a number of alternatives to strict compositional phrase structure. In the last chapter, we looked at dependency-based alternatives to constituent representations, in this chapter, we surveyed a number of alternatives where restrictions on the form of constituency have been relaxed to allow line crossing, multi-domination, multidimensionality, and multiplanar structures, looking at evidence from discontinuous constituents, scrambling, argument sharing, and cross-modular bracketing paradoxes. In the next chapter, we address one further way in which phrase-structure systems might be modified, focusing on the content and nature of various major constituent types both from a categorial and semantic perspective.

11

Phrasal Categories and Cartography

11.1 Introduction

The previous ten chapters of this book have focused on the mechanisms for forming, describing, or licensing constituent structure(s). Up to now, wherever possible, I have tried to abstract away from the content of those structures. Needless to say, the question of the nature of the content or category of constituents is vital to understanding constituent-structure systems. This much should be clear from the role played by heads in most recent theories of syntax. In this chapter, I survey the different proposals about the categories of various constituent types. I also consider evidence for their arrangement in the clause. In the Chomskyan paradigm, the endeavor of finding the correct arrangement of the right categories has come to be known as the "cartographic approach" (largely by the community of Italian linguists headed by Luigi Rizzi, who are investigating this question). I will extend the cartographic label to other approaches to the effort to understand the contentful structure of phrase structure, seeking out commonalities among these approaches. This is an extremely large topic, and could easily be the topic of several book-length treatments. Here, we sketch only the rough outline of the debates. Interested readers should follow up on the citations listed throughout this chapter.

This chapter starts with perhaps one of the most interesting discoveries of twentieth-century linguistics: the layered tripartite nature of the clauses. Here I look at how a number of approaches to syntactic structure have converged on the idea that, cross-linguistically, clauses have at their heart a core predication, which is inside a structure of operators that locate that predication in time and space relative to the speech time, and finally are closed by a structure that relates the proposition to the speaker's perspective. I address the structure of

each of these in turn. The categories that represent arguments (typically nominals) such as NP, DP, PP, and various functional items such as
number and gender are the topic of the next section. Finally, I address
the question of how predicational modificational relationships (as
typically expressed through adverbs and adjectives) are expressed in
the constituent structure.

An orthogonal issue that will run through the chapter concerns the
nature of "mixed categories" or constituents that appear to have the
properties of more than one category.[1] For example, in many languages
we find cases where there are elements that express relations that we
might characterize as verbal, and are cognate to verbs, but have a
syntactic form that is more nominal in character (i.e. they take possessive

---

[1] There are two sides to an adequate description of syntactic categories of constituents.
Obviously, if the categories are syntactic, then the description should be based at least
partly on syntactic evidence of distribution. For example, if we find a context where a word
X appears and not word Y or a phrase headed by X and never by Y, we might conclude that
X and Y do not belong to the same category. When formalist linguists like myself teach
introductory syntax (see for example Carnie 2006c), we often hold up such an approach as
scientifically superior to the traditional semantically based descriptions of categories (such
as a noun is a "person, place or thing") which are vague and rarely helpful in syntactic
description. There are problems with a purely distributional system, however. Using it, one
often gets circular argumentation. For example, take the criterion of morphological
distribution. We might define verbs as those things that can take past-tense inflectional
morphology such as -ed. But when asked to define the characteristics of a suffix such as -ed,
we are reduced to the circular characterization that they are the things that attach to verbs.
In practical terms, we might be able to use such characteristics 99 percent of the time, but
they do not really get at the deeper "why" question of categorization. Inconsistent
argumentation is also a consequence of such an approach. Take a typical textbook
characterization of the difference between nouns and verbs in English. These two categories appear in different syntactic environments in English so they must be separate categories. At the same time we sometimes find invocation of the principle of complementary
distribution, where on analogy with phonology, when two forms appear in totally distinct
environments they must be members of the same category. Such argumentation is found
in Radford (1988) and Carnie (2006c). While inconsistencies and circularities can be
controlled by the researcher, it shows that there are some significant problems with a
purely syntactic characterization of categories.

I think it is clear that some hybrid approach to the problem is required. To understand
the distributional properties of constituents we cannot appeal only to syntactic criteria (as
is common in formalist linguistics) or to primarily semantic criteria (as is common in
many versions of functionalist linguistics), nor can we assume that syntactic criteria are
derived from semantic ones (as in dependency grammars) or vice versa. We need to give
significant weight to each criterium, understanding that they may give us different kinds of
information (and may indeed lead to multiple labels or even multiple constituencies—see
Ch. 10). This is the approach I will attempt to take here. Syntactic and morphological
distribution will play a significant role in the cartographic project as described in this
chapter, but at the same time we must recognize that semantic criteria are also frequently
used to characterize and justify syntactic forms.

pronouns or assign genitive case to their complements) or we find items that are modified by adjectives and express characteristics of an individual but bear tense and appear in the position typically associated with verbs. This of course leads us to the question of whether categorial descriptions of a constituent are even appropriate. I won't address this question directly in this chapter, but will point to it when appropriate.

11.2 The tripartite structure of the clause

A colleague of mine (Heidi Harley) and I were discussing a posting by Daniel Everett on the Linguist List (http://linguistlist.org/issues/17/17–2277.html) about the major discoveries of modern syntactic theory. In particular, we were concerned with those discoveries that could truly be called universals of clause structure. We agreed that almost every major constituency-based theory—whether formalist or functionalist—seems to have converged on the idea that the "backbone" of clauses consist of at least three major parts. The first part represents the predication or lexical relations of the event/state that is being described. This idea first appears in print in Foley and Van Valin (1984). In most approaches (P&P, LFG, HPSG, TAG, Categorial Grammar) this corresponds to the VP (with or without a VP internal subject); in other approaches it goes by other names, including the nuclear predication (Dik's Functional Grammar) and the CORE (RRG). This unit expresses the basic predicational relation with at least one (or more) of the arguments associated with that predication. This structure sometimes also includes aspect and information about aktionsart.

The next layer of structure reflects the context of that predication relative to some speech time (i.e. tense and perhaps other related inflections). In formalist theories, this layer is also associated with the notion of subjecthood. The universality of a tense layer is more controversial than the predicational layer. In LFG, for example, the subject NP is not connected to the VP via tense unless there is an auxiliary in the string. Nevertheless the subject is outside the predication domain (in an unheaded S layer). This layer seems to very loosely correspond to the CLAUSE constituent of RRG as this is the layer in which temporal adverbs and related material occurs.

Finally, the outermost layer of the clause relates the tensed predication to the speaker's attitude and intentions about the event and includes such notions as mood, focus, topic, and illocution. In various formal theories this is the CP or S′ constituent. Such a structure exists in RRG as well, except it represents a separate plane of description.

(1)

Speaker Attitude/Force/Informational structure (CP Layer)
Location of the event relative to speech time (S/IP layer)
Internal properties of the event/predication (VP layer)

We might even think of these layers corresponding to the three distinct types of semantic interface: the lexical properties of the event correspond to the predicational structure (i.e. the "content" of the expression in terms of truth conditions, independent of any assignment). The temporal properties and notions of subjecthood correspond to the logical interpretation (i.e. the truth-conditional denotation of the event relative to some specific world). Finally the outermost layer corresponds to pragmatic information beyond the truth-conditional semantics. See Butler (2004) for a slightly different characterization of the tripartite structure of the clause.

It appears that there is a convergence of evidence for this rough outline of clause structure, even if there are significant debates about the internal structure of each layer and how the layers are related to one another. In the next three sections we look at the evidence for and against each of these layers.

11.3 The VP

The verb phrase (VP) category has at least three major realizations in modern syntactic theory. The first, and more traditional, view of the VP consists of the verb, any direct and indirect objects, and modifiers of the verbs, such as aspectual markers, manner adverbials, and locative markers. It does not include the external argument. The second view of the VP holds that subjects are also part of the structure at some level of representation (Koopman and Sportiche 1991). Although explicitly not equivalent, this seems very similar to the notion of CORE in RRG. The third view is a compromise alternative to these views found in many recent versions of MP. Here the VP is split into two parts: a lower part, which corresponds to the traditional view of VPs, and a higher part (a light vP) that includes the external argument.

When discussing the evidence for and against VPs, it's important to distinguish between these three versions of the VP hypothesis as they make clearly distinct predictions. I will refer to the first version as the traditional VP, to the second as the VP-Internal Subject Hypothesis (VPISH), and to the third as the split VP.

11.3.1 Classic constituency tests

Let us start with the evidence for and against traditional VPs. Leaving aside coordination, we find the following tests for a verb-object constituent (see also Ch. 7 for discussion of V′ categories and Speas (1990) for a slightly different list and discussion):

(2) (a) It was eating peanuts that Bill did.   *Cleft*
     (b) Eat peanuts is what Bill did.   *Pseudocleft*
     (c) Q: What did you do? A: Eat peanuts.   *Stand alone*
     (d) Susan hasn't eaten peanuts, but Bill has. *Ellipsis*[2]
     (e) Susan ate peanuts and Bill did so too.   *Pro-verb replacement*

Van Valin (1993) notes that all of these tests have particular information-structure effects. For example, clefting and stand-alone tests identify elements that are in focus. Ellipsis and pro-verb replacement are typical of deaccented topic structures. Van Valin argues that this is evidence against a VP. Instead he argues, within RRG, for a flat constituent structure with VP-constituency effects following from a lexically/constructionally determined (Van Valin 2003) pragmatic focus layer. In the following diagram, the dotted lines represent the potential focus domain tied to the speech act, the solid triangle represents the actual focus domain which gives us VP effects. The CORE is the flat predicate structure without a verb–object unit.

(3)

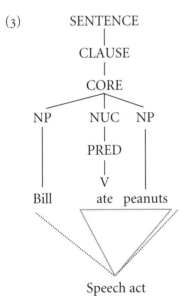

² For an illuminating discussion of ellipsis, see Johnson (2001).

The empirical observation here seems to be a good one. VPs are typically focal. When expressing a simple declarative sentence, unless contrastive stress interferes, the topical information is typically the subject and new focal information is in the verb–object sequence. Van Valin argues that, all other things equal, evidence for VPs disappears since topic–comment structures are independently required for communicative reasons. This is an interesting argument, but I think it may well be of the chicken-and-the-egg variety. Consider an alternative view of the mapping of clause structure into semantic/information structure, the one proposed by Diesing (1992). Diesing claims that a wide variety of effects, including scrambling of specifics in German and case marking effects of indefinites in Turkish follow from a bifurcation of the clause into two domains. Presupposed elements (informationally topical) are mapped to the IP/TP portion of the tree. Without exception, focal information is mapped to the VP. This includes non-specific indefinites, which are existentially quantified under a VP delimited operation of Existential Closure.

(4)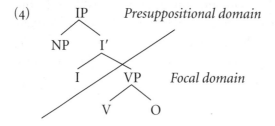

A wide variety of effects have been seen to follow from this kind of bifurcation, including object cliticization (Diesing and Jelinek 1995), person hierarchies (Jelinek 1993), animacy and definiteness effects in split case marking (Jelinek and Carnie 2003, Carnie 2005), definiteness effects in impersonal passives (Carnie and Harley 2005), and many others.

Compare this hypothesis to Van Valin's. In the tree splitting approach, we can directly predict where informational focus will appear: it corresponds exactly to the VP. In Van Valin's system, this is either constructionally stipulated or derived through a series of complicated principles from the argument structure (Van Valin 2003). The RRG system also predicts the existence of focus systems that do not exist. For example, one would predict the possibility of subject + verb focus domains in some language. To my knowledge no such language exists.[3]

---

[3] Although this might be a reasonable interpretation of syntactically ergative–absolutive systems as defined by Dixon (1994), I think other descriptions of such phenomena are

Van Valin (p.c) has pointed out to me that there are a number of VP-like effects that do not lend themselves to an account in terms of focus (in either a Diesing style account with a VP or in an RRG account without one). These include VP ellipsis, VP fronting, and VP anaphora where the VP material is topical rather than focal. In hierarchical approaches these follow directly from having a VP constituent. In RRG, these are claimed to follow from other phenomena, such as constructional templates.

Van Valin (1987)—a paper written in the GB framework—also raises the problem that there are languages that seem to exhibit no VP constituency effects at all. He points to Lakhota as an example. This is the class of languages that Jelinek (1984) called Pronominal Argument languages (see also Van Valin's 1977 dissertation). In this class of languages, in which many Native American languages are found, full NPs are never directly part of the argument structure. Only pronominals (frequently encoded as agreement morphology or incorporated nominals) can be arguments, full NPs are adjuncts to the sentence. The fact that these NPs neither form constituents with the verb nor are ever focal follows from the fact that they are never part of the VP. See Van Valin (1985) and Faltz (1995) for some discussion of Lakhota that shows it is a Pronominal Argument language. See also Baker (2001b) for related discussion of other "non-configurational" languages.

The structure of languages which exhibit pronominal-argument effects are part of a larger phenomenon that has been used to argue against universal VPs. This is the class of non-configurational languages (see Hale 1983 for an explicit characterization of this class), which are supposed to include scrambling and fixed word-order languages where either there is no clear VP structure or where the surface word order mitigates against a verb–object constituent, such as VSO or OSV order languages. In the next section, I will focus on the arguments about VSO languages. For extensive discussion of the other types of non-configurational language and the evidence for and against VPs, see Mohanan (1982), Fukui (1995), Speas (1990), Nordlinger (1998), Baker (2001b), and Bresnan (2002).

---

more explanatory; see for example Murasugi (1993). Van Valin (p.c.) has suggested that constructions such as Q: "What happened to the car?" A: "John wrecked it" exhibit subject + verb informational focus. These are "thetic" constructions where plausibly the entire clause is potentially under focus, but the topicality of the object is indicated by pronominalization of *car* to *it*.

11.3.2 VSO languages as evidence against VPs[4]

Early work in the generative grammar of VSO languages, such as Schwartz (1972), Awberry (1976), McCloskey (1979, 1980), Stenson (1981), Chung (1983), Anderson (1984), and Tallerman (1990), assumed that VSO languages differed from SOV and SVO languages in lacking a VP phrase structure rule:

(5)　(a)　SVO:　S → NP VP
　　　　　　　　VP → V NP
　　　(b)　VSO:　S → V NP NP

This class of languages, then, was claimed to have a flat, VP-less, clausal architecture:[5]

(6)

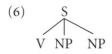

Such a structure makes very clear predictions about the behavior of the subject and object arguments. As noted by Berman (1974), who was replying to McCawley's (1970) VSO analysis of English, it predicts that subject and object NPs, since they are both post-verbal, should not be distinguishable in contexts where only one NP argument appears. In other words, verb–object and verb–subject sequences should behave identically with respect to various syntactic processes if they are not distinguished hierarchically. Anderson and Chung (1977) argue that Samoan and Tongan, two VSO languages of the South Pacific, show differences between VO and VS sequences in the interaction of Equi-NP Deletion and Subject-to-Object Raising[6]—two rules that

---

[4] Parts of the discussion on VSO order are based on an unpublished book manuscript by myself and Heidi Harley. The discussion here has been simplified from the relatively technical analysis presented there.

[5] We do not discuss here the two arguments that have been advanced in favor of flat structure for VSO languages, since, as will be seen below, the evidence against such an approach is fairly convincing. One such argument in favor of flat structure is found in Chung (1983), where she argues that the subject position in Chamorro is properly governed, thus accounting for the lack of *that*-trace effects and Sentential Subject Constraints in that language. See Sproat (1985) for extensive criticism of this approach, and Chung (1990) for a reinterpretation of these facts. The second argument has to do with the binding facts of Jacaltec discussed in Woolford (1991); this will be discussed briefly below.

[6] In more modern terminology these are Subject Control and Exceptional Case Marking (ECM). In order for their argument to follow, we are required to assume the pre-Principles and Parameters characterization of these processes, in other words, that there are not any null arguments, such as PRO, in the representation that could disambiguate VS from VO

make reference to subjects and not to objects. If the VO and VS sequences are structurally indistinguishable, then verbs that allow both Equi and Subject-to-Object Raising to apply should allow Subject-to-Object Raising to apply to objects, provided Equi has applied to delete the subject in an embedded context. This prediction is false, as seen in the following Samoan data.

(7) (a) 'Ua mānana'o tagata e mālō i le pālota.
      PERF want-PL people FUT win in the election
      "People wanted to win in the election."

     (b) E mānana'o tagata i le pālota 'ia manuia.
      FUT want-PL people at the election IRREAL be-well
      "People want the election to turn out well."

     (c) *Sā mānana'o tagata i le gaoi e pu'e.
      PAST want-PL people at the burglar FUT catch
      "People wanted to catch the burglar."

The Samoan verb *mānana'o* 'want' allows Equi-NP Deletion, as in (7a), as well as Subject-to-Object Raising, as in (7b). Given that we could create a control context in which the subject of an embedded transitive clause was deleted via Equi-NP Deletion, the order VO would result in the embedded clause. If VO and VS sequences are not distinguished in the grammar of a language, then this should act as a valid input to the rule of Subject-to-Object Raising. As shown in (7c) this is incorrect, the object cannot undergo Subject-to-Object Raising; thus, it is clear that Samoan does, indeed, distinguish subjects from objects. Anderson and Chung present similar evidence from Tongan clitic marking and Breton object marking to show that these languages also distinguish subjects and objects.[7]

Typological arguments against a VP-less analysis (like that in (6)) of VSO languages were first presented in Emonds (1980), based on Greenberg's (1966) universals. In particular, Emonds argued that VSO languages are all derived from SVO structures. His observations based on

(in the form of V PRO O). Their argument, then, is not really consistent with more recent assumptions. However, the empirical facts do show, as will be seen below, that VSO languages distinguish subjects from objects, contra Berman (1974).

  [7] It should be noted, as an aside, that in fact Anderson and Chung do not argue against a flat representation of VSO languages. Instead, they argue for a model which, like that of Relational Grammar, distinguishes subjects from objects as a primitive of the grammar, rather than trying to derive these relations from linear order with respect to the verb (cf. Berman 1974).

the typology of VSO languages are quite insightful and foreshadow much later work on the head movement of verbal predicates. First, he notes that VSO languages are much rarer than SVO languages. This, he claims, follows directly from the fact that VSO order is always derived, and SVO is a base order; the more derivation, he claims, the rarer the word-order type. Woolford (1991) argues against this argument, pointing out that current Chomskyan thinking on SVO languages also has significant derivation in these languages (see e.g. Pollock 1989).

Emonds's second typological argument is harder to dispute. Greenberg's Sixth Universal says that all languages with a VSO order also have an alternate SVO order.[8] The alternations between SVO and VSO would be entirely arbitrary under a flat structure analysis. However, if VSO is derived from SVO, then the correlation between the two orders is direct: SVO alternates are simply the cases where the verb-fronting rule has failed to apply.

Greenberg's universal 12 is:

> If a language has dominant order VSO in declarative sentences, it always puts interrogative words or phrases first in interrogative word questions; if it has dominant order SOV in declarative sentences, there is never such an invariant rule.   (Greenberg 1966: 83)

In other words, in VSO languages, complementizers—especially interrogatives—(and frequently inflectional elements as well) are initial in their clause. Emonds correlates this property to what he considers to be the cause of verb movement in VSO languages. Foreshadowing much later work, he claims that verb fronting is due to some morphological feature of the Complementizer head. He bases this on a principle he attributes to den Besten (1981):

---

[8] It is unclear to me what exactly "an alternate SVO" order means here. We may end up comparing structures that are totally unlike. For example, clauses that involve *wh*-movement, or tenseless clauses, rarely have the same word order as tensed clauses. Do these count as "alternate" orders? Or do only ordering alternations in clauses of a like-type count as "alternate orders"? We must be careful with such claims not to compare apples and oranges. Some languages—such as Arabic—appear to allow some type of SVO–VSO alternation in root clauses. Irish, on the other hand, never allows SVO in simple tensed root clauses—these must always be VSO. It does allow SVO order in tensed clauses, but only where the subject has been demonstrably fronted via A-bar movement for some kind of topicalization (as is shown by the presence of a [+wh] complementizer). SVO order is also found in tenseless clauses in some dialects. A related issue concerns what constitutes a "V". For example, with auxiliaries, do participles constitute "V"s or not? If they do, then Irish allows an Aux SVO order. If they do not, then this clause type is clearly VSO. A more careful examination of Greenberg's universal is in order here, determining, in more rigorous terms, what is being compared before we draw any strong conclusions about the theory based upon it.

> All instances of movement to pre-subject position by a grammatical transform-
> ation are attractions to a sentence-initial Comp.

Given this type of principle, the strong correlation between VSO order and clause initial complementizer particles is obvious: VSO order is caused by the clause initial particles. If we were to have a base VSO order, then the correlation between the order and clause initial particles would be mysterious; there would be no direct link between VSO order and clause initial particles.

Now turning away from typology, a great body of empirical evidence has surfaced showing that many VSO languages do not have a flat, underived VSO order. In a great many languages, there are sequences of untensed verbs or participles and objects that function as syntactic constituents, reminiscent of VPs. McCloskey (1983) shows that participles and objects in Irish form syntactic constituents. This constituent consists of the progressive participle and object (**bold** in (8)):

(8) Tá   na teangeolaí **ag**   **ól an beorach**.
     be.PRES   the linguists   PROG   drink the beer-GEN
     "The linguists are drinking the beer."

These sequences obey several standard tests for constituency in Irish. Only maximal projections may be clefted, and more specifically only one maximal projection may be clefted at a time. For example, a direct object and an indirect object may not be clefted together:

(9) *[Ull][don ghasúr] a thug sé.
     apple to-the boy WH gave he
     "It was an apple to the boy that he gave."

In contrast, the progressive participle and the direct object can be clefted together:

(10) Má's **ag cuartughadh leanbh do dhearbhrathra** a tá   tú ...
      if+C PROG seek   child   your brother   WH-are you
      "If it is seeking your brother's child that you are..." (McCloskey
      1983: 14)

Similar facts are found in Breton (11) and Welsh (12):

(11) **Lenn eul levr brezhoneg** a ran bembez.
      to-read a book Breton   WH do-1SG everyday
      "Read a Breton book is what I do everyday." (Anderson and Chung
      1977: 22)

(12) **Gweld** y ci   y   mae'r dyn.
          see   the dog   WH be-the man
          "It is seeing the dog that the man is." (Sproat 1985: 178)

McCloskey also notes that the participle and object can be the focus of the *ach* "only" particle, an honor reserved only for constituents in Irish (McCloskey 1983):

(13) Ní raibh mé ach **ag déanamh grinn**.
          NEG be.PAST I only PROG make fun
          "I was only making fun." (McCloskey 1983: 20)

There thus seem to be numerous examples of VP-like constituents in VSO languages, lending some support to the idea that VSO order is derived from some structure that has a VP constituent.

There are, however, some problems with such an analysis. It is not at all clear that these structures are headed by verbs. In the traditional grammar of Irish, all of the constructions discussed above involve a "verbal noun" (see Willis 1988, Borsley 1993, 1997, Duffield 1996, Guilfoyle 1997, Borsley and Kornfilt 2000, Carnie 2006b for a discussion of these "mixed" categories in Celtic). Within the LFG framework, I argue in Carnie (2006a) that if these structures are analyzed as NPs then some otherwise baffling properties of Irish copular constructions follow naturally. I claim there that Irish has a full NP structure but a flat clausal structure. Irish is not only verb initial but more generally predicate initial:

(14) Is[9] dlíodóir (é) Liam
          DECL lawyer (AGR) Liam
          "Will is a lawyer."

What is surprising is that when the predicate is a noun, it may be complex[10] (15a, b). This is in contrast to verbal structures where the object may not be adjacent to the tensed verb[11] (15c).

---

[9] I assume here, following Ó Sé (1990), Doherty (1992), and Carnie (1995, 1997) that *Is* here is not a true verb but a complementizer indicating declarative mood. See the above-mentioned work for evidence in that regard.

[10] See Carnie (1995, 2000), Doherty (1996, 1997), Legate (1997), Lee (2000), Massam (2000), Travis and Rackowski (2000), and Adger and Ramchand (2003) for alternative analyses of these kinds of construction.

[11] Kroeger (1993) presents remarkably similar data from Tagalog predicate-initial structures and uses this to argue that Tagalog is non-configurational, and has a completely flat structure both in verbal and non-verbal constructions. Kroeger's analysis cannot be extended to Irish which differs in some significant ways from Tagalog, including the fact that Irish has strict VSO order.

(15) (a) Is [amhrán a^L bhuailfidh an píobaire] "Màiri's Wedding".
            DECL song WH play.FUT. the piper
            "Màiri's Wedding' is a song which the piper is going to play."

      (b) Is   [fear   alainn]   Liam.
            DECL   man   handsome   Liam
            "Liam is a handsome man."

      (c) *D'   [ól   tae] Seán.
            PAST   drink   tea   Seán
            "Sean drank tea."

I proposed that a system like LFG allows a straightforward explanation of the differences among verbal and non-verbal predicates in these constructions. Following Nordlinger (1998), I proposed that phrase structure categories vary not only over category (as is standard in X-bar theory) but also over phrase-level. These elements vary both in terms of category (N, V, A, P, etc.) *and* in terms of phrasal level (word/head, phrase, etc.). I notate this variable as X^P.[12] This variable will interact with the set of phrase structure rules to produce situations where verbal predicates can only be heads, but nominal predicates can be heads or phrases. In particular, this will occur because Irish has an NP rule, but not a VP rule. Consider the following Irish c-structure rules:

(16) (a) S → $\quad$ X^P $\qquad$ NP $\qquad$ $\left(\begin{array}{c} \text{NP} \\ (\uparrow\text{OBJ})=\downarrow \end{array}\right)$
            $\qquad\qquad$ ↑=↓ $\quad$ (↑SUBJ)=↓

      (b) NP → $\;$ Det $\;$ N $\qquad$ $\left(\begin{array}{c} \text{NP} \\ (\uparrow\text{OBJ})=\downarrow \end{array}\right)$
            $\qquad\qquad$ ↑=↓ $\;$ ↑=↓

The head (↑=↓) of the sentence rule is variable in terms of both phrasality and category: X^P, meaning that either a phrase or word can be inserted into this position. There is no VP rule,[13] so an N, NP, or V can all feed into this position. Because of the phrasal variable X^P, either words or phrases may appear in the predicate position. Nominal predicates are allowed to surface either as simple nouns or as complex NPs. By contrast, with verbal predicates, only the verb with no modifiers or complements is allowed in this position. This is because Irish

---

[12] Nordlinger (1998) uses C, Bresnan (2001) uses X (italicized).

[13] See Borsley (1989, 1996) for the claim that the subject argument with finite predicates in the VSO language Welsh is a second complement, rather than a subject, which provides some support for the lack of a VP proposed here.

has an NP rule (as attested in other positions, such as the subject position), but no VP rule. Returning now to the constituency tests from Irish participle constructions, since these are at least partly nominal in character, the fact that such a constituent exists follows from the NP rule does not necessarily argue for a VP.

Other arguments against a flat, VP-less, structure for VSO languages comes from tests of the relative prominence of subjects and objects. This of course assumes that subject–object asymmetries are defined over tree structure (using, for example c-command) rather than over argument structure or functional structures as in HPSG, LFG, and RRG. If one does not accept that subject–object asymmetries are best expressed by c-command then the following arguments evaporate.

In flat structure, subjects and object are each other's sisters. Given this, we expect that there will be no structure-dependent subject–object asymmetries in VSO languages. The evidence seems to point away from this. For example, in Irish, a reciprocal[14] in subject position cannot be bound[15] by an object (17b), but the reverse is grammatical (17a).[16]

(17) (a) Chonaic Seán agus Máire lena   chéile.
           saw   John   and   Mary   with.their other
           "John and Mary saw each other."

     (b) *Chonaic lena   chéile Seán agus Máire.
           saw   with their other   John and   Mary
           "Each other saw John and Mary."

---

[14] A brief comment about reflexives in Irish is in order here. Strangely, Irish seems to allow completely unbound instances of the reflexive particle in emphatic contexts:

(i)   Chonaic sé fein an réaltlong.
      saw   he self the starship
      "Himself saw the starship." (referring to a particular person in the discourse setting)

Because of this emphatic use of the reflexive morpheme, which in such contexts seems to have little or nothing to do with true anaphora, I avoid using reflexives as examples of anaphora in this book and use reciprocals, which do not have this emphatic reading, instead. See Ó Baoill (1995) for discussion.

[15] Here, we operate under the standard, but not incontrovertible, assumption of Reinhart (1981, 1983) that binding theory makes reference to the relations of c-command, rather than simple linear precedence.

[16] Duffield (1995) presents similar evidence of subject–object asymmetries which are not dependent upon binding theory. He notes that, in Irish, resumptive pronouns are allowed in object position, but are not allowed in subject position.

Similar effects are seen in Niuean (Seiter 1980, Woolford 1991) and Berber (Choe 1987). Sproat (1985) and Hendrick (1988, 1990) show that subject and object arguments in Welsh and Breton differ with respect to parasitic-gap effects. Anderson (1984) presents evidence from control in relative clauses in Kwakwala (Kwakiutl) that show similar effects. On the other hand, Craig (1977) and Woolford (1991) present data from argument prominence in Jacaltec Mayan in favor of a flat structure. The binding facts in Jacaltec seem to indicate that the object does indeed mutually c-command the subject, as would be predicted in a flat-structure analysis. An R-expression embedded in the subject NP cannot be co-referent with an object pronoun:[17]

(18) (a) Xil   [smami   naj pel]   Ø_i.
           saw   POSS-father CL   Peter   him
           "Peter_i's father saw him_j".
           *"Peter_i's father saw him_i."

This data could be analyzed as a condition-C effect (Chomsky 1981), where the object c-commands the R-expression in the subject NP:

(19)

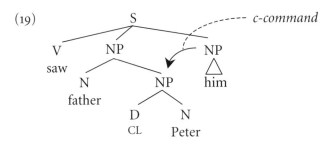

Thus, Jacaltec might well be a candidate for a flat-structure VSO language, as Woolford claims. The problem with such an analysis, however, is that Jacaltec does show standard subject–object asymmetries. For example, just as in English, reflexives are not permitted in subject position (Craig 1977). Similarly, only subjects are available for the rule of Promotion discussed by Craig. This phenomenon, similar to subject-to-subject raising, is seen in the following example:

(20) X'iche   smunla   naj.
      ASP.ABS.3.began   ERG.3.work   CL
      "He began to work."

---

[17] Due to constraints on disjoint reference, the object pronoun must surface as null in this construction; see Craig (1977: 158).

Perhaps, then, the effect seen in (18) is due to something other than condition C. The ungrammaticality of (18) with the coreferent reading could be due to a condition-B violation on the object pronoun. The R-expression possessor of the subject NP is functioning like the secondary head of that NP,[18] thus its features percolate to the higher NP node and trigger a condition-B violation. The subject NP c-commands the object. Note that this kind of head-like behavior of possessors is found in many languages; for example, Japanese allows passivization of possessor NP (Terada 1991). This kind of analysis is too complex to elaborate on here; it can be concluded that it is more consistent with the other evidence from Jacaltec, which suggests that subject–object asymmetries do occur in the language. Aissen (2000) presents a different analysis of these facts; she claims that they are not due to the binding theory at all, but that they are due to effects of obviation, where the head of the genitive (*father*) is forced to be marked as an obviative, which in turn is incompatible with a subject position. Under both these analyses, these facts cease to be evidence in favor of the flat structure approach.

Borsley (1989) argues that VP constituents exist in VSO languages at an abstract level. Working in GPSG (although see Borsley 1996 for an update of this analysis in HPSG, using a lexical rule), he proposes there is a metarule, similar to the Subject–Aux-inversion rule, which licenses a verbal projection with two NP complements from rules with a single complement. VPs in this system never exist in the constituent structure, only in the licensing rules; see Dowty (1996) for a discussion of VSO languages using categorial grammar. In this system, VP constituents also exist only at the abstract tectogrammatical level.

11.3.3 The VP-Internal Subject Hypothesis (VPISH)

On the basis of the discussion above in sections 11.3.1 and 11.3.2, let us adopt the idea that there is at least a constituent that corresponds to the verb and its complement. The traditional view was that this was the

---

[18] See Napoli (1989) for a related discussion of how the embedded PP in NPs like *that flower of a girl* is the semantic head of the NP. This is shown by the fact that verbs selecting [+human] complements can select for such NPs, despite the fact that the syntactic head of the NP is [−human]. For example, the verb *marry* can only take [+human] complements, yet the sentence *I want to marry that flower of a girl* is (sexism aside) grammatical.

VP. Building on Kitagawa (1986), Koopman and Sportiche (1991)[19] claim that the verb + complement constituent is actually V'. Further, they claim that the specifier of the VP category is the underlying position of the agent, building on Stowell's claim that subjecthood is a property of specifiers. Surface order in languages like English (where the subject precedes tensed auxiliaries) is accomplished by movement of the agent to the specifier of TP (IP):

(21)

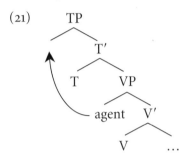

The evidence for this is both conceptual and empirical. On a conceptual level it allows us to unify (or at least more tightly constrain) the thematic properties of agents and themes. Under the VPISH, these roles are both assigned locally within the VP.[20] Empirically, this kind of structure provides a straightforward account of both post-auxiliary subjects in English and for the position of subjects in VSO languages. In existential impersonal constructions[21] in English such as (22), the subject NP *four men* follows the tense auxiliary. If the agent of the verb *sit* is VP-internal, then this order follows straightforwardly:

(22)   (a)   There were four men sitting on the floor.

   (b)

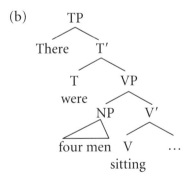

---

[19] See also Guilfoyle, Hung, and Travis (1992).

[20] In GB theory, the V governs (under m-command) both the arguments in the clause and theta role assignment happens under government.

[21] See Carnie and Harley (2005) for a fuller treatment of existential impersonal constructions.

Assuming a rule of verb movement, where tensed verbs raise to T to check their inflection (or are inserted there because of head mobility as in LFG), then VSO order also falls out from the VPISH.[22]

(23)

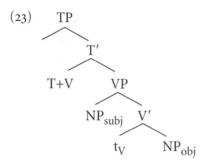

McCloskey (1991), building on research by Chung and McCloskey (1987), provides strong evidence for this kind of approach, using data from Modern Irish. One net effect of this kind of analysis is that there is a putative subject + object surface constituent in VSO languages, the VP less the moved verb. We thus expect to find constituency tests that target this constituent. The element that appears in the rightmost position in right node raising constructions must be a constituent in Irish. The S–O sequence obeys this test:

(24)   Níor   thug,   nó   is   beag   má   thug,   [an
       NEG   gave,   or   C   small   if   gave,   the

       pobal   aon   aird   ar   an   bhean   bhocht].
       people   any   attention   on   the   woman   poor
       "The community paid no attention or almost no attention
       to the poor woman." (McCloskey 1991)

Other evidence for such a constituent comes from ellipsis phenomena in Irish. Irish has a process of VP ellipsis which parallels English VP ellipsis in many ways. It applies under identity to a linguistic (i.e. non-pragmatically defined) antecedent. It is immune to island constraints. It may apply "backwards" (with the antecedent following the elided material). It tolerates antecedent contained deletion. Finally, it shows strict/sloppy pronominal interpretations. McCloskey thus claims that this phenomenon is the Irish equivalent of English VP

---

[22] We also require some principle to explain why the subject does not raise to the specifier of the TP as in English. This could be rightward case assignment (Koopman and Sportiche 1991), or covert movement (Bobaljik and Carnie 1996) or some other system.

ellipsis. It differs from English VP ellipsis, however, in what is deleted. In English, the subject obligatorily remains, but the verb and the object (and any other VP internal material) is elided and replaced with *did* (*too*). In Irish on the other hand, the verb is the one element which is not elided, rather, it is the VP constituent which is elided:

(25)   English: S   V   O   and   S   ~~V   O~~
        Irish: V   S   O   and   V   ~~S   O~~

(26)   Duirt mé go   gceannódh sí   é agus cheannaigh ~~subj object~~.
        said   I   that would.buy   she   it and   bought
        "I said that she would buy it and she did."

The VPISH coupled with a process that moves the verb higher in the clause provides us with an elegant account of these facts. The verb has raised outside of the domain of the ellipsis process, whereas the subject and object remain within the VP constituent, which is elided.[23]

11.3.4 Stacked VPs, Split VPs, vP

While the evidence is fairly convincing that subject arguments start lower in the constituent structure than their final position, there are reasons to doubt that they are as low in the tree as the VP. In fact, some converging evidence has led to the idea (now widely accepted in the P&P literature) that agent and other subject arguments are not directly introduced by predication with the verb. Instead the VP structure is

---

[23] One possible objection to this is the lack of other types of constituency effects such as focus under *ach* "only" (i) or clefting (ii)

(i)   *Ní fhaca ach [beirt an duine].
        NEG saw but two-people the man
        "Only two people saw the man."

(ii)   *[Seán teach i nDoire] a cheannaigh.
        John house in Derry C bought
        Lit.: "It was John a house in Derry that bought."

McCloskey claims, however, that these violations should not be taken as evidence against the constituency of the remnant VP. Instead, he argues that the ungrammaticality of (i) and (ii) follows a violation of the Empty Category Principle. Recall that the VP has the trace of the verb movement in it. If the VP is fronted to the beginning of a clause in a cleft (higher than the verb), or is right-adjoined to the clause in an *ach* focus, then this trace is not antecedent-governed by the verb, accounting for the ungrammaticality of the forms.

composed of two distinct structures,[24] one which represents the lexical verb, its modifiers and a single complement, and a higher structure variously called μP (Johnson 1991), PredP (Bowers 1993), vP (Chomsky 1995a) and VoiceP (Kratzer 1995). I will use the vP category here since it is by far the most common abbreviation. The head of the vP is the category v, which is called either "light verb" or "little v".

(27)

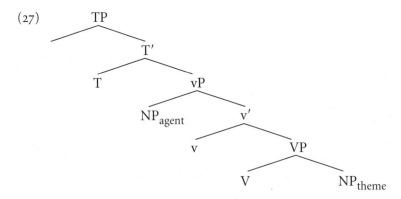

With this "split" or "stacked" verbal projection system we have a hybrid between the traditional VP and the VPISH. The agent argument is generated low, thus giving us all the benefit of the VPISH but also gives a privileged status to the subject.

There are a surprising number of arguments in favor of splitting the agent off of the VP this way. Marantz (1984) observes that external arguments do have several distinct properties. While we find sentential idioms and V+O idioms, there are no V+S idioms. The meaning of the verb can be more directly affected by the object than by the subject. The examples Marantz gives are in (28) and (29). The (a) examples represent the canonical meaning of the verb. Metaphorical meanings are forced on the verb by the objects in the other examples. So *throwing a party* does not actually involve swinging the arm and releasing an object. The particular meaning of the verb here is determined by the object. This can be contrasted to (30) where the subject does not seem to alter the meaning of the verb in the same way.[25] For a contrasting view of these facts, see Bresnan (1982) and Grimshaw (1992).

---

[24] The two predicates are linked to one another semantically, not through predicate argument composition, but through a rule of Davidsonian event identification; see Kratzer (1995).

[25] There may be a couple of apparent exceptions to this. For example, *The death of his father threw John*, where *throw* is taken to mean "emotional destabilize." However, notice that such interpretations are only available with an animate theme, so the metaphorical content of this construction might be tied to just the object, or be fully sentential in nature.

(28)   (a) throw a baseball
       (b) throw support behind a candidate
       (c) throw a boxing match
       (d) throw a party
       (e) throw a fit

(29)   (a) kill a cockroach
       (b) kill a conversation
       (c) kill an evening watching TV
       (d) kill a bottle
       (e) kill an audience (wow them)

(30)   (a) The policeman threw the ball
       (b) The boxer threw the ball
       (c) The social director threw the ball

If Marantz is correct about this, then we do not want to tie the agent too closely to the verb. Separating the agent argument out using the v category is one way to do this.

A variety of little v heads have been proposed, which vary in their semantic content (a causative, a form that means *become*, and various forms associated with voice). There is morphological evidence to support this. Many of the Austronesian languages have overt morphology on the verb corresponding to these forms. Sentence (31) is an example from Malagasy.

(31)   M+an+sasa   ny lamba   (amin   ny   savony)   Rasoa.
       T+v+wash   the clothes with   the   soap   Rasoa
       "Rasoa washes the clothes with the soap."

Stacked light verbs also can explain the fact that English allows multiple auxiliaries. Multiply stacked vPs provide a head for each of these (32). A similar analysis of auxiliaries is found in HPSG (Sag, Wasow, and Bender 2003).

(32)   (a) Mike is playing bridge.
       (b) Mike had played bridge.
       (c) Mike must play bridge.
       (d) Mike was beaten.
       (e) Mike has been playing bridge.
       (f) Mike was being beaten.
       (g) Mike must be playing bridge.

(h) (if) Mike had have played, then . . .
     (If Mike would have played . . .)

(i) Mike had been beaten.

(j) Mike had been playing bridge.

(k) Mike must have played bridge.

(l)

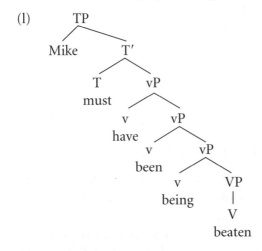

The origins of the little v approach lie in the proper treatment of double-object constructions like (33a). X-bar theory allows only one complement position in the tree, so the two obligatory complement NPs in (33a) are mysterious.

(33) (a) John gave Mary a book.
      (b) John gave a book to Mary.

Further, Barss and Lasnik (1986) show that in goal–theme orders (33a), goals c-command themes (34a, a'), and in theme–goal orders (33b), themes c-command goals (33b, b'):

(34) (a)   Mary showed John himself (in the mirror).
      (a') *Mary showed himself John (in the mirror).
      (b)   Mary showed John to himself.
      (b') ??Mary showed himself to John.

This means that the leftmost argument is higher in the tree than the one on the right. Larson (1988) argues that a split-VP approach solves this problem. There are two verbs *give*, one with two NPs and the other with an NP and a PP. With the addition of the vP to host the agent, we have a place for both the theme and the goal such that the first c-commands the second. Surface order is derived by movement of the V into the v.

(35) (a)   (b)

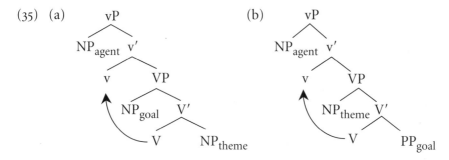

Having a split-VP structure then accounts for a wide variety of data, while capturing both the locality of the VPISH and the distance of the traditional VP. Other little v-like categories have been proposed in the literature, including ApplP which, is tied to applicative constructions (McGinnis 2001; Pylkkänen 2001, 2002). See also Harley and Noyer (1998) for a discussion of the role of little v in nominalizations.

There is one further aspect of the split VP that remains to be mentioned. Travis (forthcoming)[26] argues using morphological evidence from a variety of Austronesian languages and syntactic evidence from languages with object shift that there is a functional category that lies between the vP and VP which represents situation aspect (roughly, aktionsart).

(36) $[_{vP}\ v\ [_{AspP}\ Asp\ [_{VP}\dots V\dots]]]$

This projection also serves to case-mark objects. There is some semantic motivation behind this projection: certain kinds of objects lead to various situational aspect distinctions. For example, if you ate an apple, the eating event ends when the apple is finished, by contrast, if you just eat, the eating event has no clear end point. An object-licensing category between vP and VP, in the guise of AgrO (object agreement) is also found in Koizumi (1994, 1995). Carnie (1995) and Carnie and Harley (1997) argue that you need both Aspect and AgrO to account for the order of elements in Irish and Scots Gaelic non-finite clauses; see also Noonan (1992, 1993, 1994) and Adger (1996). The claim that Aspect is tied to the VP (or the domain of predication) is also consistent with (under very different assumptions) the views of Dik (1989) and Role and Reference Grammar.

---

[26] See also Ramchand (1993) and MacDonald (2006).

11.4 The clausal layer

Much of the discussion in the following two sections concerns what is known in the P&P framework as "functional categories". The literature on functional categories is vast; so vast that I cannot hope to even expose the tip of the iceberg. I give here some of the leading questions and some of the matter that has the most consensus behind it, but the reader should not consider these sections even remotely authoritative or complete about the topic. In this section, we consider the nature of the clause, that is, the structure traditionally labeled S in early generative grammar (and is still labeled as such in many approaches, including LFG, GPSG, and HPSG).

There are three major classes of treatments for the clausal layer. There are those views that have S as an unheaded category, whose function is simply to license the predication between the subject and the VP. This was the view of early transformational grammar and survives to a lesser degree in some versions LFG but only in clauses where there is no auxiliary to head an IP (Inflectional Phrase).[27] Far more approaches adopt one of the other two approaches. In HPSG and GPSG, the clause is a projection of the predicate of the clause, usually the V. In GPSG this is because Inflection is usually part of the verb, and since the theory is meant to be "surface-true" it cannot express a more abstract category like Infl. In HPSG, the S category is simply the feature structure that has all of its argument features fully resolved. A significant portion of the literature in the Principles and Parameters tradition (both GB and MP) focuses on the third treatment: the clausal layer is made up by one or more projections of functional categories, which are headed by grammatical properties. Abney (1987) and Grimshaw (1992) suggest hybrids of the second and third approaches. They have functional categories, but these are viewed as extended projections of the V. See Bury (2003) for a more up-to-date version of this claim.

For the most part, we will focus on the functional category approach and make reference to the others as necessary. I will largely assume that the whole premise of functional categories (or something like them, such as the operators in RRG) is well motivated; see Hudson (1996) for a criticism of this assumption and of the entire functional-projection

---

[27] This is part of a larger programmatic restriction of "economy of expression", where forms appear only in the c-structure of the sentence if they have overt expression as words. See Falk (1983) for more discussion.

endeavor. I will also assume that functional categories and their relative order to each other is universal. This too is controversial. For example, Fukui (1995) claims that Japanese lacks functional categories, which explains why *wh*-phrases in the language are in situ. Lebeaux (1996) claims that functional categories are only present if they are required for licensing. Ouhalla (1991, 1994) argues that SVO languages differ from VSO languages in precisely the order in which the TP and AgrSP functional projections are found. He claims that VSO languages have TP over AgrSP (which licenses nominative case) and SVO languages have AgrSP dominating TP. These claims aside, a universal hierarchy of functional categories—if it can be found—is to be preferred on economy grounds.

Within transformational grammar and related approaches in the 1960s and 1970s (see for example Chomsky 1965), the S category was unheaded, but often included an AUX category to host auxiliaries. This category was thought to contain two elements, tense and agreement. With the widespread adoption of X-bar theory for other categories, the existence of an unheaded S category seemed suspicious. Jackendoff (1977) proposed that S was a verbal projection (V‴ or a higher bar level). This view was (and is) still widely adopted in the GPSG and HPSG approaches to syntax.

(37)

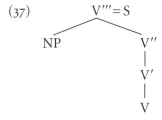

Auxiliaries and temporal adverbs were placed in the specifier of V″.

Emonds (1978) proposed instead that there is a category Infl (for inflection) that hosts auxiliaries, and, in their absence, the features associated with tense and inflection (37). Ken Hale suggested that Infl was the head of the S category in class lectures and an unpublished paper in 1979. Stowell (1981) proposes that this category be assimilated to the X-bar approach giving us Infl, I′, and IP. Pesetsky (1982), Huang (1982), and Falk (1983) all pursue and argue for this kind of approach. When an auxiliary appeared, it occupied this head (38a). When the inflection appeared on the verb, the Infl category lowered to the V (38b):

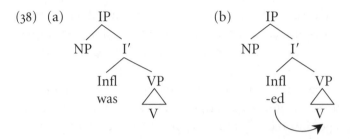

(38) (a)   IP   (b)   IP

Koopman (1984) (see also Emonds 1978) argued that variation in the position of the verb relative to various elements, such as negation or adverbs, between languages like French and English (and other languages including Vata) could be attributed to whether the V moved to Infl (41a) or the Infl lowered to the V (41b) (for the LFG equivalent to this—head mobility—see Kroeger 1993):

(39) (a) I often eat apples.   Adv V Obj

      (b) Je mange souvent des pommes.   V Adv Obj
           I   eat   often   of.the apples
           "I often eat apples."

(40) (a) I do not eat apples.   *not* V object

      (b) Je ne mange pas des pommes.   V *not* object
           I   NEG eat   not   of.the apples
           "I do not eat apples."

(41) (a)   TP   (b)   TP

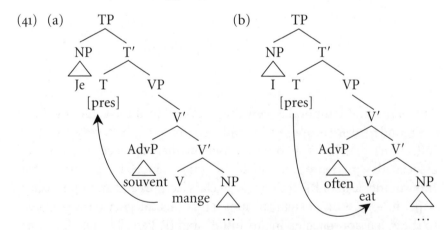

With the addition of the VP internal subject hypothesis V → Infl movement can also explain VSO order (see section 11.3). Positing an Infl head, even in contexts where there is no overt auxiliary, thus provides a mechanism for explaining variation in word order across languages.

Pollock (1989) argues that a single functional category like IP is not enough to solve various problems of word order. He suggests splitting Infl into the two subcomponents of the old Aux category T and Agr. The evidence comes from French non-finite clauses. Consider first a finite clause with both negation and an adverb (42a), where the adverb is adjoined to the projection of the verb, and *pas* "not" is in some functional category lower than Infl. Next consider the infinitive in (43a) the verb appears in some position between the negation and the adverb. There is no obvious head position in (42b) for the verb to land in.

(42) (a) Je n'ai   pas souvent arrivé   en   retard.
          I NEG-have not often   arrived in   late
          "I have not often arrived late."

      (b) [$_{IP}$ Infl [$_{NegP}$ not [$_{VP}$ [$_{V'}$ often [$_{V'}$ V]]]]]

(43) Ne   pas   arriver   souvent en   retard c'est triste.
      NEG not   arrive-INF often   in   late   it's   sad
      "It's sad not to arrive late often".

To account for this, Pollock proposes that the Infl category is more correctly identified as T (explaining why the verb does not move to it in tenseless non-finite clauses), and that the position the verb lands in in (43) is Agr (44).

(44) [$_{TP}$ T [$_{NegP}$ not [$_{AgrP}$ Agr [$_{VP}$ [$_{V'}$ often [$_{V'}$ V]]]]]].

Chomsky (1991, 1993) extends this approach. Considering the nature of the category Agr, he proposes that this category is fundamentally part of the mechanism for assigning Case (for a contrasting view see Massam 1994). The intuition behind this approach is that both case and agreement are mechanisms for expressing grammatical relations. As such he proposes that there are really two Agr categories,[28] one for assigning nominative case (AgrS) and one for accusative case (AgrO). These straddle the TP:

(45) [$_{AgrSP}$ *Nominative* AgrS [$_{TP}$ T [$_{AgrOP}$ *Accusative* AgrO [$_{VP}$...

Case assignment is not solely the domain of AgrPs. Since nominative case is often tied to tense, T and AgrS jointly assign the case when T has head-moved to AgrS. Since accusative case is typically tied to the

---

[28] See Belletti (2001) and Rizzi (2004) for illuminating surveys of the literature on AgrPs.

argument structure of the verb, AgrO serves as a host for case assignment only when the V has head moved into it.

Obviously, this architecture is challenged by the wide variety of word
orders expressed in language. However, Chomsky (1993) provides a
unique explanation for word-order variation given this clausal structure.
He suggests that all movement of the subject to the specifier of AgrS, the
object to the specifier of AgrO and the movement of the V head through
all of the head positions are universal. However, the universality of the
movement holds only at the abstract level of logical form, where a
condition requiring that all features be checked must hold (the principle
of full interpretation).[29] Cross-linguistic variation follows from variation
in timing of these operations relative to a rule of Spell-out which creates
the PF (or phenogrammatical structure) of the sentence. The positioning of elements in the surface string is due to movements that occur
overtly, or before Spell-out. Those that are not seen in the language
occur covertly, or after Spellout. For example, since English verbs and
objects appear to be low in the tree movement to these positions is
covert. As strange as the idea of a "covert" movement operation might
be, this provides a very constrained model of acquisition: children need
only learn the timings of operations to learn the grammar of their
language. It also predicts a limited number of permutations of order,
which should correspond to the overt expression of the tense and
agreement morphology of the language.

Let us consider some of the evidence that has been proposed in this
line of argumentation. Bobaljik and Jonas (1996) argue that three
argument positions are needed to account for each of the arguments
in the transitive expletive construction:

(46) Það   hafa   margir   jólasveinar   borðað búðing.
      there have   many   christmas.trolls eaten   pudding
      "Many Christmas trolls have eaten pudding."

Evidence from languages with object-positioning alternations also
points to the existence of an AgrO position below TP. As a typical
example, consider the facts in (47) from Irish. (See Bobaljik and Carnie
1996 among many other sources).

---

[29] The ideas here find correlates in other approaches. The Principle of Full Interpretation is similar to the requirement in LFG and GSPG that the structure represents a
unification of features, and the requirement in HPSG that all features are resolved. The
idea of an abstract LF is quite tightly related to the notion of a tectogrammatical structure
(see Ch. 10).

(47) (a) Tá   Seán   ag   scríobh   na   habairte.   **VO**
          be   John   PROG   write   the   sentence.GEN
          "I want John to write the sentence."

    (b) Ba mhaith liom [Seán   an abairt a^L scríobh].**OV**
          c good with.1.s   John.ACC   the sentence.ACC   PRT write
          "I want John to write the sentence."

In some circumstances (in the progressive aspect, or in non-finite clauses in the literary Munster dialect), the object follows non-finite verbs and takes an inherent genitive case (47a); in other circumstances (such as non-finite clauses in Northern dialects, or in other periphrastic aspects such as the perfective) the object precedes the non-finite verb and takes accusative case. In such cases, a particle homophonous with the third-person possessive pronoun appears between the object and the verb. Bobaljik and Carnie (1996) identify this pronoun as an overt instantiation of AgrO. In Irish, when an overt subject is present verbal agreement takes the default third-person form; when the subject is null, by contrast, the agreement expresses the person relations. The same pattern seems to hold of the particle in (46b), when the object is null, the form of the particle is identical to the possessive pronoun that agrees in person and number with the object (48).

(48) Ba mhaith liom *pro* $mo^L/do^L/a^L/a/ar^N/bhúr^N/a^N$ (m)b(h)ualadh.
     c   good   with.me   1s/2s/3MS/3FS/1PL/2PL/3PL   strike
     "I would like to strike me/you/him/her/us/you/them."

It thus seems not unreasonable to claim that in Irish, VSO order involves overt movement of the V to AgrS; overt movement of the subject to the specifier of the TP to check the EPP requirements—the formalization of the idea that all clauses must have subjects—of the clause; Objects appear in the specifier of the AgrO category. The specifier of the AgrS category is used only covertly, distinguishing Irish from languages like English or French (Duffield 1995; Bobaljik and Carnie 1996).

(49) $[_{AgrSP}$ AgrS-T-AgrO-V $[_{TP}$ Subject t_T $[_{AgrOP}$ Object
     t_{AgrO} $[_{VP}$ t_{Subj} t_V $t_{Obj}]]]]$.

Splitting the Infl category into three thus provides three positions for the arguments to appear in.

    Nevertheless, there is evidence that the AgrS-T-AgrO-V cartography of the clausal layer is not entirely correct. First, again from Irish consider the position of the VP adverb *ariamh* "always" relative to the subject (50), taken from McCloskey (1996b). If this adverb is VP adjoined, then the subject must be outside the VP (cf. the discussion in section 11.3 where we showed that McCloskey 1991 uses evidence from ellipsis to argue that both the subject and object in Irish are VP-internal). The presence of the TP category provides a simple analysis for this subject placement. However, the position of the object relative to the adverb is more surprising. It follows an element we are proposing is at the left edge of the VP.

(50)   Níor   shaothraigh   Eoghan   **ariamh**   pingin.
　　　　　V　　　　　　　　　S　　　　　adv　　　　O
　　　　NEG   earned   　　　Owen   　ever   　　penny
　　　　"Eogan never earned a penny."

This suggests that the accusative-case position is not in an AgrOP that dominates VP. Recall however, the discussion of inner aspect and AgrPs, in section 11.3, that appear in a layered VP. Carnie (1995), following Koizumi (1995) and Harley (1995), argues that the AgrO category is between the vP and the VP, allowing it to follow the vP adjoined temporal adverb.

(51)   [$_{vP}$ *agent* v [$_{AgrOP}$ *Accusative* AgrO [$_{VP}$ V *theme*]]].

Adding in Travis's inner aspect, a VP internal AgrOP provides a position for each element in the sentence (52), which—although pragmatically odd—is grammatical.

(52)   Níl   [$_{TP}$ Aindriú [$_{vP}$ ariamh [$_{AspP}$ tar-éis [$_{AgrOP}$ a thrachtas a^{L}
　　　　Neg.be   Andrew   ever　　　　　ASP　　　　　　　his thesis AgrO

　　　　[$_{VP}$ chríochnú]]]]]]
　　　　　　finish.VN
　　　　"Andrew has never just finished his thesis."

The order of elements at the top end of the clausal layer is also suspect. AgrS is linked to case, T to the EPP. In a language like Irish, where the subject is supposed to appear in the specifier of the TP[30] we expect to

---

[30] I assume here that the verb in is not in C following Duffield (1995) and McCloskey (1996a), based on co-occurrence with overt complementizers and the behavior of TP adjoined adverbs. This contrasts with the older analysis of VSO as movement of the V to C first proposed by Emonds (1980), and also found in Déprez and Hale (1986), Hale (1989) and Stowell (1989). Watanabe (1993), Clack (1994), Carnie, Pyatt, and Harley (1994) and Carnie, Harley and Pyatt (2000).

find EPP effects, and not Case effects. The opposite however, is true. Irish has movement for case in the perfective passive (53).

(53) Beidh   **an**   **trachtas**   críochnaithe   agam   amárach.
      be.FUT   the   thesis   finished   at.me   tomorrow
      "The thesis will have been finished by me tomorrow."

By contrast, McCloskey (1996b) shows that Irish does not display EPP effects. Not only does it not have any overt expletives in subject position, but in one kind of unaccusative in the language, where the theme is quirkily marked with a preposition so does not require case, the sole argument behaves as if it is a complement with respect to positioning in non-finite contexts, and with respect to various tests for constituency. If the EPP holds in Irish, then we would expect these unaccusative subjects to appear in subject position, but they do not. McCloskey (1996b, 1997) argues that the higher of the two functional categories is the EPP licensor,[31] and the lower one is associated with nominative Case.

(54) [$_{F_1P}$ *EPP* F1 [$_{F_2P}$*Nom* F2P...

Carnie (1995) identifies these two positions as TP and AgrSP, respectively. Taking this together with the layered VP we get the following interleaved clausal and VP layers:

(55) [$_{TP}$ *EPP* T [$_{AgrSP}$ *Nom* AgrS [$_{vP}$ *agent* v [$_{AspP}$ Asp [$_{AgrOP}$ *Acc* AgrO
      [$_{VP}$...]]]]]].

See Carnie and Harley (1997), who examine some of the consequences of this approach. For an alternative view of the architecture of the clausal layer, see Dooley (1990), Guilfoyle (1990, 1993, 1994), Rouveret (1991), Fassi-Fehri (1993), Roberts (1994), Duffield (1995), Roberts and Shlonsky (1996)

The whole AgrP endeavor was questioned on conceptual grounds by Chomsky (1995a), who argued that AgrPs have a different status from other functional projections such as TP (see also Iatridou 1991 for arguments against AgrO). For Chomsky (1995a), an element in the syntactic tree must be a legitimate object of interpretation (i.e. have an interpretation at LF). He claims that while TP has a clear semantic function, AgrPs do not, so should not be part of the clausal cartography.

---

[31] For a very different view of the EPP, where the effects are not due to a particular head but follow from general principles of structure formation, see Mohr (2005).

Instead, following Ura (1994), he claims that TP and vP should allow multiple specifiers (by this, he actually means Chomsky-adjoined structures) and these heads serve the purpose of AgrS and AgrO, respectively. AgrPs are widely absent from the current minimalist literature. I personally think this is a mistake. Although the original motivations for two AgrPs were weak (in Chomsky 1993 they were purely conceptual), subsequent work has shown that they can account for a wide variety of agreement particles (such as the AgrO particle in Irish). Sportiche (1996) also showed they were an important mechanism for explaining the properties of Romance pronominal clitics. While it is true that the Agrs have no clear function in the LF, they do have such a function at the other interface (PF). One might counter Chomsky's objections to the Agr categories by claiming that items in the tree must have an interpretation at either of the two interfaces, in which case AgrPs can be construed as legitimate objects.

A number of other functional projections in the clausal layer have been proposed. Beghelli (1995) and Beghelli and Stowell (1997) put forth three new functional categories (DistP, ShareP, and RefP) to account for scope ambiguity among quantified DPs. Roberts (2005) proposes splitting AgrPs into PersP (person) and NumP (Number) on the basis of data from Welsh and various Italian dialects. Cardinaletti (2004) suggests that in addition to AgrP and TP, two other subject related functional categories are required: SubjP hosts "subject of predication" arguments and EPPP hosts arguments that satisfy EPP effects. Spencer (1992) proposes the Full Functional Projection Hypothesis,[32] which argues that each feature associated with the verbal projection gets its own functional projection. This idea is echoed more recently in the work of Kayne (2005), who claims that all variation is ultimately controlled by microparameters, each associated with a particular functional category and every functional element is the locus of some distinct parametric variation. Behind this proposal is the idea that parametric variation has to do with the pronunciation or non-pronunciation of a wide variety of functional items.

11.5 The informational layer

The informational layer contains constituent structure associated with finiteness, illocutionary force, negation, mood, and topic and focus

---

[32] See also Mohr (2005).

structures. I will start with the arguments that distinguish an unheaded S' analysis from a CP structure, with some pointers to other approaches. Then I will turn to the internal structure of CPs to discuss the evidence that CP should be expanded into several different categories the way IP expanded into TP and AgrPs.

11.5.1 S' and CP[33]

In the 1960s and 1970s, the structure that provided means of subordinating one clause into another was the S', which had S and Comp (complementizer) daughters:

(56)

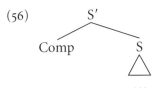

Like S, S' was often viewed as a projection or extended projection of the V head. Bresnan (1972) provides the first detailed probe into the nature of complementizers and their grammatical function and suggested that Comp (later shortened to C) was the head of the S' category. The argument came from the fact that various verbs select for the form of the complementizer that follows. For example, a verb like *ask* allows an *if* complementizer, but a verb like *think* does not. Grimshaw (1977) argues that the selectional restrictions of this type are for the logical type of the sentence rather than the form of the complementizers. Stowell (1981) provides extensive evidence in favor of the idea that C is the head of S' from Case theory. See Fassi-Fehri (1981), Koopman (1984), and Chomsky (1986a) for apparently independent proposals to implement the headedness of C into X-bar theoretic terms giving the CP category; see Pollard and Sag (1994) for arguments[34] that C is not the head of CP.

---

[33] Thanks to Anne Abeillé, John Beavers, Bob Borsley, Aaron Broadwell, Stan Dubinsky, David Pesetsky, and Stephen Wechsler for helping me track down the origins of the CP analysis.

[34] Pollard and Sag point out that verbs like *demand* select bare verbs:

(i)   I *demand* that he leave (*leaves).

If C is the head of the embedded clause then we have no means of doing local selection for the form of the verb. But if the V is the head of S' then *demand* can select a bare form of the verb. There is, however, an easy way around this in the C-as-head theory. English must have two *thats*; one is for declarative contexts, the other for subjunctives. *Demand* selects the subjective *that*, which in turn selects a defective IP, which triggers the bare form of the verb.

Beyond selection for a particular type of C, there is evidence from a variety of constructions that point towards an X-bar-theoretic CP. The structure of *wh*-questions is a good starting point. Early characterizations of *wh*-movement suggested moving the *wh*-phrase into the Comp position itself (see for example Ross 1967). There are several reasons to be suspicious of this account. First, it implies the idea that Comp is a position in the tree rather than a word or head; for example, we can move quite a complex phrase to the beginning of the sentence:

(57)   [Which Pictures of Bill] did Susan like?

Movement of a phrase into a head is unusual (see, however, the discussion of Carnie 1995 in Ch. 8). Second, the position of the inverted auxiliary in these questions is quite mysterious. In the CP analysis, by contrast, a straightforward analysis of these facts is available. *Wh*-phrases appear in a specifier position—specifiers typically being filled by phrases, and the inverted auxiliary appears in the C head itself. The *wh*-movement is triggered by a *wh*-feature on the C, the head movement is motivated by a [+Q] feature on the C.[35] (For a very different view of subject–aux inversion, see the literature from GPSG including GKPS.)

(58)

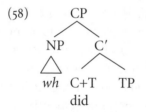

A similar account can be given to the discourse-related V2 effects in languages like German. In tensed clauses without an overt complementizer, the verb must appear in "second position". The first position in the sentence is occupied by a topicalized constituent. In example (59) (data from Haegeman 1994), the verb *kaufte* always appears in the second position, and any of the other elements (the subject *Karl*, the object *dieses Buch*, or the temporal adverb *gestern*) can appear in the first position. The remaining constituents follow the verb.

(59)   (a) Karl   kaufte   gestern   dieses   Buch.
           Karl   bought   yesterday this   book
           "Karl bought this book yesterday."

---

[35] The [+Q] complementizer is realized by particles in many languages including Japanese and Irish.

(b) Dieses Buch kaufte Karl gestern.
    "Karl bought this book yesterday."

(c) Gestern kaufte Karl dieses Buch.
    "Karl bought this book yesterday."

In clauses with overt complementizers, by contrast, there is no V2 ordering. The verb appears in final position:

(60) Ich dachte daß Karl gestern   das Buch gekauft hat.
      I   thought that Karl yesterday the book bought has
      "I thought that Karl bought the book yesterday."

The standard analysis within the P&P framework (den Besten 1981; Taraldsen 1985; Thráinsson 1985; Platzack 1986a, b, 1987, 1995; Schwartz and Vikner 1989, 1996) holds that there is a requirement that the complementizer position be filled in tensed clauses. The verb raises to the empty complementizer position in matrix clauses via Infl. There is then an additional requirement that the specifier of a matrix complementizer be filled by some element, giving the V2 order.

(61)

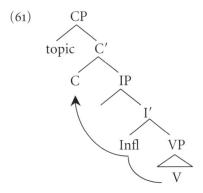

In embedded clauses, however, the complementizer position is filled, and the verb cannot raise to it. Simultaneously, the requirement that Spec of CP be filled by some XP is removed. Thus V2 ordering is blocked. Carnie, Pyatt, and Harley (1994) and Carnie, Harley, and Pyatt (2000) propose a similar analysis for Old Irish.

11.5.2 Expanded CP

Rizzi (1997) argues that the left edge of the clause (i.e. the CP system) is more finely grained than a single projection.[36] In this, he follows some

---

[36] See Iatridou and Kroch (1992) for earlier arguments that clauses have multiple CPs stacked on top of them.

earlier work that proposed MoodP (Zanuttini 1997) and Polarity (Culicover 1991; Laka 1991; Branigan 1992); we will return to the latter briefly below in section 11.6. Rizzi argues that on the inside of the CP system we have a functional head that represents finiteness. Finiteness is not tense, but has temporal properties; for example, many languages have finiteness particles that depend partly on the tense system for their form, but do not express the full range of tense morphology found on verbs. On the outside edge of the CP system, we have a category that represents illocutionary force (is the sentence a proposition, an interrogative, a command, or, alternatively, is it a declarative clause, a question, or an imperative?). Between the two, Rizzi argues for three positions directly tied to the information structure of the clause. In the very middle is a focus position, which is associated with new information in the clause. Straddling this focus position are two positions associated with old information or topics. This gives rise to the structure in (62)

(62) [$_{ForceP}$ Force [$_{TopP}$ Top [$_{FocP}$ Foc [$_{TopP}$ Top [$_{FinP}$ Fin [$_{TP}$...

Rizzi presents evidence from the positioning of topics, focus, inverted auxiliaries, adverbials, and complementizers in Italian and English. The results also provide an interesting account of some mysterious adverbial effects in Irish. McCloskey (1996a) observes that the order of adverbial elements and complementizers in English is different in embedded and matrix contexts.

(63) (a) I said next Christmas that we should see Frank. (*interpretation where the seeing occurs next Christmas. Only a matrix interpretation is allowed)

    (b) Next Christmas, who should we see? (*next Christmas* can be interpreted with *see*)

In Irish, surprisingly, the order of adverbials and complementizers is different. Adverbials appear to the left of both complementizers and subjects in both matrix and embedded CPs (data from McCloskey 1996a):

(64)   Adverb   C   V
      Líonaim d'eagla **dá dtógfainn   mo radharc dóibh**   go   dtitfinn.
      fill.1s   of fear if lift-1s.COND my sight   from.3s that fall.1s
      "I fill up with fear that, were I to take my eyes off, then
      I would fall."

Thus Irish shows the converse pattern to English.

McCloskey suggests that the solution to this paradox is that the adverbs in (64) are IP adjoined, thus explaining their embedded scope, despite the fact they appear to the left of the complementizer. He claims that the C° in Modern Irish lowers to attach to the verb because it requires support as a clitic, as illustrated in (65).

(65) [$_{CP}$ C [$_{IP}$ Adv [$_{IP}$ I+V [...]]]]

Roberts (2005) presents an alternative analysis that makes use of Rizzi's expanded CP without resorting to lowering rules. He argues that the difference between Irish and English lies in the nature of the complementizer. Sentential adverbs of the relevant type are Topics, and appear in one of the two Top positions. The English *that* complementizer is Force and appears above the adverb; Irish *go* is Fin and appears below the adverb:

(66) [$_{ForcP}$ [$_{force}$ *that*] ... [$_{Top}$ Adv ... [$_{FinP}$ [$_{Fin}$ *go*] IP]]].

He extends this to explain the relative ordering of two different types of complementizer in Welsh, and their relation to focal elements. See also Hendrick (2000), who provides a different expanded CP typology for initial particles in Celtic.

There are a number of other proposals for the content of the expanded CP system. Many of the articles in Rizzi (2004) are particularly informative about this. Benincà and Polleto (2004) argue for splitting up the higher TopicP into multiple positions. Taking a card from the deck where the VP is interleaved with Agr and AspP, Belletti (2004) argues—using evidence from different kinds of inversion in Romance—that there is also a Topic and Focus structure inside the clausal layer (under T). Polleto and Pollock (2004) argue for a different split CP. These are only a few of the works on this topic.

Outside of the P&P tradition (and to a lesser degree the LFG tradition where functional categories are also extensively used), we see different approaches to the material that is proposed to be in the informational layer of the clause. The operator structure of Dik's functionalist grammar is surprisingly similar to the split CP system, but not identical to it. In Role and Reference Grammar this kind of information is not included in the main constituent structure of the clause (with the exception of material that appears in two positions on the right of the tree: the LDP and PCS which have properties similar to the TopP and FocP mentioned above. However, the identification of these positions with these semantic functions is not one-to-one. The kind of information represented by Fin and Force appear on the separate operator tier, focal information itself has its own tier. In HPSG, all of this information is contained in the feature structure of the clause and may or may not be represented positionally.

11.6 Negation and adverbials

We move away from the tripartite clause structure now to consider other elements that appear in the clause. We start with the positioning of negation and adverbials. The categorial status and position of these elements is far more controversial than that of the tripartite clausal backbone. Take negation for example: is it an adjunct to some other category or is it a fully functional element that heads its own phrase? Are there different kinds of negation? How does negation positionally interact with the functional categories discussed in sections 11.4 and 11.5? These are huge questions. Nearly identical questions can be asked about adverbs and other categories that function adverbially. I will try to point out a few major lines of thought here, but as in other sections, the reader should not assume that what is described here is definitive or even representative.

11.6.1 Negation

An excellent summary of the issues concerning negation can be found in Zanuttini (2001), which this section draws upon liberally. Let us start with the question of whether negation is a functional head or an operator in some non-head position including specifiers and adjunction positions. All three possibilities (adverbial, specifier, head) are found. Indeed, most analyses of negation assume that different negative elements may well be positioned in different X-bar theoretic positions. Early analyses have negations adjoined to the VP. The spirit of this kind of account lives on in HPSG where negation is a modifier licensed by a special modification rule like adverbs and adjectives, and in approaches like RRG, where negation is an operator in the operator structure, typically tied to the CORE structure (although can appear at different levels). Certainly it is the case that some negatives, such as *never*, have the flavor of adverbs and other adjuncts as they appear in the same basic positions as other adverbs such as *ever* or *always*.

Kayne (1991) claims that French *ne* is a head. It moves with a verb that head-moves to T, it also blocks clitic climbing from an embedded clause:

(67) (a) Jean   l'a   fait   manger   à   Paul.
           John   it-has   made   eat   to   Paul
           John made Paul eat it.

      (b) *Jean l'a   fait   ne   pas   manger   à   Paul
           John   it-has   made   NEG   not   eat   to   Paul
           John made Paul not eat it.

By contrast, Pollock (1989) relies on the idea that French *pas* "not" is a specifier to explain why it does not block head-movement. See also Schafer (1995), who argues that Breton *ket* "not" is a negation in an A-bar specifier position and thus blocks *wh*-movement around it. English *not* blocks adjacency between Infl and V as if it were a head, accounting for why *do* support is required in its context (see Bobaljik 1994 for one possible explanation). Holmberg and Platzack (1988) claim that negation in Swedish is not a head because it does not block head movement to Infl:

(68) Jan köpte   inte boken.
      Jan bought not books
      "Jan didn't buy books."

It follows, then, that either negation can vary in its status as a head, adjunct, or specifier from language to language or that we have multiple kinds of negation X-bar theoretically.

Even under the assumption that negation has some status as a functional head, there is a fair amount of controversy about the position of the NegP relative to the other elements in the clausal cartography. VSO languages presumably have their verb in T, yet in almost every such language, negation precedes the V. By contrast, in languages like English and French the negation seems to be between T and the VP (either between auxiliaries and the verb or between the raised verb and auxiliaries and the object). Ouhalla (1991) proposes that languages parameterize whether negation selects TP or VP; Watanabe (1993) shows that Pembrokeshire Welsh has negation in both places; Laka (1991) argues that there really are two different kinds of negation. Predicate negation is low in the tree and scopes over the VP (like English *not*). The higher negation position is associated with the more general notion of propositional polarity. Laka calls this ΣP. The same projection is called PolP by Culicover (1991) and Koizumi (1995) and ΠP by Branigan (1992). Zanuttini (1997) uses evidence from Italian dialects to argue for four different negation positions interspersed through the clausal layer.

11.6.2 Adverbs

Adverbs are often the poor cousins in syntactic analysis. Despite the fact that they make important semantic contributions to the clause, they are often optional and their semantics and subcategories are not well understood. Worse, their positioning in the sentence is often relatively free (although usually with subtle effects on the meaning of the expression).

In generative grammar, there are roughly two major camps concerning the organization of adverbs relative to other elements in the clause. One, which we might label the "scopal view", holds that Adverb (or more precisely, adverb phrases) are adjoined to the projection of the head they most closely modify. Jackendoff (1972) is the earliest version of this view, see also McConnell-Ginet (1982), Frey and Pittner (1998) and Ernst (2003, 2004). Variants of this approach have adverbs as real adjuncts (sister and daughter of bar levels) or as Chomsky-adjoined to the phrase. Although there are particular differences among different scholars, these are grouped into at least three major categories, which correspond roughly to the tripartite structure of the clause. Manner adverbs (like *loudly*) are adjoined to the VP, temporal adverbs (such as *previously*) appear in the IP/TP clausal domain, and speaker oriented adverbs (such as *obviously*) appear in the CP domain. See Ernst (2004) for a far more refined view of adverb types and semantic considerations.

A variant on this approach is found in the HPSG and GPSG literature, where adverbs are licensed by a special modifier rule. The semantics of the adverb combine with the semantics of the constituent it combines with to form a composite function. In LFG (see e.g. the detailed discussion in Cobb 2006), the position of adjectives is restricted by functions (features) that correspond to different classes of adjectives. The c-structure rules contain annotations (sometimes underspecified) that restrict which kind of adverb can appear where in the c-structure.

The alternative approach is to associate particular adverbs with particular functional categories that are related to the semantics of the adverb itself. The most explicit version of this is found in Cinque

(1999), but see also Laenzlinger (1996, 2002) and Alexiadou (1997). Cinque claims that adverbs are elements that are licensed in the specifier position of different kinds of functional categories, including specific types of Asp, T, and Mood. The arguments come from the ordering of adverbs with respect to each other and inflectional elements. One version of Cinque's hierarchy is shown in (69):

(69) [*frankly* Mood$_{speech\ act}$ [*fortunately* Mood$_{evaluative}$ [*allegedly* Mood$_{evidential}$ [*probably* Mod$_{epistemic}$ [*once* T$_{past}$ [*then* T$_{fut}$ [*perhaps* Mood$_{irrealis}$ [*necessarily* Mod$_{necessity}$ [*possibly* Mod$_{possbility}$ [*usually* Asp$_{habitually}$ [*again* Asp$_{repetitive}$ [*often* Asp$_{frequentative}$ [*intentionally* Mod$_{volitional}$ [*quickly* Asp$_{celerative}$ [*already* T$_{anterior}$ [*no longer* Asp$_{terminative}$ [*still* Asp$_{continuative}$ [*always* Asp$_{perfect}$ [*just* Asp$_{retrospective}$ [*soon* Asp$_{proximative}$ [*briefly* Asp$_{durative}$ [*characteristically* Asp$_{generic}$ [*almost* Asp$_{prospective}$ [*completely* Asp$_{completive}$ [*well* Voice $_{[fast/early}$ Asp$_{celerativeII}$ [*again* Asp$_{repetitiveII}$ [*often* Asp$_{frequentiveII}$ [*completely* Asp$_{completiveII}$ ···

Languages vary in terms of which categories are realized adverbally and which are realized in terms of an inflectional head (or both). Ordering variation is due to variations in the movement of the verb (and other elements) through this functional structure.

11.7 NPs and DPs

Finally, we turn briefly to the cartography of nominal constructions. We start with a quick look at the question of what the head of nominal arguments is including a discussion of the functional structure of the determiner.

The oldest tradition both inside generative grammar and outside, is that nouns head nominal constituents. Selectional restrictions seem to bear this out. The oddness of #*John ate the rock* has to do with the fact that rocks are not the kinds of things that can be eaten. This is a property of the noun. Brame (1982), however, raised the possibility that the determiner was head of the nominal constituent; see also Szabolcsi (1983) and, in the dependency tradition, Hudson (1984). The work credited with popularizing this notion in P&P syntax was Abney (1987). Abney built on Chomsky's original (1970) observations about the parallelisms between clauses and nominals (such as *Rome destroyed the city* and *Rome's destruction of the city*); if we take it that clauses are headed by Infl, then it should not be a big stretch to conclude that some functional category is also the head of the nominal. See Stowell (1989) for a semantic argument that splits nominals into DP and NP. Ritter (1988) argues using evidence from construct-state nominals in Hebrew that a rule of N→ D movement, parallel to V→ T movement, explains the complementarity between construct state nominals and overt determiners, and explains the order of elements in the NP (see also Mohammed 1988). Ritter (1991, 1992) proposes splitting the DP into two categories, DP (which is the rough equivalent of the CP) and NumP, to account for alternations in order between two types of possessive construction in Hebrew. Picallo (1991) proposed a GenderP, but Ritter (1993) presented a number of a arguments against it. Several scholars, most prominently Baltin (1980), have suggested that a Quantifier Phrase (QP) dominates the DP (in order to account for phrases like *all the men*). A very articulated DP structure is proposed in Manzini and Savoia (2004); an earlier proposal is in Zamparelli (1995). For good summaries of the literature on DPs and their internal structure, see Bernstein (2001) and Longobardi (2001) and more recent work cited in Roberts (2005).

11.8 Concluding remarks

I started this chapter with the warning that the topic of the content of constituents was a massive one. I have attempted to provide here an outline of some of the arguments for one particular view of phrase structure cartography with occasional pointers to other approaches. I have tried to provide arguments for a tripartite organized clause which makes extensive use of functional categories at all levels. But I have barely scratched the surface of this intricate topic. Scholars working in other traditions will no doubt be frustrated that I have not given more space to their views, but I feel that's inevitable in a survey like this.

There is also a significant number of topics that I did not even attempt to cover here. For example, I have not discussed the question of how prepositional phrases (PPs) and adjective phrases (AdjP) fit into the system. Nor have I addressed any questions about analyses of honorifics, empty categories, classifiers, degree modifiers, small clause constructions, conjunctions, secondary predications, copular constructions, relative clauses, and other adjunct clauses. Nevertheless, I hope this chapter has given a taste of the flavor of debate over the content of phrasal constituents.

12

New Advances

12.1 Introduction

The material in Chapters 1–11 is largely the material that appeared in the first edition of this book, modulo many important corrections and a few minor additions. This chapter is new to this revised edition of *Constituent Structure*. It contains discussion of some important ideas that have emerged since the original version of this book was submitted for publication in 2007. The material discussed here largely supplements the material in Chapter 8 and concerns innovations in the Minimalist approach to constituent structure. I start with the description of a recent proposal by López (2009) of a simplified and weaker version of Kayne's (1994) Linear Correspondence Axiom. Then we turn to a discussion of the origins of X-bar-like relations as proposed by Medeiros (2008). This in turn is followed by a brief description of two approaches that decompose the Merge operation (Boeckx (2008) and Hornstein and Nuñes (2008)) and finally a very brief description of a version of Minimalism that I've been developing that takes seriously the idea behind dependency grammars: constituent structure takes a back seat to feature checking.

12.2 López (2009): The violable Two-Step LCA

For Kayne (1994), the LCA (cf. section 8.3) is an absolute constraint holding over phrase structure representations. López (2009) proposes an interesting variation. He argues that rather than being an absolute constraint, the LCA is a soft (i.e. violable) constraint, which can be overridden by prosodic considerations. As the operation of linearization is part of the mapping of syntactic structure to Phonetic Form (PF), we might expect that the LCA can interact with other operations involved in this mapping, including the construction of prosodic phonological phrasing (such as the constraint that requires the alignment of the right edge of syntactic constituents with the right edge of intonational phrases, and the constraint that heads and their extended projections (i.e. a head and the functional categories associated with it) should form a contiguous prosodic phrase). The evidence for this proposal comes from Clitic Right Dislocation (CLRD) in Spanish. These constructions are a challenge for the LCA because, as López shows, they clearly involve movement to a rightwards specifier which c-commands—as evidenced by binding and scope—the direct object (which appears to its left). The LCA predicts this to be impossible, as c-commanders have to precede their complements. López demonstrates that remnant movement approaches to this apparent rightward specifier fail on empirical grounds.

Kayne's version of the LCA requires that there is a distinction between the terminal word and its category. López notes that this is not consistent with current understandings of constituency (such as BPS), so instead proposes a different version of the LCA which, while drawing on the same basic intuition as the original (that is, if a terminal asymmetrically c-commands another, then it precedes it), is simpler and doesn't rely on the terminal/category distinction. Based on Epstein's definition of c-command (see Chapter 4), López proposes the Two-Step LCA (TLCA) (so called because it involves first a simple relationship between terminals and then a second step looking at projections):

(1)   *Two-Step Linear Correspondence Axiom*

Given terminals x, y:

a. if x c-commands y, then x precedes y

b. if x and y do not stand in a c-command relationship, then if x^{max} commands y then x precedes y (López 2009)

This constraint seems to derive all the cases of the LCA.[1] López proposes that this constraint holds of linearized structures, but can be overridden by other prosodic constraints. He claims that clitic-right dislocated elements bear special discourse-anaphoric features that trigger special prosodic alignments. CLRD elements project their own right-edged intonational phrase. But the projection of this intonational phrase interrupts the intonational phrase of the verb and its

---

[1] With one important exception not discussed by López: the case of two terminals which mutually c-command one another.

projections. The only way to linearize this while meeting intonational constraints is to order the specifier occupied by the CLRD element to the right, in violation of the TLCA. In Spanish then, the constraint that requires that intonational phrases be contiguous outranks the LCA, thus allowing a rightward specifier. The important lesson to take away from this is that the LCA, while an important advance in understanding linearization, fails in some crucial cases. We return to this briefly in section 12.5.

12.3 "Third factor" effects on constituency:[2] Carnie and Medeiros (2005), Medeiros (2008)

In a short working paper (Carnie and Medeiros 2005), David Medeiros and I made the observation that when an X-bar structure is fully spelled out with filled specifiers and complement positions, the structure exhibits a pattern consistent with the Fibonacci sequence of numbers. Consider a tree, generated by MERGE from the numeration {A, B, C, D, E, F, G, H, I, J, K, L} where every specifier and every complement position has been filled,[3] and each item has been merged only once. Further, let's annotate this tree with the maximal categories as defined by Chomsky (1995b)—where a label that is immediately dominated by the projection of another category is an XP[4]—and for ease of exposition we annotate other non-terminal nodes as X'. One possible version of such a tree is given in (2). Nodes that are ambiguous between terminal and maximal categories are annotated XP/X.

(2)

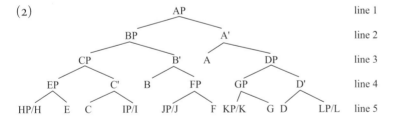

	line 1
	line 2
	line 3
	line 4
	line 5

---

[2] Thanks to Dave Medeiros for helpful discussion of this section.

[3] At the bottom-most layer of such a tree, some nodes may be ambiguous between specifier and complement status. For example, HP/H in (2) is simultaneously a specifier and a complement, in the traditional sense of X-bar theory (cf. Chomsky's (1995b) slightly different definitions); further branching below this level would disambiguate these structures.

[4] See also the principles of determining maximal and minimal status discussed in Speas (1990).

If we count the number of XPs in each line of this derivation, counting XP/X° ambiguous cases as XPs, we see a partial Fibonacci sequence (1, 1, 2, 3, 5). This property is true of all trees that are maximized in this way. The first (top) level—the root node—consists of one XP node. The next level contains one XP (the specifier of the root) and one X′. Thereafter, in the nth level there is one XP for each YP in the $(n-1)$th level (the specifier of that YP), and one XP for each YP in level $n-2$ (complement of that YP); no other XPs occur in the nth level. Letting the function $XP(n)$ represent the number of XPs in the nth level, we see that $XP(1) = 1$, $XP(2) = 1$, and for $n > 2$, $XP(n) = XP(n-1) + XP(n-2)$. Then $XP(n) = Fib(n)$, the Fibonacci function which yields the familiar sequence (1, 1, 2, 3, 5, 8...). The number of X′ categories, counted in the same way, forms the Fibonacci sequence as well, as does the number of heads, though the sequences begin at the second and third levels of the tree, respectively. Carnie and Medeiros speculate that the Extended Project Principle (Chomsky 1981), reinterpreted as a requirement that specifiers be filled, is correlated in some way with this observation, although directions of causality are not clear. In other words, it is precisely having specifiers (cf. Starke 2004) that makes tree structures Fibonacci-like. If the relevant pattern in phrase structure arises for reasons related to optimality in some sense—as seems to be the case for some related patterns in nature—then the deeply mysterious EPP may find a naturalistic explanation.

The observation that X-bar theoretic trees exhibit Fibonacci-like organization should not be surprising, as similar patterns are found in many natural systems. The fact that it appears in X-bar theory, however, leads to an interesting observation about the origins of X-bar theoretic phrase-structural relations. Medeiros (2008) provides a more nuanced and sophisticated view of this phenomenon than Carnie and Medeiros (2005): he claims that the fact such a pattern emerges in syntactic structures is evidence that it is, perhaps, a consequence of what Chomsky (2005) calls a "third factor."[5] He constructs an explicit optimality argument for X-bar-like organization, of the sort hinted at in Carnie and Medeiros (2005). His idea is that X-bar organization—and endocentricity more generally—need not be explicitly encoded in the computational system. In particular they are not directly encoded in the operation that generates constituent structures. That is, X-bar structures are not explicit in the nature of the merge operation,

---

[5] The other two factors being genetics and environment. See also Soschen (2008).

precisely because they are the best solution to the problem of access to the information in the tree. Medeiros provides a proof that X-bar theory-like trees are the best solution to ensure optimal packing of information in a way that c-command relationships are efficiently expressed. He explains that kind of phrasal organization independently in terms of computational optimality. Specifically, such phrasal formats minimize the "search space" for c-command computations. The suggestion is that this optimal organization plausibly "comes for free" from some analogue of least action in the cognitive domain. As such, X-bar theory isn't part of our genetic endowment, nor does it result from exposure to input. Instead it is a consequence of general organizational principles that phenotypically trump genotypes in such a wide variety of domains as the organization of tiger stripes, the positioning of leafs on a stem, etc. (Douady and Couder 1992; Uriagereka 1998, among others). The discovery that such a fundamental part of constituent structure as X-bar theoretic relations may, in fact, be due to something purely non-linguistic is part of a general trend in minimalist thinking these days; it is also found in the work discussed in the next section.

12.4 Decomposing Merge: Boeckx (2008), Hornstein and Nuñes (2008), and Hornstein (2009)

Next, we consider the work of Hornstein (2009), Hornstein and Nuñes (2008) (henceforth H&N), and Boeckx (2008), all of whom attempt to derive parts of the Merge operation from non-language-specific computational operations. In particular, all these works argue that the Merge operation can be composed into two parts: an operation available to general cognition called COMBINE by Boeckx and CONCATENATE[6] by H&N and Hornstein (2009), and a separate language-specific operation which imposes a label on the structure (accomplished by the operation LABEL for H&N and Hornstein (2009), and the Probe-Label Correspondence Axiom[7] (PLCA) in Boeckx).

---

[6] H&N's use of the term "concatenate" is confusing. In Chapter 2, we argued that syntactic structure is not simply concatenation. H&N, however, use the term in a slightly more sophisticated way. Under their conception, the output of concatenation results in an atomic unit, essentially constituents (although that notion also requires labeling) which themselves can be concatenated with other elements.

[7] Definition of the PLCA from Boeckx (2008: 96): "The label of $\{\alpha, \beta\}$ is which ever of α or β probes the other. Where the probe = lexical item whose uF [AC: uninterpretable feature] gets valued."

One important argument in favor of this disassociation of the two parts comes from adjunction structures. H&N claim that adjuncts, unless stressed or moved, are not labeled—only concatenated. They essentially "dangle off" the constituent structure (cf. the discussions of three-dimensional structures in Chapter 10). To be precise, the combination of concatenate and label operations applies in the context of head–complement structures resulting in labeled sets such as: [$_V$ ate$^\wedge$apples]. If a structure has an adverb adjoined to it we get [$_V$ ate$^\wedge$apples]$^\wedge$quickly. This cleverly captures the intuition—discussed at length in Chapters 8 and 10—that adjuncts are somehow "outside" the main body of the sentence. This explains why adjuncts, but not complements, can be stranded with movement or ellipsis, and don't participate in a variety of c-command-sensitive phenomena (see chapter 8 for further discussion).[8]

Hornstein (2009) takes us down other paths which lie well outside the scope of this book, but I will mention one very briefly as an important motivation for decomposing Merge. Building on recent work that suggests that language is a relatively recent and very rapid innovation in modern humans (see Hinzen 2006), he observes that the genetic shift between linguistic and non-linguistic hominids probably was not the effect of Darwinian selection over time. Instead, following Hauser, Chomsky, and Fitch (2002), he suggests that it was a rapid and simple mutation. This mutation resulted in the ability to turn symmetric concatenated objects into the asymmetric labeled objects we now identify as syntactic structures. Dividing the operation into two parts allows a simple solution to why human language is distinct from animal communication systems and general cognition, again in line with the recent trend in minimalist thinking that I observed above in the discussion of Medeiros (2008).

Boeckx (2008) also divides the Merge operation up into two parts, like H&N and Hornstein (2009). For H&N, the labeling is triggered by

---

[8] Following Epstein's (1999) intuition that c-command follows from the Merge operation, but adding the additional stipulation that Merge is always an asymmetric process (see also Di Sciullo and Isac 2008), H&N suggest that c-command emerges precisely in situations where the Merge (or Move) operation has applied. Hornstein (2009) extends a movement approach to binding and control: since movement is a special kind of merger, it follows that antecedents will always c-command their bindees/controllees. Hornstein also addresses two other areas where c-command is thought to play a role: Linearization falls out from the asymmetric nature of Hornstein's Merge operation (although this amounts to a retreat to the notion of word-order parameters). Minimality falls out from a particular vision of "paths" (i.e. the set of nodes that dominate the trace of the movement). Minimality is calculated by comparing the membership of these path-sets.

selection. Boeckx broadens this so that labeling applies when an element checks an uninterpretable feature[9] (i.e. a purely grammatical rather than semantically interpretable feature). When this happens, the element bearing the uninterpretable feature (α) (the locus in Collins 2002) is the label, and the set created is an ordered set with the head as the first member and the checker (β) as the second: $<\alpha, \beta>$. This notation is of course identical to that of Langendoen (2003) discussed in Chapter 8. As discussed in Chapter 9 and in section 12.5 below, these ordered pairings actually give rise to something more like a dependency grammar than a phrase structure grammar. With respect to adjuncts, Boeckx—like H&N and Hornstein (2009)—claims these are concatenates, but are unordered (unlabeled).[10]

The reason for broadening the range of triggers for labeling to include not only selectional relations but all uninterpretable features is Boeckx's radical claim that merger for movement (Chomsky's (2004b) "internal merge") is really of a kind with more traditional Merge, in that it establishes a relationship between some functional/uninterpretable element and some element that checks that grammatical feature. As such, in cases where internal Merge applies, the moved element is (re)merged into a specifier position, and the triggering head labels the new constituent (i.e. projects to the phrasal level). For example, if a wh-word is internally merged to check some feature with a C, then the C projects/labels the constituent. Under this conception, "movement chains" amount to the same thing as constituent structures (i.e. in the sentence "what did you eat" we have both a "VP" constituent $<eat, what>$, and a chained constituent $<C, what>$). This results in a multidomination structure (see Chapter 10). A word like "what" is simultaneously ordered with and paired to V and C. The payout for this is that we can reduce locality conditions on chains to

---

[9] For a third alternative determinant for the labeling operation, see Di Sciullo and Isac (2008) (henceforth D&I). They propose that the labels are uniquely determined by an inclusion relation: where the label's features must properly include those of the non-label. The problem that D&I attempt to address is the issue of how the very simple Merge operation ensures that, for example, heads that select for both complements and specifiers merge with these elements in the correct order (first complements, then specifiers). As in all such proposals, the devil is in the details. D&I make a distinction between categorial features (N, V, etc.) and "operator features" such as [+wh]. The later govern internal Merge (movement). External Merge ignores the operator features for the purpose of determining featural inclusion.

[10] H&N's notation [v eat^apples] is roughly equivalent to Boeckx's $<eat, apples>$, and H&N's eat^quickly would be equivalent to Boeckx's {eat, quickly}.

nothing more than the search space restrictions that Medeiros (2008) suggests, i.e. X-bar theory. Chains are allowed to have a base position (X°), an intermediate stop (X'), and a maximal projection (XP) (where X°, X', and XP are positions in the chain rather than phrasal projections). Boeckx attempts a theory of locality restrictions based on this intuition, in order to explain a variety of island effects cross-linguistically.

12.5 Minimalist Dependency Grammar

The take-home lesson from H&N, Hornstein (2009), and Boeckx (2008) is that the Merge operation might be better viewed as a combination of a very general cognitive operation that allows us to combine things (combine or concatenate) with a specific operation that allows us to identify a more prominent member of the pairing, which acts as the head or label for the constituent. This is nearly identical in conception to the view of dependency grammars, as discussed in Chapter 9 (section 9.3)—an intuition first noted by Brody (1998, 2000) and explored in some detail by Collins and Ura (2004).[11] I hope you will allow me to close this revised survey of constituent structure with a personal indulgence. In some recent, as yet unpublished work,[12] I have been pursuing a version of this notion of dependencies but based within a Minimalist theory of feature checking. The empirical motivation behind this move is the phenomenon of light pronoun post-posing in Scottish Gaelic, which seems to be largely determined by prosodic concerns (Adger 2007). The rule, surprisingly, pays attention to some aspects of constituency (for example, it never inserts the pronoun in the middle of an adjunct), but it ignores organizational constituency among complements and adjuncts of the head it is an argument of. This has two consequences: first, the phonological nature of the rule casts some doubt on the LCA as the sole determinant of linearization (cf. the discussion of López (2009) in section 12.2 above). Second, it suggests that constituency relationships need to be looser than those imposed by traditional tree and set notations, but not too loose. Following Collins and Ura (2004), I suggest that feature-checking relationships establish simple dependencies between heads. My

---

[11] See also Jayaseelan's (2008) implementation of Starke's (2004) "Specifierless Syntax."

[12] Presented at the Belgian Conference on Generative Linguistics 3 and currently available in Powerpoint and handout form on my personal website.

innovation is that these dependencies are sorted into relations based on which feature is checked. So there is a set of dependencies between heads and their complements (called INTERNAL), a set of dependencies between heads and their specifiers (called EXTERNAL), and a set of relationships between modifiers (adjuncts) and the head they modify (called MOD).[13] These relations are determined explicitly by the features that are involved in a pairwise checking relationship between words. So complement selection is accomplished by saturating an INTERNAL feature on a head, etc. Constituent structure, as in traditional dependency grammars, is an epiphenomenon that emerges from subordinate dependencies. This is easiest to see in an example. Let's start with the sentence *The cat kissed a puppy.* The representation of this sentence in Minimalist dependency grammar is the set of dependencies expressed by each feature (relation):

(3) $S_1 = \{R_1, R_2\}$

   R1: INTERNAL $= \{$ <THE, CAT>, <A, PUPPY>, <KISS, A> $\}$

   R2: EXTERNAL $= \{$ <KISS, THE> $\}$

Note that there is no BPS-like structure that directly represents constituency (i.e. nothing like ≪kiss, <a, puppy≫, <the, cat≫ or the BPS {kiss, {{the,{the, cat}}, {kiss, {kiss, {a {a, puppy}}}}}}); instead we have a much looser set of relationships, which allows operations like Scottish Gaelic pronoun post-posing to apply. It also allows for a very straightforward mechanism for representing multidomination: such situations arise precisely when a word is the second member of more than one dependency pairing. Ordering in this system is stipulated through a set of rules stated over these dependency relations including rules tied to specific lexical items like Scottish Gaelic light pronouns, which may or may not include some weakened version of the LCA like that proposed by López (2009).

12.6 Postscript

The too-short sketch of Minimalist dependency grammar given in section 12.5 above is no doubt very unsatisfying and leaves more questions asked than answered. However, I think it serves a purpose beyond sketching some ideas germin in the head of the current author.

---

[13] Note that by doing this, however, I fail to capitalize on the insights of Medeiros and stipulate X-bar theory instead.

I think it reveals some of the important ways in which fundamental questions about the most basic relationships in syntactic theory are still very open and poorly understood. For example, it is still unclear what precisely constituency tests reveal. Are constituents real? Are multi-dominant and three-dimensional structures valid? How are structural relationships defined? What is the role of headedness? Are syntactic representations proofs, derivations, real linguistic objects, or epiphenomena? What information is coded into these representations and what information flows from lexical entries? What is the nature of the principles that assemble, generate, or license syntactic constituent structures? These are very basic and fundamental questions for a theory of syntax. The discipline has made progress on all of these fronts, as seen by the work that is surveyed in this book, However, I think we're embarrassingly far away from understanding or coming to a consensus about the details of constituent structure.

If you are a student, I hope you take away from this book a snapshot of what the important questions and issues are in constituent-structure theorizing and have developed a sense of the ways in which scholars have approached these questions. If you are a more established scholar, I hope you find that I have cast some light on the dark recesses of these issues, leading ideas, and relationships among approaches to constituent structure. It's my sincere hope that this work will facilitate more cross-fertilization of ideas about constituency between people working in different frameworks, even if the current work doesn't take a specific stand on the nature of its central subjects.

References

Abeillé, Anne and Owen Rambow (2000). "Tree Adjoining Grammar: An Overview." In Anne Abeillé and Owen Rambow (eds.) *Tree Adjoining Grammars: Formalisms, Linguistic Analysis and Processing.* Stanford: CSLI Publications, 1–68.

Abney, Steve (1987). *The English Noun Phrase in its Sentential Aspect.* Ph.D. dissertation, MIT.

Aczel, Peter (1988). *Non-Well-Founded Sets.* Stanford: CSLI Publications.

Adger, David (1996). "Aspect, Agreement and Measure Phrases in Scottish Gaelic." In Robert Borsley and Ian Roberts (eds.) *The Syntax of the Celtic Languages.* Cambridge: Cambridge University Press, 200–22.

—— (2007). "Pronouns Post-pose at PF." *Linguistic Inquiry* 38: 343–9.

—— and Gillian Ramchand (2003). "Predication and Equation." *Linguistic Inquiry* 34: 325–59.

Aissen, Judith (2000). "Prosodic Conditions on Anaphora and Clitics in Jakaltek." In Andrew Carnie and Eithne Guilfoyle (eds.) *The Syntax of Verb Initial Languages.* Oxford: Oxford University Press, 185–200.

Ajdukiewicz, Kazimierz (1935). "Die Syntaktische Konnexitat." *Studia Philosophica* 1: 1–27.

Alexiadou, Artemis (1997). *Adverb Placement: A Case Study in Antisymmetric Syntax.* Amsterdam: John Benjamins.

Anderson, Stephen (1984). "Kwakwala Syntax and the Government-Binding Theory." In E.-D. Cook and Donna Gerdts (eds.) *The Syntax of Native American Indian Languages.* [Syntax and Semantics, 16]. New York: Academic Press, 21–75.

—— and Sandra Chung (1977). "On Grammatical Relations and Clause Structure in Verb Initial Languages." In P. Cole and J. Saddock (eds.) *Grammatical Relations* [Syntax and Semantics, 8]. New York: Academic Press, 1–25.

Aoun, Joseph and Dominique Sportiche (1983). "On the Formal Theory of Government." *Linguistic Review* 2: 211–36.

Awbery, G. M. (1976). *The Syntax of Welsh: A Transformational Study of the Passive.* Cambridge: Cambridge University Press.

Bach, Emmon (1979). "Control in Montague Grammar." *Linguistic Inquiry* 10: 515–31.

Backofen, Rolf, James Rogers, and K. Vijay-Shanker (1995). "A First Order Axiomatization of the Theory of Finite Trees." *Journal of Logic, Language and Information* 4: 5–39.

Bailyn, Robert (2003). "Does Russian Scrambling Exist?" In Simin Karimi (ed.) *Word Order and Scrambling.* Oxford: Blackwell, 156–76.

Baker, Mark (2001a). "Phrase Structure as a Representation of 'Primitive' Grammatical Relations." In William Davies and Stan Dubinsky (eds.) *Objects and Other Subjects: Grammatical Functions, Functional Categories and Configurationality*. Dordrecht: Kluwer, 21–51.

—— (2001b). "The Nature of Non-configurationality." In Mark Baltin and Chris Collins (eds.) *Handbook of Syntax*. Oxford: Blackwell, 407–38.

—— (2003). *Lexical Categories: Verbs, Nouns and Adjectives*. Cambridge: Cambridge University Press.

Baltin, Mark (1980). "On the notion 'Quantifier Phrase'." *Linguistic Inquiry* 11: 247–9.

—— (1987). "Degree Complements." In G. Huck and A. Ojeda (eds.) *Discontinuous Constituency*. San Diego: Academic Press, 11–26.

—— (1989). "Heads and Projections." In Mark Baltin and Anthony Kroch (eds.) *Alternative Conceptions of Phrase Structure*. Chicago: University of Chicago Press, 1–16.

—— (2006). "The Non-Unity of VP Preposing." *Language* 82: 734–66.

—— and Anthony Kroch (1989). *Alternative Conceptions of Phrase Structure*. Chicago: University of Chicago Press.

Bar-Hillel, Yehoshua (1964). *Language and Information: Selected Essays on their Theory Theory and Application*. Reading, MA: Addison Wesley Publishing Company.

Barker, Chris and Geoffrey Pullum (1990). "A Theory of Command Relations." *Linguistics and Philosophy* 13: 1–34.

Barss, Andrew (2002). *Anaphora: A Reference Guide*. Oxford: Blackwell.

—— and Howard Lasnik (1986). "A Note on Anaphora and Double Objects." *Linguistic Inquiry* 17: 347–54.

Barton, Ellen (1991). "Non-sentential Constituents and Theories of Phrase Structure." In Katherine Leffel and Denis Bouchard (eds.) *Views on Phrase Structure*. Dordrecht: Kluwer, 193–214.

Beghelli, Filippo (1995). *The Phase Structure of Quantifier Scope*. Ph.D. dissertation, UCLA.

—— and Timothy Stowell (1997). "Distributivity and Negation." In A. Szabolcsi (ed.) *Ways of Scope Taking*. Dordrecht: Kluwer, 71–107.

Belletti, Adriana (2001). "Agreement Projections." In Chris Collins and Mark Baltin (eds.) *Handbook of Contemporary Syntactic Theory*. Oxford: Blackwell, 483–510.

—— (2004). "Aspects of the Low IP Area." In Luigi Rizzi (ed.) *The Structure of CP and IP: The Cartography of Syntactic Structures*, ii. Oxford: Oxford University Press, 16–51.

Benincà, Paola and Cecilia Polleto (2004). "Topic, Focus and V2: Defining the CP Sublayers." In Luigi Rizzi (ed.) *The Structure of CP and IP: The Cartography of Syntactic Structures*, ii. Oxford: Oxford University Press, 52–75.

Bennett, Paul (1995). *A Course in Generalized Phrase Structure Grammar*. London: UCL Press.

Berman, Ann (1974). "On the VSO hypothesis." *Linguistic Inquiry* 5: 1–38.

Bernstein, Judy (2001). "The DP Hypothesis: Identifying Clausal Properties in the Nominal Domain." In Chris Collins and Mark Baltin (eds.) *Handbook of Contemporary Syntactic Theory*. Oxford: Blackwell, 536–61.

Blackburn, Patrick, Claire Gardent, and Wilfired Meyer-Viol (1993). "Talking About Trees." In *Proceedings of the 6th conference of the European Chapter of the Association for Computational Linguistics*, 21–29.

Blevins, James (1990). *Syntactic Complexity: Evidence for discontinuity and Multidomination*. Ph.D. dissertation, University of Massachusetts, Amherst.

Bloomfield, Leonard (1933). *Language*. New York: Henry Holt (republished in 1984 by University of Chicago Press).

Bobaljik, Jonathan David (1994). "What Does Adjacency Do?" *MIT Working Papers in Linguistics* 22: 1–32.

—— and Andrew Carnie (1996). "A Minimalist Approach to Some Problems of Irish Word Order." In Ian Roberts and Robert Borsley (eds.) *The Syntax of the Celtic Languages*. Cambridge: Cambridge University Press, 223–40.

—— and Dianne Jonas (1996). "Subject Positions and the Roles of TP." *Linguistic Inquiry* 27(2): 195–236.

Boeckx, Cedric (2008). *Bare Syntax*. Oxford: Oxford University Press.

Borsley, Robert (1980). "In Defense of Single Mothers." *Journal of Linguistics* 16: 95–101.

—— (1989). "An HPSG Approach to Welsh." *Journal of Linguistics* 25: 333–54.

—— (1993). "On So-called 'Verb Nouns' in Welsh." *Journal of Celtic Linguistics* 2: 35–64.

—— (1996). *Modern Phrase Structure Grammar*. Oxford: Blackwell.

—— (1997). "On a Nominal Analysis of Welsh Verb-Nouns." In Anders Ahlqvist and Vera Capkova (eds.) *Dán do Oide: Essays in memory of Conn R. Ó Cleirigh*. Dublin: Institiúid Teangeolaíochta Éirinn, 39–47.

—— and Jaklin Kornfilt (2000). "Mixed Extended Projections." In R. Borsley (ed.) *The Nature and Function of Syntactic categories* [Syntax and Semantics, 32]. New York: Academic Press, 101–32.

Bošković, Željko and Howard Lasnik (1999). "How Strict is the Cycle?" *Linguistic Inquiry* 30: 691–703.

Bouchard, Denis (1995). *The Semantics of Syntax: A Minimalist Approach to Grammar*. Chicago. University of Chicago Press.

Bowers, John (1993). "The Syntax of Predication." *Linguistic Inquiry* 24(4): 591–656.

Brame, Martin (1982). "The Head-Selector Theory of Lexical Specifications and the Nonexistence of Coarse Categories." *Linguistic Analysis* 10: 321–5.

Branigan, Phil (1992). *Subjects and Complementizers*. Ph.D. dissertation, MIT.

Bresnan, Joan (1972). *The Theory of Complementation in English Syntax*. Ph.D. dissertation, MIT.

—— (1976). "On the Form and Functioning of Transformations." *Linguistic Inquiry* 7: 3–40.

Bresnan, Joan (1982). "The Passive in Lexical Theory." In Joan Bresnan (ed.) *The Representation of Grammatical Relations*. Cambridge MA: MIT Press.

—— (2001). *Lexical Functional Syntax*. Oxford: Blackwell.

—— Ronald Kaplan, Stanley Peters, and Annie Zaenen (1982). "Cross-Serial Dependencies in Dutch." *Linguistic Inquiry* 13: 513–35.

Brody, Michael (1998). "Projection and Phrase Structure." *Linguistic Inquiry* 29: 367–98.

—— (2000). "Mirror Theory: Syntactic Representation in Perfect Syntax." *Linguistic Inquiry* 31: 29–56.

Bunt, Harry (1996a). "Discontinuous Constituency: Introduction." In H. Bunt and A. van Horck (eds.) *Discontinuous Constituency*. Berlin: Mouton de Gruyter, 1–10.

—— (1996b). "Formal Tools for Describing and Processing Discontinuous Constituent Structure." In H. Bunt and A. van Horck (eds.) *Discontinuous Constituency*. Berlin: Mouton de Gruyter, 63–83.

Bury, Dirk (2003). *Phrase Structure and Derived Heads*. Ph.D. dissertation, University College London.

—— (2005). "Preverbal Particles in Verb-Initial Languages." In Andrew Carnie, Heidi Harley, and Sheila Dooley (eds.) *Verb First*. Amsterdam: John Benjamins, 135–54.

Butler, Jonny (2004). *Phase Structure, Phrase Structure and Quantification*. Ph. D. dissertation, University of York.

Cardinaletti, Anna (2004). "Toward a Cartography of Subject Positions." *The Structure of CP and IP: The Cartography of Syntactic Structures*, ii. Oxford: Oxford University Press, 115–65.

Carnap, Rudolf (1952). "Meaning Postulates." *Philosophical Studies* 3: 65–73.

Carnie, Andrew (1995). *Head Movement and Non-Verbal Predication*. Ph.D. dissertation, MIT.

—— (1997). "Two Types of Non-Verbal Predication in Modern Irish." *Canadian Journal of Linguistics* 42(1–2): 57–74.

—— (2000). "On the Notions XP and X⁰." *Syntax* 3(2): 59–106.

—— (2005). "A Phase-Geometric Approach to Multiple Marking Systems." Martha McGinnis and Norvin Richards (eds.) *Perspectives on Phases. MIT Working Papers in Linguistics* 49: 87–102.

—— (2006a). "Celtic Mixed Categories: A Phase-bounded Approach." Syracuse/Cornell Workshop on the Internal Syntax of Nominalized Clauses, 25 Mar. 2006.

—— (2006b). "Flat Structure, Categorial Uncertainty and Non-Verbal Predication in Irish." *Journal of Celtic Linguistics* 9: 13–31.

—— (2006c). *Syntax: A Generative Introduction*, (2nd edn). Oxford: Blackwell.

—— and Eithne Guilfoyle (eds.) (2000). *The Syntax of Verb Initial Languages*. Oxford: Oxford University Press.

—— and Heidi Harley (1997). "Distinguishing the EPP and Nominative case." *Penn Working Papers in Linguistics* 4(3): 71–86.

—— —— (2005). "Existential Impersonals." *Studia Linguistica* 59: 46–65.

—— —— and Elizabeth Pyatt (2000). "VSO Order as Raising to out of IP." In A. Carnie and E. Guilfoyle (ed.) *The Syntax of Verb Initial Languages.* Oxford: Oxford University Press, 39–60.

—— —— and Sheila Dooley (2005). *Verb First.* Amsterdam: John Benjamins.

—— and David Medeiros (2005). "Tree maximization and the Extended Projection Principle." *Coyote Working Papers in Linguistics* 14: 51–5.

—— Elizabeth Pyatt, and Heidi Harley (1994). "The Resurrection: Raising to Comp, Evidence from Old Irish." *Studies in the Linguistic Sciences* 24: 85–100.

Chametzky, Robert (1994). "Chomsky Adjunction." *Lingua* 93: 245–64.

—— (1995). "Dominance, Precedence and Parameterization." *Lingua* 96: 163–78.

—— (1996). *A Theory of Phrase Markers and the Extended Base.* Albany: SUNY Press.

—— (2000). *Phrase Structure: From GB to Minimalism.* Oxford: Blackwell.

Chen-Main, Joan (2006). *The Generation and Linearization of Multi-Dominance Structures.* Ph.D. dissertation, Johns Hopkins University.

Choe, Hyon Sook (1987). "An SVO Analysis of VSO Languages and Parameterization: A Study of Berber." In Mohammed Guerssel and Kenneth L. Hale (eds.) *Studies in Berber Syntax. Lexicon Project Working Paper* 14: 121–58.

Chomsky, Noam (1957). *Syntactic Structures.* The Hague: Mouton.

—— (1963). "Formal Properties of Grammars." In R. Duncan Luce and E. Galanter (eds.) *Handbook in Mathematical Psychology,* ii. New York: Wiley, 323–418.

—— (1965). *Aspects of the Theory of Syntax.* Cambridge, MA: MIT Press.

—— (1970). "Remarks on Nominalization." In R. Jacobs and P. Rosenbaum (eds.) *Readings in English Transformational Grammar.* Waltham: Ginn, 184–221.

—— (1973). "Conditions on Transformations." In Stephen R. Anderson and Paul Kiparsky (eds.) *A Festschrift for Morris Halle.* New York: Holt, Rinehart & Winston, 232–86.

—— (1975). *The Logical Structure of Linguistic Theory.* New York: Plenum.

—— (1981). *Lectures on Government and Binding.* Dordrecht: Foris.

—— (1986a). *Barriers.* Cambridge, MA: MIT Press.

—— (1986b). *Knowledge of Language: Its Nature, Origins and Use.* New York: Praeger.

—— (1991). "Some Notes on Economy of Derivation and Representation." In R. Friedin (ed.) *Principles and Parameters in Comparative Grammar.* Cambridge, MA: MIT Press, 417–54.

—— (1993). "A Minimalist Program for Linguistic Theory." In Kenneth Hale and Samuel J. Keyser (eds.) *The View From Building 20.* Cambridge, MA: MIT Press, 1–49.

Chomsky, Noam (1995a). *The Minimalist Program.* Cambridge, MA: MIT Press.

—— (1995b). "Bare Phrase Structure." In Gert Webelhuth (ed.) *The Principles and Parameters Approach to Syntactic Theory: A Synopsis.* Oxford: Blackwell, 385–439.

—— (2000). "Minimalist Inquiries: The Framework." In Roger Martin, David Michael, and Juan Uriagereka (eds.) *Step by Step: In Honor of Howard Lasnik.* Cambridge, MA: MIT Press, 89–155.

—— (2001). "Derivation by Phase." In *Ken Hale: A Life in Language.* Cambridge, MA: MIT Press, 1–52.

—— (2004a). "Beyond Explanatory Adequacy." In Adriana Belletii (ed.) *Structure and Beyond: The Cartography of Syntactic Structures,* iii. Oxford: Oxford University Press, 104–31.

—— (2004b). "On Phases." MS, MIT.

—— (2005). "Three Factors in Language Design." *Linguistic Inquiry* 36: 1–22.

—— and Howard Lasnik (1977). "Filters and Control." *Linguistic Inquiry* 8: 425–504.

Chung, Sandra (1983). "The ECP and Government in Chamorro." *Natural Language and Linguistic Theory* 1: 209–44.

—— (1990). "VPs and Verb Movement in Chamorro." *Natural Language and Linguistic Theory* 8: 559–619.

—— and James McCloskey (1987). "Government, Barriers and Small Clauses in Modern Irish." *Linguistic Inquiry* 18: 173–237.

Cinque, Guiglemo (1999). *Adverbs and Functional Heads: A Crosslinguistic Perspective.* Oxford: Oxford University Press.

Citko, Barbara (2005). "On the Nature of Merge: External Merge, Internal Merge and Parallel Merge. *Linguistic Inquiry* 36: 476–96.

Clack, Susan (1994). "A Consideration of V2 in Relation to Middle Welsh." In Ian Roberts (ed.) *Research Papers in Welsh Syntax. Bangor Research Papers in Linguistics* 5: 38–77.

Clements, G. N. (1985). "The Geometry of Phonological Features." *Phonology Yearbook* 2: 225–52.

Cobb, Carolina (2006). *The Syntax of Adverbs: An LFG Approach.* M.Phil. thesis, Oxford University.

Collins, Chris (1997). *Local Economy.* Cambridge, MA: MIT Press.

—— (2002). "Eliminating Labels." In Samuel Epstein and Daniel Seeley (eds.) *Derivation and Explanation in the Minimalist Program.* Oxford: Blackwell, 2–64.

—— and Hiroyuki Ura (2004). "Eliminating Phrase Structure." MS, Cornell University and Kwansei Gaikuin University.

Cowper, Elizabeth (1992). *A Concise Introduction to Syntactic Theory.* Chicago: Chicago University Press.

Craig, Colette (1977). *The Structure of Jacaltec.* Austin: University of Texas Press.

Croft, William (1996). "What's a Head." In Johan Rooryk and Laurie Zaring (eds.) *Phrase Structure and the Lexicon*. Dordrecht: Kluwer, 35–75.

—— (1999). "What (Some) Functionalists Can Learn from (Some) Formalists." In Michael Darnell, Edith Moravcsik, Frederick Newmeyer, Michael Noonan, and Kathleen Wheatley (eds.) *Functionalism and Formalism in Linguistics*. Amsterdam: John Benjamins, 85–108.

—— (2001). *Radical Construction Grammar: Syntactic Theory in Typological Perspective*. Oxford: Oxford University Press.

Culicover, Peter (1991). "Topicalization Inversion and Complementizers in English." MS, The Ohio State University.

—— and Ray Jackendoff (2005). *Simpler Syntax*. Oxford: Oxford University Press.

Curry, Haskell (1961). "Some Logical Aspects of Grammatical Structure." In Roman Jakobson (ed.) *Structure of Language and its Mathematical Aspects* [Symposia on Applied Mathematics, 12]. Providence, RI: American Mathematical Society, 56–68.

Dayal, Veneeta (1993). "Binding Facts in Hindi and the Scrambling Phenomenon." In Miriam Butt, Tracy Holloway King, and Gillian Ramchand (eds.) *Theoretical Perspectives on Word Order in South Asian Languages*. Stanford: CSLI, 237–61.

de Saussure, Ferdinand (1966). *Course in General Linguistics*. New York: McGraw Hill.

de Vries, Mark (2003). "Three-Dimensional Grammar." In L. Cornips and P. Fikkert (eds.) *Linguistics in the Netherlands* 20. Amsterdam: John Benjamins: 201–13.

—— (2004). "Parataxis: The Third Dimension in Syntactical Space." MS, Utrecht.

—— (2005). "Coordination and Syntactic Hierarchy." *Studia Linguistica* 59: 83–105.

den Besten, Hans (1981). "On the Interaction of Root Transformations and Lexical Deletive Rules." *Groninger Arbeiten zur Germanistischen Linguistik* 20: 1–78.

Déprez, Viviane (1994). "Parameters of Object Movement." In N. Corver and Henk van Riemsdijk (eds.) *Studies on Scrambling: Movement and Non-Movement Approaches to Free Word-Order Phenomena*. Berlin: Mouton de Gruyter, 101–52.

—— and Kenneth Hale (1986). "Resumptive Pronouns in Irish." *Proceedings of the Harvard Celtic Colloquium* 5: 38–48.

Di Sciullo, Anna Maria and Daniela Isac (2008). "The Asymmetry of Merge." *Biolinguistics* 2: 260–90.

Diesing, Molly (1992). *Indefinites*. Cambridge, MA: MIT Press.

—— and Eloise Jelinek (1995). "Distributing Arguments." *Natural Language Semantics* 3: 123–76.

Dik, Simon (1989). *The Theory of Functional Grammar.* Part I: *The Structure of the Clause.* Dordrecht: Foris.

Dixon, R. M. W. (1994). *Ergativity.* Cambridge: Cambridge University Press.

Doherty, Cathal (1992). "Clausal Structure and the Modern Irish Copula." *Syntax at Santa Cruz* 1: 65–91.

—— (1996). "Clausal Structure and the Modern Irish Copula." *Natural Language and Linguistic Theory* 14: 1–46.

—— (1997). "Predicate Initial Constructions in Irish." In *Proceedings of West Coast Conference on Formal Linguistics* 15: 81–95. Stanford: CSLI.

Dooley, Sheila Collberg (1990). "An Expanded INFL Syntax for Modern Irish." *Lund University Working Papers* 36: 1–17.

Douady, S. and Y. Couder. (1992). "Phyllotaxis as a Physical Self-organized Growth Process." *Physical Review Letters* 68: 2098–101.

Dowty, David (1982). "Grammatical Relations and Montague Grammar." In Pauline Jacobson and Geoffrey Pullum (eds.) *The Nature of Syntactic Representations.* Dordrecht: Reidel, 79–130.

—— (1989). "Notes on Categorial Grammar and X′ Syntax: Some Fundamental Differences and Similarities." In J. Powers, U. Subramania, and A. Zwicky (eds.) *Papers in Morphology and Syntax.* The Ohio State University.

—— (1996). "Towards a Minimalist Theory of Syntactic Structure." In H. Bunt and A. van Hock (eds.) *Discontinuous Constituency.* Berlin: Mouton de Gruyter, 11–62.

Duffield, Nigel (1995). *Particles and Projections in Irish Syntax.* Dordrecht: Kluwer.

—— (1996). "On Structural Invariance and Lexical Diversity." In Robert Borsley and Ian Roberts (eds.) *The Syntax of the Celtic Languages: A Comparative Perspective.* Cambridge: Cambridge University Press, 214–40.

Emonds, Joseph (1973). "Constraints on Phrase Structure Configurations." *Stanford Occasional Papers in Linguistics* 115–36.

—— (1976). *A Transformational Approach to English Syntax.* San Diego: Academic Press.

—— (1978). "The Verbal Complex V′-V in French." *Linguistic Inquiry* 9: 151–75.

—— (1980). "Word Order and Generative Grammar." *Journal of Linguistic Research* 1: 33–54.

—— (1985). *A Unified Theory of Syntactic Categories.* Dordrecht: Foris.

Enderton, H. B. (1972). *A Mathematical Introduction to Logic.* New York: Academic Press.

Engdahl, Elisabet (1986). *Constituent Questions: The Syntax and Semantics of Questions with Special Reference to Swedish.* Dordrecht: Reidel.

Epstein, Samuel (1999). "Unprincipled Syntax: The Derivation of Syntactic Relations." In Sam Epstien and Norbert Hornstein (eds.) *Working Minimalism.* Cambridge, MA: MIT Press, 317–45.

—— Erich Groat, Ruriko Kawashima, and Hisatsugu Kitahara (1998). *A Derivational Approach to Syntactic Relations.* Oxford: Oxford University Press.

Ernst, Thomas (2003). "Semantic Features and the Distribution of Adverbs." In Ewald Lang, Claudia Maienborn, and Catherine Fabricius-Hansen (eds.), *Modifying Adjuncts* [Interface Explorations, 4]. Berlin: Mouton de Gruyter, 307–34.

—— (2004). *The Syntax of Adjuncts*. Cambridge: Cambridge University Press.

Falk, Yehuda (1983). "Constituency, Word Order and Phrase Structure Rules." *Linguistic Analysis* 11: 331–60.

—— (2001). *Lexical Functional Grammar: An Introduction to Parallel Constraint Based Syntax*. Stanford: CSLI.

Faltz, Leonard (1995). "Towards a Typology of Natural Logic." In Eloise Jelinek, Angelika Krazer, and Emmon Bach (eds.) *Quantification in Natural Language*. Dordrecht: Kluwer, 271–320.

Farrell, Patrick (2005). *Grammatical Relations*. Oxford: Oxford University Press.

Fassi-Fehri, Abdelkader (1981). *Complémentation et anaphore en arabe moderne, une approche lexical fonctionelle*. Ph.D dissertation, University de Paris III.

—— (1993). *Issues in the Structure of Arabic Clauses and Words*. Dordrecht: Kluwer.

Fillmore, Charles (1963). "The Position of Embedding Transfromations in a Grammar." *Word* 19: 208–31.

Fodor, Janet Dean and Stephen Crain (1990). "Phrase Structure Parameters." *Linguistics and Philosophy* 13: 619–59.

Foley, William and Robert Van Valin (1984). *Functional Syntax and Universal Grammar*. Cambridge: Cambridge University Press.

Fong, Sandiway and Robert Berwick (1985). "New Approaches to Parsing Conjunctions using Prolog." *Proceedings of the 23rd Annual Meeting of the Association for Computational Linguistics* 118–26.

Frank, Robert (2002). *Phrase Structure Composition and Syntactic Dependencies*. Cambridge, MA: MIT Press.

—— and Fero Kuminiak (2000). "Primitive Asymmetric C-command Derives X-Bar Theory." In M. Hirotani, A. Coetzee, N. Hall, and J.-Y. Kim (eds.) *Proceedings from the Thirtieth Meeting of the North East Linguistic Society (NELS)* 30: 203–17.

—— and K. Vijay-Shankar (2001). "Primitive c-command." *Syntax* 4: 164–204.

—— Paul Hagstrom, and K. Vijay-Shanker (2002). "Roots Constituents and C-command." In Alexis Alexiadou (ed.) *Theoretical Approaches to Universals*. Amsterdam: John Benjamins, 109–37.

Frege, G. (1891). "Function and Concept." In *Collected Papers*, transl. P. Geach. Oxford: Blackwell, 137–56.

—— (1923). "Gedankengefüge." In G. Patzig (ed.) (1976) *Frege, Logische Untersuchungen*. Göttingen, 72–91.

Freidin, Robert (1992). *Foundations of Generative Syntax*. Cambridge, MA: MIT Press.

Frey, Werner and Karin Pittner (1998). "Zur Positionierung der Adverbiale im deutschen Mittelfeld." *Linguistische Berichte* 176: 489–539.

Fukui, Naoki (1995). *The Theory of Projection in Syntax.* Stanford: CSLI (first pub. 1988, Ph.D. dissertation, MIT).

—— (2001). "Phrase Structure." In Mark Baltin and Chris Collins (eds.) *Handbook of Contemporary Syntactic Theory.* Oxford: Blackwell, 374–406.

—— and Margaret Speas (1986). "Specifiers and Projection." In N. Fukui, T. Rapoport, and E. Sagey, (eds.) *Papers in Theoretical Linguistics: MIT Working Papers in Linguistics* 8: 128–72.

—— and Yuji Takano (1998). "Symmetry in Syntax: Merge and Demerge." *Journal of East Asian Linguistics* 7: 27–86.

Gaifman, Haim (1965). "Dependency Systems of Phrase Structure Systems." *Information and Control* 8: 304–7.

Garrett, Merrill (1967). *Syntactic Structures and Judgments of Auditory Events.* Ph.D. dissertation, University of Illinois.

Gärtner, Hans-Martin (1999). "Phrase-Linking Meets Minimalist Syntax." *Proceedings of the West Coast Conference on Formal Linguistics (WCCFL)* 18: 159–69.

—— (2002). *Generalized Transformations and Beyond.* Berlin: Akademie Verlag.

Gazdar, Gerald (1982). "Phrase Structure Grammar." In Pauline Jacobson and Geoffrey K. Pullum (eds.) *The Nature of Syntactic Representation.* Dordrecht: Reidel.

—— and Geoffrey Pullum (1981). "Subcategorization, Constituent Order, and the Notion 'Head'." In Michael Moortgat, Harry van der Hulst, and Teun Hoekstra (eds.) *The Scope of Lexical Rules.* Dordrecht: Foris, 107–23.

—— —— (1982). *Generalized Phrase Structure Grammar: A Theoretical Synopsis.* Bloomington: Indiana University Linguistics Club.

—— Ewan Klein, Geoffrey Pullum, and Ivan Sag (1985). *Generalized Phrase Structure Grammar.* Cambridge, MA: Harvard University Press.

GKPS, *see* Gazdar, Klein, Pullum, and Sag (1985).

Goldberg, Adele (1995). *Constructions: A Construction Grammar Approach to Argument Structure.* University of Chicago Press.

—— (2006). *Constructions at Work: The Nature of Generalization in Language.* Oxford: Oxford University Press.

Goldsmith, John (1976). *Autosegmental Phonology.* Ph.D. dissertation, MIT.

Goodall, Grant (1987). *Parallel Structures in Syntax: Coordination, Causatives and Restructuring.* Cambridge: Cambridge University Press.

Greenberg, Joseph (1966). "Some Universals of Grammar With Particular Reference to the Order of Meaningful Elements." In J. Greenberg (ed.) *Universals of Language.* Cambridge, MA: MIT Press, 73–113.

Grimshaw, Jane (1977). *English Wh-Constructions and the Theory of Grammar.* Ph.D. dissertation, University of Massachusetts, Amherst.

—— (1992). *Argument Structure.* Cambridge, MA: MIT Press.

Grootveld, Marjon (1992). "On the Representation of Coordination." In Reineke Bok-Bennema and Roeland van Hout (eds.) *Linguistics in the Netherlands 1992*. Amsterdam: John Benjamins, 61–73.

Gruber, Jeffrey (1967). "Functions of the Lexicon in Formal Descriptive Grammars." *Technical Memorandum TM-3770/000/00*. Systems Development Corporation. Santa Monica.

Guilfoyle, Eithne (1990). *Functional Categories and Phrase Structure Parameters*. Ph.D. dissertation, McGill University.

—— (1993). "Nonfinite Clause in Modern Irish and Old English." *Proceedings of the Chicago Linguistic Society* 29(1): 199–214.

—— (1994). "VNPs, Finiteness and External Arguments." In M. Gonzalez (ed.) *Papers from the Twenty-Fourth Annual Meeting of the North Eastern Linguistics Society (NELS)* 24: 141–55.

—— (1997). "The Verbal Noun in Irish Non-finite Clauses." In Vera Capková and Anders Ahlqvist (eds.) *Dán do Oide, Essays in Memory of Conn Ó Cléirigh*. Dublin: Institiúid Teangeolaíochta Éireann, 187–200.

—— Henrietta Hung, and Lisa Travis (1992). "Spec of IP and Spec of VP: Two Subjects in Austronesian Languages. *Natural Language and Linguistic Theory* 10: 375–414.

Haegeman, Liliane (1988). Review of Goodall, "Parallel Structures in Syntax". *Lingua* 75, 273–87.

—— (1994). *Introduction to Government and Binding Theory* (2nd edn). Oxford: Blackwell.

—— (2001). "X-bar Theory." In *MIT Encyclopedia of Cognitive Science*. Cambridge, MA: MIT Press, 892–5.

—— and Henk van Riemsdijk (1986). "Verb Projection Raising, Scope and the Typology of Rules Affecting Verbs." *Linguistic Inquiry* 17: 417–66.

Hale, Kenneth L. (1983). "Warlpiri and the Grammar of Non-Configurational Languages." *Natural Language and Linguistic Theory* 1: 5–47.

—— and Samuel J. Keyser (1991). "On the Syntax of Argument Structure." *Lexicon Project Working Paper 34*. Cambridge, MA: MIT Center for Cognitive Science.

Halitsky, David (1975). "Left Branch Ss and NPs in English: A Bar Notation Analysis." *Linguistic Analysis* 1: 279–96.

Hammond, Michael (1988). "On Deriving the Well-formedness Condition." *Linguistic Inquiry* 19: 319–25.

—— (2005). "A Mereological Approach to Autosegmental Well-formedness." MS, University of Arizona.

Harley, Heidi (1995). *Subjects, Events and Licensing*, Ph.D. dissertation, MIT.

—— (2005). "Bare Phrase Structure, Acategorial Roots, One- Replacement and Unaccusativity." *Harvard Working Papers on Linguistics* 11: 59–78.

Harley, Heidi and Rolf Noyer (1998). "Mixed Nominalizations, Short Verb Movement and Object Shift in English." In Pius N. Tamanji (ed.) *Papers from the Twenty-Eighth Annual Meeting of the North Eastern Linguistics Society (NELS)* 28, 143–57.

Harman, Gilbert (1963). "Generative Grammars Without Transformation Rules." Language 39: 597–616.

Harris, Randy Allen (1993). *The Linguistics Wars.* Oxford: Oxford University Press.

Harris, Zellig (1946). "From Morpheme to Utterance." *Language* 22: 151–83.

—— (1951). *Methods in Structural Linguistics.* Chicago: University of Chicago Press.

—— (1957). "Co-Occurrence and Transformations." *Language* 33: 283–340.

Harwood, F. W. (1955). "Axiomatic Syntax: The Construction and Evaluation of a Syntactic Calculus." *Language* 31: 409–13.

Hauser, Mark, Noam Chomsky and Tecumseh Fitch (2002). "The Faculty of Language: What Is It, Who Has It, and How did it Evolve?" *Science* 298: 159–79.

Hays, David (1964). "Dependency Theory: A Formalism and Some Observations." *Language* 40: 511–25.

Heim, Irene and Angelika Kratzer (1997). *Semantics in Generative Grammar.* Oxford: Blackwell.

Hendrick, Randall (1988). *Anaphora in Celtic and Universal Grammar.* Dordrecht: Kluwer.

—— (1990). "Breton Pronominals, Binding and Barriers." In R. Hendrick (ed.) *The Syntax of the Modern Celtic Languages* [Syntax and Semantics, 23.] New York: Academic Press, 121–65.

—— (2000). "Celtic Initials." In A. Carnie and E. Guilfoyle (ed.) *The Syntax of Verb Initial Languages.* Oxford: Oxford University Press, 13–38.

Heny, Frank (1979). Review of Chomsky 1975. *Synthese* 40: 317–59.

Higginbotham, James (1985). "A Note on Phrase Markers." *MIT Working Papers in Linguistics* 6: 87–101 (first pub. as Higginbotham 1982, "A Note on Phrase Markers." *Revue Québecoise de linguistique* 13: 147–66).

Hinton, G. E. (1981). "Implementing Semantic Networks in Parallel Hardware." In G. E. Hinton and J. A. Anderson (eds.) *Parallel Models of Associative Memory.* Hillsdale NJ: Erlbaum, 161–81.

Hinzen, Wolfram (2006). *Minimal Mind Design.* Oxford: Oxford University Press.

Holmberg, Anders and Christer Platzack (1988). "The Role of Agr and Finiteness in some European VO languages." Paper presented at GLOW 1989, Utrecht.

Hopcroft, John, Rajeev Motwani, and Jeffrey Ullman (2001). *Introduction to Automata Theory, Languages and Computation.* Boston: Addison Wesley.

Hornstein, Norbert (1977). "S and X-bar Convention." *Linguistic Analysis* 3: 137–76.

—— (2009). *A Theory of Syntax: Minimal Operations and Universal Grammar*. Cambridge: Cambridge University Press.

—— and Jairo Nuñes (2008). "Adjunction, Labeling and Bare Phrase Structure." *Biolinguistics* 2: 57–86.

Huang, C.-T. James (1982). *Logical Relations in Chinese and the Theory of Grammar*. Ph.D. dissertation, MIT.

Huck, Geoffrey (1985). "Exclusivity and Discontinuity in Phrase Structure Grammar." *Proceedings of the West Coast Conference on Formal Linguistics* 4: 92–3.

—— and John A. Goldsmith (1996). *Ideology and Linguistic Theory: Noam Chomsky and the Deep Structure Debates*. London: Routledge.

—— and Alejandro Ojeda (1987). "Introduction." In G. Huck and A. Ojeda (eds.) *Discontinuous Constituency*. San Diego: Academic Press, 1–9.

Hudson, Richard (1984). *Word Grammar*. Oxford: Basil Blackwell.

—— (1987). "Zwicky on Heads." *Journal of Linguistics* 23: 109–32.

—— (1990). *English Word Grammar*. Oxford: Basil Blackwell.

—— (1996). "Grammar Without Functional Categories." MS, University College London.

—— (2007). *Language Networks: The New Word Grammar*. Oxford: Oxford University Press.

Huybregts, R. A. C. (1984). "The Weak Inadequacy of Context Free Phrase Structure Grammars." In G. de Haan (ed.) *Van Periferie naar Kern*. Dordrecht: Foris.

Iatridou, Sabine (1991). "About Agr(P)." *Linguistic Inquiry* 21: 551.

—— and Anthony Kroch (1992). "The Licensing of CP Recursion and Its Relevance to the Germanic Verb-Second Phenomenon." *Working Papers in Scandinavian Syntax* 50: 1–24.

Jackendoff, Ray (1972). *Semantic Interpretation in Generative Grammar*. Cambridge, MA: MIT Press.

—— (1977). *X-bar Syntax: A Theory of Phrase Structure*. Cambridge, MA: MIT Press.

—— (2002). *Foundations of Language: Brain, Meaning, Grammar, Evolution*. Oxford: Oxford University Press.

Jayaseelan, K. A. (2008). "Bare Phrase Structure and Specifier-less Syntax." *Biolinguistics* 2: 87–106.

Jelinek, Eloise (1984). "Empty Categories, Case and Configurationality." *Natural Language and Linguistic Theory* 2: 39–76.

—— (1993). "Ergative Splits and Argument Type." *MIT Working Papers* 18: 15–42.

—— and Andrew Carnie (2003). "Argument Hierarchies and the Mapping Principle." In A. Carnie, H. Harley, and M. Willie (eds.) *Formal Approaches to Function*. Amsterdam: John Benjamins, 265–96.

Johnson, Kyle (1991). "Object Positions." *Natural Language and Linguistic Theory* 9: 577–636.

—— (2001). "What VP Ellipsis Can Do, What It Can't, But Not Why." In Chris Collins and Mark Baltin (eds.) *Handbook of Contemporary Syntactic Theory*. Oxford: Blackwell, 439–79.

Joshi, Aravind (1985). "How Much Context-Sensitivity is Necessary for Characterizing Structural Descriptions: Tree Adjoining Grammars." In D. Dowty, L. Karttunen, and A. Zwicky (eds.) *Natural Language Processing: Theoretical, Computational and Psychological Perspectives*. Cambridge: Cambridge University Press.

Joshi, Aravind and Yves Schabes (1996). "Tree-adjoining Grammars." In Grzegorz Rosenberg and Arto Salomaa (eds.) *Handbook of Formal Languages*, iii. New York: Springer, 69–123.

—— L. Levy, and M. Takahashi (1975). "Tree Adjunct Grammars." *Journal of Computer and System Science* 10: 136–63.

Kaneko, Yoshiaki (1999). "Toward Eliminating C-command from Linguistic Theory." *Explorations in English Linguistics* 14 (http://www.sal.tohoku.ac.jp/eng/eel1.htm).

Karimi, Simin (2003). "Word Order and Scrambling." Oxford: Blackwell.

Karttunen, Lauri (1989). "Radical Lexicalism." In Mark Baltin and Anthony Kroch (eds.) *Alternative Conceptions of Phrase Structure*. Chicago: University of Chicago Press, 43–65.

Kathol, Andreas (2000). *Linear Syntax*. Oxford: Oxford University Press.

—— and Robert Levine (1993). "Inversion as a Linearization Effect." *Proceedings of the North Eastern Linguistic Society Meeting* 23: 207–1.

Kayne, Richard (1984). "Unambiguous Paths." In Richard Kayne (ed.) *Connectedness and Binary Branching*. Dordrecht: Foris, 129–63. (Originally published in R. May and J. Koster (eds.) 1981, *Levels of Syntactic Representation*. Dordrecht: Foris, 143–83.)

—— (1989). "Notes on English Agreement." *CIEFL Bulletin* 1: 40–67.

—— (1991). "Romance Clitics, Verb Movement and PRO." *Linguistic Inquiry* 22: 647–86.

—— (1994). *The Antisymmetry of Syntax*. Cambridge, MA: MIT Press.

—— (2005). "Some Notes on Comparative Syntax with Special Reference to English and French." In Richard Kayne and Gugliemo Cinque (eds.) *Oxford Handbook of Comparative Syntax*. Oxford: Oxford University Press, 3–69.

Kim, D.-B. (1992). *The Specificity–Non-specificity Distinction and Scrambling Theory*. Ph.D. dissertation, University of Wisconson.

Kitagawa, Yoshi (1986). *Subjects in Japanese and English*. Ph.D. dissertation, University of Massachusetts.

Klima, Edward (1964). "Relatedness Between Grammatical Systems." *Language* 40: 1–20.

Koizumi, Masatoshi (1994). "Object Agreement Phrases and the Split VP Hypothesis." In Jonathan Bobaljik and Colin Phillips (eds.) *Papers on Case and Agreement I. MIT Working Papers in Linguistics* 18: 99–148.

—— (1995). *Phrase Structure in Minimalist Syntax*. Ph.D. dissertation, MIT.

Kolb, Hans-Peter (1999). "Macros for Minimalism? Towards Weak Descriptions of Strong Structures." In Hans-Peter Kolb and Uwe Mönnich (eds.) *The Mathematics of Syntactic Structures: Trees and Their Logics*. Berlin: Mouton de Gruyter, 231–58.

Koopman, Hilda (1984). *The Syntax of Verbs*. Dordrecht: Foris.

—— and Anna Szabolcsi (2000). *Verbal Complexes*. Cambridge, MA: MIT Press.

—— and Dominique Sportiche (1991). "The Position of Subjects." *Lingua* 85: 211–58.

Kornai, Andras and Geoffrey Pullum (1990). "The X-bar Theory of Phrase Structure." *Language* 66: 24–50.

Kracht, Marcus (1993). "Mathematical Aspects of Command Relations." In *Proceedings of the 6th conference of the European Chapter of the Association for Computational Linguistics* 240–9.

Kratzer, Angelika (1995). "Stage-level and Individual-level Predicates." G. Carlson and F. Pelletier (eds.) *The Generic Book*. Chicago: Chicago University Press, 125–75.

Kroch, Anthony and Aravind Joshi (1985). "The Linguistic Relevance of Tree Adjoining Grammar." *University of Pennsylvania Department of Computer and Information Science Technical Report no. MS-CIS-85-16*.

—— —— (1987). "Extraposition in a Tree Adjoining Grammar." In G. Huck and A. Ojeda (eds.) *Discontinuous Constituents* [Syntax and Semantics, 20]. New York: Academic Press, 107–49.

Kroeger, Paul (1993). *Phrase Structure and Grammatical Relations in Tagalog*. Stanford: CSLI Publications.

Kupin, Joseph (1978). "A Motivated Alternative to Phrase Markers." *Linguistic Inquiry* 9: 302–8.

Kural, Murat (2005). "Tree Traversal and Word Order." *Linguistic Inquiry* 36: 367–87.

Laenzlinger, C. (2002). "A Feature Based Theory of Adverb Syntax." *Generative Grammar in Geneva* 3: 67–106.

—— (1996). *Comparative Studies in Word Order Variations: Adverbs, Pronouns, and Clause Structure in Romance and Germanic*. Ph.D. dissertation, University of Geneva.

Laka Mugarza, Miren Itziar (1991). *Negation in Syntax. On the Nature of Functional Categories and Projections*. Ph.D. dissertation, MIT.

Lamb, Sydney (1966). *Outline of Stratificational Grammar*. Washington, DC: Georgetown University Press.

Lambek, Joachim (1958). "The Mathematics of Sentence Structure." *American Mathematical Monthly* 65: 154–70 (repr. in W. Buszkowski, W. Marciszewski, and J. van Benthem (eds.) *Categorial Grammar.* Amsterdam: John Benjamins, 153–72).

Langacker, Ronald (1966). "On Pronominalization and the Chain of Command." In W. Reibel and S. Schane (eds.) *Modern Studies in English.* Englewood Cliffs, NJ; Prentice Hall, 160–86.

—— (1987). *Foundations of Cognitive Grammar,* i: *Theoretical Prerequisites.* Stanford: Stanford University Press.

Langendoen, D. Terence (1975). "Finite State Parsing of Phrase-Structure Languages and the Status of Readjustment Rules in Grammar." *Linguistic Inquiry* 6: 533–4.

Langendoen, D. Terence (2003). "Merge." In Andrew Carnie, Heidi Harley, and MaryAnn Willie (eds.) *Formal Approaches to Function in Grammar.* Amsterdam: John Benjamins, 307–18.

—— and Paul Postal (1984). *The Vastness of Natural Language.* Oxford: Basil Blackwell.

Larson, Richard (1988). "On the Double Object Construction." *Linguistic Inquiry* 19(3): 335–91.

Lasnik, Howard (1976). "Remarks on Coreference." *Linguistic Analysis* 2: 1–22.

—— (1998). "Some Reconstruction Riddles." *University of Pennsylvania Working Papers in Linguistics* 5(1): 83–98.

—— (2000). *Syntactic Structures Revisited.* Cambridge, MA: MIT Press.

—— and Joseph Kupin (1977). "A Restrictive Theory of Transformational Grammar." *Theoretical Linguistics* 4: 173–96.

—— Juan Uriagereka, and Cedric Boeckx (2005). *Course in Minimalist Syntax: Foundations and Prospects.* Oxford: Blackwell.

Lebeaux, David (1988). *Language Acquisition and the Form of the Grammar,* Ph.D. dissertation, University of Massachusetts.

—— (1996). "Determining the Kernel." In Johan Rooryck and Laurie Zaring (eds.) *Phrase Structure and the Lexicon.* Dordrecht: Kluwer Academic, 139–72.

Lee, Felicia (2000). "VP Remnant Movement and VSO in Quiaviní Zapotec." In A. Carnie and E. Guilfoyle (ed.) *The Syntax of Verb Initial Languages.* Oxford: Oxford University Press, 143–62.

Leffel, Katherine and Denis Bouchard (1991). *Views on Phrase Structure.* Dordrecht: Kluwer.

Legate, Julie (1997). *Irish Predication: A Minimalist Analysis.* Master's Thesis, University of Toronto.

Lewis, Harry and Christos Papadimitriou (1981). *Elements of the Theory of Computation.* New York: Prentice Hall.

Lightfoot, David (1979). *Principles of Diachronic Syntax.* Cambridge: Cambridge University Press.

Lockwood, David (1972). *Introduction to Stratificational Linguistics.* New York: Harcourt, Brace, Jovanovich.

Longacre, Robert E. (1960). "String Constituent Analysis." *Language* 36: 63–88.

Longobardi, Giuseppi (1994). "Proper Names and the Theory of N-Movement in Syntax and Logical Form." *Linguistic Inquiry* 25: 609–5.

—— (2001). "The Structure of DPs: Some Principles, Parameters and Problems." In Chris Collins and Mark Baltin (eds.) *Handbook of Contemporary Syntactic Theory.* Oxford: Blackwell.

López, Luis (2009). "Ranking the Linear Correspondence Axiom." *Linguistic Inquiry* 40: 239–76.

McCarthy, John (1979). *Formal Problems in Semitic Phonology and Morphology.* Ph.D. dissertation, MIT.

McCawley, James (1973). "Concerning the Base Component of a Transformational Grammar." In James McCawley (ed.) *Grammar and Meaning.* Taishukan Publishing, 35–58 (first pub. 1968, *Foundations of Language* 4: 248–69).

—— (1970). "English as a VSO Language." *Language* 46: 286–99.

—— (1982). "Parentheticals and discontinuous constituent structure." *Linguistic Inquiry* 13: 91–106.

—— (1987). "Some Additional Evidence for Discontinuity." In G. Huck and A. Ojeda (eds.) *Discontinuous Constituents.* San Diego: Academic Press, 185–200.

—— (1988). *The Syntactic Phenomena of English.* Chicago: University of Chicago Press.

—— (1989). "Individuation in and of Syntactic Structures." In Mark Baltin and Anthony Kroch (eds.) *Alternative Conceptions of Phrase Structure.* Chicago: University of Chicago Press, 117–38.

McCloskey, James (1979). *Transformational Syntax and Model Theoretic Semantics: A Case Study in Modern Irish.* Dordrecht: Reidel.

—— (1980). "Is There Raising in Modern Irish?" *Eriú* 31: 59–99.

—— (1983). "A VP in a VSO Language." In Gerald Gazdar, Geoffrey Pullam, and Ivan Sag (eds.) *Order, Concord and Constituency.* Dordrecht: Foris, 9–55.

—— (1991). "Clause Structure, Ellipsis and Proper Government in Irish." *Lingua* 85: 259–302.

—— (1996a). "On the Scope of Verb Movement in Modern Irish." *Natural Language and Linguistic Theory* 14: 47–104.

—— (1996b). "Subjects and Subject Positions in Modern Irish." In Robert Borsley and Ian Roberts (eds.) *The Syntax of the Celtic Languages.* Cambridge: Cambridge University Press, 241–83.

—— (1997). "Subjecthood and Subject Positions." In Liliane Haegeman (ed.) *Elements of Grammar: Handbook in Generative Grammar.* Dordrecht: Kluwer, 197–236.

McCloskey, James (2005). "A Note on Predicates and Heads in Irish Clausal Syntax." In Andrew Carnie, Heidi Harley, and Sheila Dooley (eds.) *Verb First*. Amsterdam: John Benjamins, 155–74.

McConnell-Ginet, Sally (1982). "Adverbs and Logical form." *Language* 58: 144–84.

MacDonald, Jonathan (2006). *The Syntax of Inner Aspect*. Ph.D. dissertation, State University of New York–Stony Brook.

McGinnis, Martha (2001). "Variation in the Phase Structure of Applicatives." In P. Pica and J. Rooryck (eds.) *Linguistic Variations Yearbook* 1. Amsterdam: John Benjamins, 101–42.

Mahajan, Anoop (1990). *The A/A-bar distinction and Movement Theory*. Ph.D. dissertation, MIT.

Manaster-Ramer, Alexis and Michael Kac (1990). "The Concept of Phrase Structure." *Linguistics and Philosophy* 13: 325–62.

Manzini, Rita and Leonardo Savoia (2004). "Clitics: Cooccurrence and Mutual Exclusion Patterns." *The Structure of CP and IP: The Cartography of Syntactic Structures*, ii. Oxford: Oxford University Press, 211–50.

Marantz, Alec (1984). *On Grammatical Relations*, MIT Press, Cambridge Mass.

Massam, Diane (1994). "Case Without Functional Categories." *Proceedings of the (1994) Canadian Linguistic Association Meeting*, 369–80.

—— (2000). "VSO and VOS: Aspects of Niuean Word Order." In A. Carnie and E. Guilfoyle (ed.) *The Syntax of Verb Initial Languages*. Oxford: Oxford University Press, 97–116.

—— (2005). "Lexical Categories, Lack of Inflection and Predicate-Fronting in Niuean." In Andrew Carnie, Heidi Harley, and Sheila Dooley (eds.) *Verb First*. Amsterdam: John Benjamins, 227–42.

Matthews, P. H. (1967). Review of Chomsky (1965), *Aspects of the Theory of Syntax*. *Journal of Linguistics* 3: 119–52.

May, Robert (1985). *Logical Form, its Structure and Derivation*. Cambridge, MA: MIT Press.

Medeiros, David (2008). "Optimal Growth in Phrase Structure." *Biolinguistics* 2: 152–95.

Miller, Philip H. (1999). *Strong Generative Capacity: The Semantics of Linguistic Formalism*. Stanford: CLSI Publications.

Miyagawa, Shigeru (2001). "EPP, Scrambling, and Wh-in-situ." In Michael Kenstowicz (ed.) *Ken Hale: A Life in Language*. Cambridge, MA: MIT Press, 293–338.

—— (2003). "A-Movement Scrambling and Options Without Optionality." In Simin Karimi (ed.) *Word Order and Scrambling*. Oxford: Blackwell, 177–200.

Mohammed, M. A. (1988). "On the Parallelism between IP and DP." *Proceedings of the West Coast Conference on Formal Linguistics* 7. Stanford. Stanford Linguistic Association, 241–54.

Mohanan, K. P. (1982). "Grammatical Relations and Clause Structure in Malayalam." Joan Bresnan (ed.) *The Mental Representation of Grammatical Relations.* Cambridge, MA: MIT Press, 504–89.

Mohr, Sabine (2005). "Clausal Architecture and Subject Positions." Amsterdam: John Benjamins.

Moltmann, Frederike (1991). "Scrambling in German and the Specificity Effect." MS, MIT.

—— (1992). *Coordination and Comparatives.* Ph.D. dissertation, MIT.

Moortgat, Michael (1989). *Categorial Investigations: Linguistic and Logical Aspects of the Lambek Calculus.* Dordrecht: Reidel.

Moravcsik, Edith (2006). *An Introduction to Syntactic Theory.* London: Continuum Press.

Moro, Andrea (1997). *The Raising of Predicates: Predicative Noun Phrsases and the Theory of Clause Structure.* Cambridge: Cambridge University Press.

—— (2000). *Dynamic Antisymmetry.* Cambridge, MA: MIT Press.

Muadz, Husni (1991). *Coordinate Structures: A Planar Representation.* Ph.D Dissertation. University of Arizona.

Murasugi, Kumiko (1993). *Crossing and Nested Paths: NP Movement in Accusative and Ergative Languages.* Ph.D. dissertation, MIT.

Muysken, Pieter (1982). "Parameterizing the Notion 'Head'." *Journal of Linguistic Research* 2: 57–75.

Napoli, Donna Jo (1989). *Predication Theory.* Cambridge: Cambridge University Press.

Newmeyer, Frederick J. (1980). *Linguistic Theory in America: The First Quarter-Century of Transformational-Generative Grammar.* Orlando, FL: Academic Press.

—— (1986). *Linguistic Theory in America.* San Diego: Academic Press.

—— (1998). *Language Form and Language Function.* Cambridge, MA: MIT Press.

Nissenbaum, Jon (1998). "Movement and Derived Predicates Evidence from Parasitic Gaps." *MIT Working Papers in Linguistics* 25: 247–95.

Noonan, Máire (1992). *Case and Syntactic Geometry.* Ph.D. dissertation, McGill University.

—— (1993). "Statives, Perfectives and Accusativity: The Importance of Being Have." In J. Mead (ed.) *Proceedings of the West Coast Conference on Formal Linguistics* 11: 354–70.

—— (1994). "VP-Internal and VP-External AgrOP: Evidence from Irish." *Proceedings of the West Coast Conference on Formal Linguistics* 13: 318–13.

Nordlinger, Rachel (1998). *Constructive Case: Evidence from Australian Languages.* Stanford : CSLI Publications.

Nuñes, Jairo (1998). "Bare X-bar Theory and Structures formed by Movement." *Linguistic Inquiry* 29: 160–7.

Ó Baoill, Donall (1995). "The Modern Irish Reflexive Form *Fein* as a Three in One Anaphor." Paper presented at the Celtic Linguistics Conference, Dublin.

Ó Sé, Diarmuid (1990). "Tense and Mood in Irish Copula Sentences." *Ériu* 41: 62–75.

Ochi, Masao (1999). "Multiple Spellout and PF adjacency." In P. Tamanji, M. Hirotani, and N. Hall (eds.) *Proceedings from the Twenty-Ninth Annual Meeting of the North Eastern Linguistic Society (NELS)* 29. Amherst, MA: GLSA Publications, 293–306.

Oehrle, Richard, Emmon Bach, and D. Wheeler (eds.) *Categorial Grammars and Natural Language Structures.* Dordrecht: Reidel.

Osborne, Timothy (2006). "Parallel Conjuncts." *Studia Linguistica* 60: 64–96.

Ouhalla, Jamal (1991). *Functional Categories and Parametric Variation.* Routledge. London.

—— (1994). "Verb Movement and Word Order in Arabic." In David Lightfoot and Norbert Hornstein (eds.) *Verb Movement.* Cambridge: Cambridge University Press, 41–72.

Palm, Adi (1999). "The Expressivity of Tree Languages for Syntactic Structures." In Hans Peter Kolb and Uwe Mönnich (eds.) *The Mathematics of Syntactic Structures: Trees and Their Logics.* Berlin: Mouton de Gruyter, 114–31.

Partee, Barbara, Alice ter Meulen, and Robert Wall (1990). *Mathematical Methods in Linguistics.* Dordrecht: Kluwer.

Pesetsky, David (1982). *Paths and Categories.* Ph.D. dissertation, MIT.

—— (1995). *Zero Syntax: Experiencers and Cascades.* Cambridge, MA: MIT Press.

Peters, Stanley and R. W. Ritchie (1973). "On the Generative Power of Transformational Grammars." *Information Sciences* 6: 59–83.

—— —— (1982). *Phrase Linking Grammars.* Technical Report, Department of Linguistics, University of Texas.

Phillips, Colin (2003). "Linear Order and Constituency." *Linguistic Inquiry* 34: 37–90.

Picallo, Carme (1991). "Nominals and Nominalization in Catalan." *Probus* 3: 279–316.

Pickering, Martin and Guy Barry (1991). "Sentence Processing Without Empty Categories." *Language and Cognitive Processes* 6: 259.

Pike, Kenneth (1943). "Taxemes and Immediate Constituents." *Language* 19: 65–82.

Platzack, Christer (1986a). "Comp, Infl, and Germanic Word Order." In Lars Hellan and Kirsti Koch Christensen (eds.) *Topics in Scandinavian Syntax.* Dordrecht: Reidel, 185–234.

—— (1986b). "The Position of the Finite Verb in Swedish." In Hubert Haider and Martin Prinzhorn (eds.) *Verb Second Phenomena in Germanic Languages.* Dordrecht: Foris, 27–47.

—— (1987). "The Scandinavian Languages and the Null Subject Parameter." *Natural Language and Linguistic Theory* 5: 377–401.

—— (1995). "The Loss of Verb Second in English and French." In Adrian Battye and Ian Roberts (eds.) *Clause Structure and Language Change.* Oxford: Oxford University Press, 200–6.

Pollard, Carl (1985). "Phrase Structure Grammar Without Metarules." *Proceedings of the West Coast Conference in Formal Linguistics* 4: 246–61.

—— (1988). "Categorial Grammar and Phrase Structure Grammar: An Excursion on the Syntax–Semantics Frontier." In Richard Oehrle, Emmon Bach, and D. Wheeler (eds.) *Categorial Grammars and Natural Language Structures*. Dordrecht: Reidel, 391–415.

—— (2004). "Higher-order Categorical Grammar." In M. Moortgat (ed.) *Proceedings of the Conference on Categorial Grammars (CG2004)*, 340–61 (Montpellier).

—— and Ivan Sag (1994). *Head Driven Phrase Structure Grammar*. Stanford: CSLI.

Polleto, Cecilia and Jean-Yves Pollock (2004). "On the Left Periphery of Some Romance Wh-Questions." In Luigi Rizzi (ed.) *The Structure of CP and IP: The Cartography of Syntactic Structures*, ii. Oxford: Oxford University Press, 251–96.

Pollock, Jean-Yves (1989). "Verb Movement, Universal Grammar, and the Structure of IP." *Linguistic Inquiry* 20: 365–424.

Postal, Paul (1967). *Constituent Structure: A Study of Contemporary Models of Syntactic Description*. Bloomington: Indiana University Linguistics Club.

Pulleyblank, Doug (1983). *Tone in Lexical Phonology*. Ph.D. dissertation, MIT.

Pullum, Geoffrey (1982). "Free Word Order and Phrase Structure Rules." In J. Pustejovsky and P. Sells (eds.) *Proceedings from the Twelfth Meeting of the North Eastern Linguistic Society Meeting (NELS)* 12: 209–20.

—— (1984). "Chomsky on the Enterprise." *Natural Language and Linguistic Theory* 2: 349–55.

—— (1985). "Assuming Some Version of the X-bar Theory." *Syntax Research Center Report SRC-85–01*. Santa Cruz: University of California.

—— (1986). "Footloose and Context Free." *Natural Language and Linguistic Theory* 4: 409–14.

—— and Barbara Scholz (2005). "Contrasting Applications of Logic in Natural Language Syntactic Description." In Petr Hajek, Luis Valdes-Villanueva, and Dag Westerstahl (eds.) *Logic, Methodology and Philosophy of Science 2003: Proceedings of the 12th International Congress*. Amsterdam: Elsevier.

Pylkkänen, Liina (2001). "What Applicative Heads Apply to." In M. Fox, A. Williams, and E. Kaiser (eds.) *Proceedings of the 24th Penn Linguistics Colloquium*. Department of Linguistics, University of Pennsylvania.

—— (2002). *Introducing Arguments*. Ph.D. dissertation, MIT.

Radford, Andrew (1988). *Introduction to Transformational Grammar*. Cambridge: Cambridge University Press.

Ramchand, Gillian (1993). *Aspect and Argument Structure in Modern Scottish Gaelic*. Ph.D. dissertation, Stanford University.

Rayward-Smith, V. J. (1995). *A First Course in Formal Language Theory* (2nd edn). London: McGraw-Hill.

Reape, Mike (1994). "Domain Union and Word Order Variation in German." In John Nerbonne, Klaus Netter, and Carl Pollard (eds.) *German in HPSG*. Stanford: CSLI Publishers, 151–97.

Reinhart, Tanya (1976). *The Syntactic Domain of Anaphora*. Ph.D. dissertation, MIT.

—— (1981). "Definite NP anaphora and C-command domains." *Linguistic Inquiry* 12: 605–36.

—— (1983). *Anaphora and Semantic Interpretation*. Croom Helm, London.

Richards, Norvin (1999). "Dependency Formation and Directionality of Tree Construction." *MIT Working Papers in Linguistics* 34: 67–105.

Richardson, John F. (1982). "Constituency and Sublexical Syntax." *Proceedings of the Chicago Linguistics Society Regional Meeting* 18: 446–76.

—— and Robert Chametzky (1985). "A String-based Reformulation of C-command." In S. Berman, J.-W. Choe, and J. McDonough (eds.) *Proceedings from the Fifteenth Meeting of the North Eastern Linguistic Society (NELS)* 15: 332–3.

Ritter, Elizabeth (1988). "A Head-Movement Approach to Construct-state Noun Phrases." *Linguistics* 26: 909–29.

—— (1991). "Two Functional Categories in Noun Phrases: Evidence from Hebrew." In S. Rothstein (ed.) *Perspectives on Phrase Structure: Heads and Licensing* [Sytnax and Semantics, 26]. San Diego: Academic Press, 37–62.

—— (1992). "Cross-Linguistic Evidence for Number Phrase." *Canadian Journal of Linguistics* 37: 197–218.

—— (1993). "Where's Gender?" *Linguistic Inquiry* 24: 795–803.

Rizzi, Luigi (1989). *Relativized Minimality*. Cambridge MA.: MIT Press.

—— (1997). "The Fine Structure of the Left Periphery." In L. Haegeman (ed.) *Elements of Grammar*. Dordrecht: Kluwer, 281–337.

—— (2004). "On the Cartography of Syntactic Structures." In Luigi Rizzi (ed.) *The Structure of CP and IP: The Cartography of Syntactic Structures*, ii. Oxford: Oxford University Press, 3–15.

Roberts, Ian (1994). "Two Types of Head Movement in Romance." In David Lightfoot and Norbert Horstein (eds.) *Verb Movement*. Cambridge: Cambridge University Press, 207–42.

—— (2005). *Principles and Parameters in a VSO Language*. Oxford: Oxford University Press.

—— and Ur Shlonsky (1996). "Pronominal Enclisis in VSO Languages." In Ian Roberts and Robert Borsley (eds.) *The Syntax of the Celtic Languages*. Cambridge: Cambridge University Press, 171–99.

Rogers, James (1994). *Studies in the Logic of Trees with Applications to Grammar Formalisms*. Ph.D. dissertation, University of Delaware.

—— (1998). *A Descriptive Approach to Language-Theoretic Complexity*. Stanford: CSLI publications.

Ross, John R. (1967). *Constraints on Variables in Syntax*. Ph.D. dissertation, MIT.

Rouveret, Alain (1991). "Functional Categories and Agreement." *The Linguistics Review* 8: 353–87.

Rubin, Edward (2003). "Determining Pair-Merge." *Linguistic Inquiry* 34: 660–68.

Rumelhart, David and James McClelland (1987). *Parallel Distributed Processing.* Cambridge, MA: MIT Press.

Sadock, Jerrold (1991). *Autolexical Syntax: A Theory of Parallel Grammatical Relations.* Chicago: University of Chicago Press.

Sag, Ivan, Tom Wasow, and Emily Bender (2003). *Syntactic Theory: A Formal Introduction* (2nd edn). Stanford: CSLI.

Sagey, Elizabeth (1986). *The Representation of Features and Relations in Non-Linear Phonology.* Ph.D. dissertation, MIT.

—— (1988). "On the Illformedness of Crossing Association Lines." *Linguistic Inquiry* 19: 109–8.

Saito, Mamoru (1984). "On the Definition of C-command and Government." In *Proceedings of the North East Linguistic Society* 14: 402–17.

—— and Naoki Fukui (1998). "Order in Phrase Structure and Movement." *Linguistic Inquiry* 29: 439–74.

Sampson, Geoffrey (1975). "The Single Mother Condition." *Journal of Linguistics* 11: 1–11.

Schafer, Robin (1995). "Negation and Verb Second in Breton."*Natural Language and Linguistic Theory* 13: 135–72.

Schwartz, Arthur (1972). "The VP Constituent of SVO Languages." In J. P. Kimball (ed.), *Syntax and Semantics* 1: 213–35.

—— and Sten Vikner (1989). "All Verb Second Clauses are CPs." *Working Papers in Scandinavian Syntax* 43: 27–49.

—— —— (1996). "The Verb Always Leaves IP in V2" In Adriana Belletti and Luigi Rizzi (eds.) *Parameters and Functional Heads: Essays in Comparative Syntax.* Oxford: Oxford University Press, 11–62.

Seely, Daniel (2004). "On Projection Free Syntax." MS, Eastern Michigan University.

Seiter, William (1980). *Studies in Niuean Syntax.* New York: Garland.

Seuren, P. A. M. (1998). "Western Linguistics: An Historical Introduction." Oxford: Blackwell.

Shieber, Stuart (1985). "Evidence Against the Context-freeness of Natural Language." *Linguistics and Philosophy* 8: 333–43.

——Susan Stucky, Hans Uszkoreit, and Jane Robinson (1983). "Formal Constraints on Metarules." *Proceedings of the Association for Computational Linguistics,* 22–7.

Siegal, Dorothy (1974). *Topics in English Morphology.* Ph.D. dissertation, MIT.

Soschen, Alona (2008). "On the Nature of Syntax." *Biolinguistics* 2: 196–224.

Speas, Margaret (1985). "Saturation and Phrase Structure." *MIT Working Papers in Linguistics* 6: 174–98.

Speas, Margaret (1990). *Phrase Structure in Natural Language*. Dordrecht: Kluwer.

—— (1991). "Generalized Transformations and the D-Structure Position of Adjuncts." In Susan Rothstein (ed.) *Perspectives on Phrase Structure: Head and Licensing* [Syntax and Semantics, 25]. San Diego: Academic Press, 241–57.

Spencer, Andrew (1992). "Nominal Inflection and the Nature of Functional Categories." *Journal of Linguistics* 28: 313–41.

Sportiche, Dominique (1996). "Clitic Constructions." In Johan Rooryk and Laurie Zaring: *Phrase Structure and the Lexicon*. Dordrecht: Kluwer, 213–76.

Sproat, Richard (1985). "Welsh Syntax and VSO Structure." *Natural Language and Linguistic Theory* 3: 173–216.

Starke, Michal (2004). "On the Inexistence of Specifiers and the Nature of Heads." In Adriana Belletti (ed.), *The Cartography of Syntactic Structures, Vol. 3: Structures and Beyond*. New York: Oxford University Press, 252–68.

Steedman, Mark (1989). "Constituency and Coordination in a Combinatory Grammar." In Mark Baltin and Anthony Kroch (eds.) *Alternative Conceptions of Phrase Structure*. Chicago: University of Chicago Press, 201–31.

—— (1996). *Surface Structure and Interpretation*. Cambridge, MA: MIT Press.

—— (2000). *The Syntactic Process*. Cambridge, MA: MIT Press.

Stenson, Nancy (1981). *Studies in Irish Syntax*. Tübingen: Gunter Narr Verlag.

Stepanov, Arthur (2001). "Late Adjunction and Minimalist Phrase Structure." *Syntax* 4: 94–125.

Stockwell, R. P., J. D. Bowen, and J. W. Martin (1965). *The Grammatical Structures of English and Spanish*. Chicago: University of Chicago Press.

Stowell, Timothy (1981). *Origins of Phrase Structure*. Ph.D. dissertation, MIT.

—— (1989). "Subjects, Specifiers and X-bar Theory." In Mark Baltin and Anthony Kroch (eds.) *Alternative Conceptions of Phrase Structure*. Chicago: University of Chicago Press, 232–62.

Stuurman, Frits (1985). *Phrase Structure Theory in Generative Grammar*. Dordrecht: Foris.

Sweet, Henry (1891). *New English Grammar*. London: Clarendon Press.

Szabolcsi, Anna (1983). "The Possessor That Ran Away from Home." *Linguistic Review* 3: 89–102.

Tallerman, Maggie (1990). "VSO Word Order and Consonantal Mutation in Welsh." *Linguistics* 28: 398–416.

Taraldsen, Tarald (1985). "On Verb Second and the Functional Content of Syntactic Categories." In Hubert Haider and Martin Prinzhorn (eds.) *Verb Second Phenomena in Germanic Languages*, Dordrecht: Foris, 7–25.

Terada, Michiko (1991). *Incorporation and Argument Structure in Japanese*. Ph. D. dissertation, University of Massachusetts.

Tesnière, Lucien (1959). *Éléments de syntaxe structurale*. Paris: Klincksieck.

Thráinsson, Höskuldur (1985). "V1, V2, V3." In Hubert Haider and Martin Prinzhorn (eds.) *Verb Second Phenomena in Germanic Languages.* Dordrecht: Foris, 169–94.

Travis, Lisa deMena (1984). *Parameters and Effects of Word Order Variation.* Ph.D. dissertation, MIT.

—— (1989). "Parameters of Phrase Structure." In Mark R. Baltin and Anthony S. Kroch (eds.) *Alternative Conceptions of Phrase Structure.* Chicago: Chicago University Press, 263–79.

—— (forthcoming). *Inner Aspect.* Springer.

—— and Andrea Rackowski (2000). "V-initial Languages: X or XP Movement and Adverb Placement." In A. Carnie and E. Guilfoyle (eds.) *The Syntax of Verb Initial Languages.* Oxford: Oxford University Press, 117–42.

Uehara, Keiko (2003). *Center-Embedding and Nominative Repretion in Japanese Sentence Processing.* Ph.D. dissertation, City University of New York.

Ura, Hiroyuki (1994). "Varieties of Raising and the Feature-Based Bare Phrase Structure Theory." *MIT Occasional Papers in Linguistics 7.*

Uriagereka, Juan (1998). *Rhyme and Reason: An Introduction to Minimalist Syntax.* Cambridge, MA: MIT Press.

—— (1999). "Multiple Spellout." In Samuel Epstein and Norbert Hornstein (eds.) *Working Minimalism.* Cambridge, MA: MIT Press, 241–82.

van Hoek, Karen (1997). *Anaphora and Conceptual Structure.* Chicago: University of Chicago Press.

van Oirsouw, Robert R. (1987). "Three-Dimensionality." In G. de Haan and W. Zonneveld (eds.) *Formal Parameters of Generative Grammar,* iii. Utrecht Institute of Linguistics (OTS), 31–46.

van Riemsdijk, Henk and Edwin Williams (1981). "NP-structure." *The Linguistic Review* 1: 171–217.

Van Valin, Robert (1977). *Aspects of Lakhota Syntax.* Ph.D. dissertation, University of California at Berkeley.

—— (1985). "Case Marking and the Structure of the Lakhota Clause." J. Nichols and A. Woodbury (eds.) *Grammar Inside and Outside the Clause.* Cambridge: Cambridge University Press, 363–413.

—— (1987). "The Role of Government in the Grammar of Head-marking Languages." *International Journal of American Linguistics,* 53: 371–97.

—— (1993). "A Synopsis of Role and Reference Grammar." In R. Van Valin (ed.) *Advances in Role and Reference Grammar.* Amsterdam: John Benjamins, 1–164.

—— (2000). "Functional Linguistics." In M. Aronoff and J. Rees-Miller (eds.) *Handbook of Linguistics,* Oxford: Blackwell, 319–16.

—— (2001). *An Introduction to Syntax.* Cambridge: Cambridge University Press.

Van Valin, Robert (2003). "Information Structure, Syntax, and Linking." Paper presented at the Role and Reference Grammar Conference. UNESP São José do Rio Preto.

—— and Randy LaPolla (1997). *Syntax: Structure, Meaning and Function.* Cambridge: Cambridge University Press.

Wall, Robert (1972). *Introduction to Mathematical Linguistics.* Englewood Cliffs, NJ: Prentice Hall.

Wasow, Thomas (1972). *Anaphoric Relations in English.* Unpublished Ph.D. dissertation, MIT.

Watanabe, Akira (1993). *Agr Based Case Theory and Its Interaction With the A-bar System*, Ph.D. dissertation, MIT.

Wells, Rulon (1947). "Immediate Constituents." *Language* 23: 81–117.

Wilder, Chris (1999). "Right-Node Raising and the LCA." *Proceedings of the West Coast Conference on Formal Linguistics* 18: 588–98.

Willis, Penny (1988). "Is the Welsh Verbal noun a verb or a Noun?" *Word* 39(3): 201–4.

Wood, Mary Magee (1993). *Categorial Grammars.* London: Routledge.

Woolford, Ellen (1991). "VP-Internal Subjects in VSO and Non-Configurational Languages" *Linguistic Inquiry* 22(3): 503–40.

Yang, Charles (1999). "Unordered Merge and its Linearization." *Syntax* 2: 38–64.

Yngve, Victor (1958). "A Programming Language for Mechanical Translation." *Mechanical Translation* 1: 25–41.

—— (1960). "A Model and an Hypothesis for Language Structure." *Proceedings of the American Philosophical Society* 104: 444–66.

Zamparelli, Roberto (1995). *Layers in the Determiner Phrase.* Ph.D. dissertation, University of Rochester.

Zanuttini, Rafaella (1997). *Negation and Clausal Structure.* Oxford: Oxford University Press.

—— (2001). "Sentential Negation." In Chris Collins and Mark Baltin (eds.) *Handbook of Contemporary Syntactic Theory.* Oxford: Blackwell.

Zepter, Alex (2000). "Specifiers and Adjuncts." MS, Rutgers (ROA 413–0900).

Zwart, Jan Wouter (2003). "On the Format of Dependency Relations." Colloquium talk, Harvard University, 10 Nov. 2003.

Zwicky, Arnold (1985). "Heads." *Journal of Linguistics* 21: 1–28.

—— (1986a). "Free Word Order in GPSG." *Ohio State University Working Papers in Linguistics* 32: 125–32.

—— (1986b). "Immediate Precedence in GPSG." *Ohio State University Working Papers in Linguistics* 32: 133–8.

—— (1986c). "Incorporating the Insights of Autolexical Syntax." *Ohio State University Working Papers in Linguistics* 32: 139–49.

—— and Stephen Isard (1963). "Some Aspects of Tree Theory." *Working Paper W-6674.* Bedford, MA: The MITRE Corporation.

Index